Andropov in Power

ANDROPOV IN POWER

From Komsomol to Kremlin

JONATHAN STEELE
and
ERIC ABRAHAM

ANCHOR PRESS/DOUBLEDAY
Garden City, New York
1984

Library of Congress Cataloging in Publication Data

Steele, Jonathan.
Andropov in power.

Bibliography: p.
Includes index.
1. Andropov, IU. V. (IUrii Vladimirovich), 1914–
2. Heads of state—Soviet Union—Biography. I. Abraham,
Eric. II. Title.
DK290.3.A53S74   1984   947.085'4'0924   83-45157
ISBN: 0-385-18911-7

Copyright © 1983 by Jonathan Steele and Eric Abraham

All Rights Reserved
Printed in the United States of America
First Edition

Contents

Preface		vi
1	The Real Andropov	1
2	Up and Almost Down	19
3	Their Man in Hungary	45
4	Ten Years in the Central Committee	64
5	Crushing Dissent 1967–82	86
6	Spymaster	109
7	The Rise to Supreme Power	136
8	Taking Charge at Home	152
9	First Steps in Foreign Policy	174
10	Conclusion	205
Select Bibliography		209
Index		211

Preface

Writing a biography of Yuri Andropov is both a daunting and an exciting experience. Articles about him littered the Western press in the first weeks after he succeeded Brezhnev. Much was written but little revealed. Speculation and rumour – much of it fed by his old department, the KGB – vastly outweighed hard, confirmable facts. Could one hope to have better luck? As the research net was extended, it soon became clear one could. Andropov turned out to be a less shadowy figure than usually imagined.

This book had been conceived within days of Andropov's appointment, after Eric Abraham produced the first television documentary on him for the BBC's *Panorama* programme. Using the initial contacts made for the film, we joined up to finish the project in time for the first anniversary of Brezhnev's death. While Eric organised the research, I wrote.

Scores of people who knew him or knew of him at various stages of his wide-ranging career were interviewed at length. In Finland our researchers talked to diplomats, politicians, and Second World War veterans about the 10-year period he served in Soviet Karelia as a partisan organiser against the Finnish forces, and later as an important Party official. In Budapest and abroad they interviewed Hungarians who worked closely with him during the Hungarian uprising when he was the Soviet Ambassador.

In Western Europe and the United States, Soviet dissidents and emigrés who remember his time at the head of the KGB recalled their experiences. In Moscow I spoke with diplomats who attended his meetings with visiting leaders, and observed him at close hand since he came to power. I also talked to Soviet officials who worked

Preface

with him in the Central Committee. In line with normal Soviet practice none was willing to be quoted by name, and their views were cautious, but they too added valuable insights to the emerging picture.

Painstaking research into the gold-mine of material published in the Soviet media produced some previously unknown details. Boring, repetitive, and interminably grey, once in a while the volumes of the Soviet press reveal a nugget which rewards the hours of searching and whets the appetite for more. The microfilm collection of the British Museum produced the 1950 account in a Karelian newspaper of the Party meeting at which Andropov was fiercely attacked for covering up corruption and being out of touch with ordinary workers' lives. From the archives of Radio Liberty in Munich, Elizabeth Teague was able to analyse Andropov's views as the historic split with China unfolded and pressures grew for a return to Stalinism in the Soviet Union.

Many people helped in this effort to portray Andropov and the background which shaped him. Special thanks to Roy Allison for his research into the Karelian period, Jonathan Haslam for help on Andropov's early life, Peter Reddaway for sharing his knowledge of the dissident scene, and Elizabeth Teague for investigating the time Andropov spent in the Central Committee and giving other useful advice. Thanks too to Renée Kraus who spent hours interviewing in Europe, and Don Larrimore who did the same in the United States. John Gittings and Geoffrey Stern made valuable comments on some of the chapters in draft. Finally, thanks to Ruth and Katya.

Jonathan Steele
October 1983

1
The Real Andropov

They had come to Moscow ostensibly for Leonid Brezhnev's funeral, to pay their respects to the memory of the departed Soviet President. But most of the four princes, fourteen Foreign Ministers, fifteen Prime Ministers, and thirty-two Heads of State who gathered in the Kremlin on November 15, 1982 were more interested in the living than the dead.

Three days earlier a special meeting of the Central Committee had chosen Yuri Vladimirovich Andropov to be the new General Secretary of the Party. As they waited in line in the Kremlin's Great Hall of St George for their first encounter with the new Soviet leader, the mood among the foreign dignitaries was one of eager curiosity. To the major Western representatives – Vice President George Bush of the United States, French Prime Minister Pierre Mauroy, West Germany's President Karl Carstens, and Britain's Foreign Secretary, Francis Pym – Yuri Andropov was an unknown figure.

On a few occasions, such as Richard Nixon's second Presidential visit to Moscow in 1974, he had appeared briefly in the welcoming party at the airport, but for most of the period of East-West detente in the 1970's he had avoided public functions. As head of the Committee for State Security (KGB) he had no place in official negotiations with foreign visitors.

Yet in spite of the significance of Andropov's job as director of the Soviet Union's vast network of espionage and counter-espionage, Western governments knew surprisingly little about him. His American counterparts, the Central Intelligence Agency, were not sure of the small but basic fact whether his wife was alive.

No Western analyst had been completely confident that Andropov would emerge as Brezhnev's successor. His views on key Soviet foreign policy decisions, like the invasion of Afghanistan, or the strength of his commitment to detente, were unknown.

To Russians as well as foreigners he was identified almost exclusively with the KGB. Muscovites nicknamed him Yuri Dolgoruki – Yuri of the Long Hands – a pun on the name of the medieval founder of Moscow, who is commemorated by a large equestrian statue on Gorky Street, the city's main shopping thoroughfare.

Now he had advanced to the country's most important post, and the world's politicians were keen to evaluate the new leader. A side door opened in the ceremonial hall, and Andropov entered. He was accompanied by Andrei Gromyko, the veteran Foreign Minister, Nikolai Tikhonov, the Prime Minister, and Vasily Kuznetsov, the Acting President. Surprise number one was the absence of Konstantin Chernenko, who had been tipped by many Western observers as the main rival to inherit Brezhnev's job. Andropov, it seemed, was well in charge. Surprise number two was his physical appearance. Pale and stooping, he peered uncertainly through heavy glasses at every step he took on the ornate carpet. His shirt collar was a size larger than necessary, the top button fastened an inch from his neck.

At sixty-eight, Andropov was taking over supreme power in the Kremlin at a more advanced age than any of his predecessors. Foreign observers inevitably wondered how strong a leader he could be. But as the guests filed slowly by for a hand-shake and brief greeting, they found that first impressions were deceptive. Andropov was animated and alert. A few were promised a longer meeting that day or the next. After a half-hour talk Vice President Bush reported that Andropov seemed "self-confident, firmly in command, clear about policy positions, and quick and concise in making points"[1]. When he received the West German President the following day, Andropov appeared even more self-assured. During a ninety-minute meeting, Andropov did not ask the Foreign Minister, Gromyko, to say a single word.

---

1. *International Herald Tribune*, November 18, 1982.

West German officials found the meeting a dramatic contrast with the last years of Brezhnev's rule. The ailing Soviet leader used to read slowly and hesitantly from a prepared statement, waiting patiently while it was translated paragraph by paragraph. When his visitor asked questions, Brezhnev would leave it to Gromyko to answer directly, or else the Foreign Minister would prompt him by whispering in his ear. "It was sad and embarrassing", as one official put it[2]. Andropov was different. His reactions were quick. He spoke eagerly and with energy. In his hurry to move on to the next point, he frequently interrupted the interpreter before he had finished.

As the months went by, Andropov grew visibly into his new job. By the time of his second meeting with a senior West German figure, the opposition candidate for Chancellor, Hans-Jochen Vogel, in January 1983, his visitors were impressed at his grasp and memory for detail, including such relatively minor points as the number of Soviet Germans permitted to emigrate over recent years. In April he took the risk of an interview with a Western journalist, Rudolf Augstein, the publisher of the weekly magazine, *Der Spiegel*. The ground rules were that written questions had to be submitted in advance. Written replies were then produced. But Andropov went a stage further. In a move that Brezhnev had never allowed himself during eighteen years of power, he answered additional oral questions while the West German's tape-recorder turned. Andropov was fluent and grammatical, talked about his musical tastes, and in a wry answer denied Western reports that he had once played a cunning game of tennis until ill-health drove him off the court. Asked if it was true that he played tennis, Andropov replied, "No. That's why it's easier to give it up"[3].

If Andropov came across as an intelligent man with a keen mind, he also seemed a colder, less emotional person than Brezhnev. France's Foreign Minister, Claude Cheysson, described him as an "unromantic man" who worked "like a computer". "He made a presentation which was cool and objective, accompanied at times by a little personal touch in his gesture, in his smile, or in the way he set out an argument. But in all this he was extraordinarily dispassionate, lacking in that human warmth I found elsewhere...

2. West German official interviewed by Jonathan Steele, Moscow, March 1983.
3. *Der Spiegel*, April 25, 1983, p. 132.

even in my talks with Gromyko"[4], Cheysson told reporters as he flew back from Moscow. "He is a sober man, and precise, who shows no emotion, sticking to the facts and to a mathematical reasoning".

The assessments of Andropov's Western visitors did not differ greatly from those of Soviet sources, whether official or not. A senior political commentator who worked closely with Andropov in the Central Committee in the 1960's portrayed Brezhnev in his later years as an avuncular man who refused to take tough decisions and tolerated incompetence and corruption around him: "For Brezhnev politics was a hobby. For Andropov it is a profession"[5]. Roy Medvedev, the dissident historian, who still retains contact with some members of the Party intelligentsia, described Brezhnev as "an open type with many friends". Andropov by contrast is "unsociable"[6]. An American diplomat who observed Andropov at the airport welcoming ceremony for Nixon in 1974 felt he seemed somewhat distanced from his Politburo colleagues, "in some ways a loner"[7].

Andropov's working style in his first months as leader was also different from Brezhnev's. He avoided any personality cult and kept pictures of himself to a minimum in the Soviet press. He received visitors in an office where the only portrait on the wall was that of his predecessor. The messages of greetings sent to foreign governments on their national days and published almost daily in the Soviet press were no longer signed by the Party leader's name, as in Brezhnev's time, but by the Politburo or the Council of Ministers anonymously. He made it clear he was not prepared to waste much time on ceremony and protocol. Andropov gave up Brezhnev's practice of greeting important visitors at the airport, and established a new routine by which another member of the Politburo goes to the airport while he meets his guests in the Kremlin yard. Flattering references to him in the Soviet media are rare. One of the few which appeared was attributed to the West German Chancellor, Helmut Kohl, whose comments on Andropov

4. *International Herald Tribune*, February 24, 1983.
5. Soviet commentator interviewed by Jonathan Steele, Moscow, March 1983.
6. Roy Medvedev, interviewed by Jonathan Steele, Moscow, March 1983.
7. American diplomat interviewed by Jonathan Steele, Moscow, March 1983.

were quoted by the official news agency Tass during his visit to Moscow in July 1983: "Our conversation was open and direct; a conversation not between diplomats but human beings. I found I was meeting a man who goes to the heart of the matter with his arguments...who discuses every circumstance, every fact, every detailed statistic"[8].

Andropov's speeches were relatively short and concise, and contained frequent touches of realism and warnings against dogma. Addressing the Central Committee for the first time after Brezhnev's funeral, he admitted that "I don't have ready recipes" to solve the country's economic problems. "You cannot get things moving by slogans alone",[9] he added. In February 1983 in a long article on Karl Marx in the theoretical journal *Kommunist*, which some Soviet sources say he wrote himself, the new leader declared that Party members would be useless followers of Marx if they "relied on the magic power of quotations"[10]. At a Central Committee meeting in June, two days before he was nominated to fill the vacant presidency, he attacked the conservative nature of the Soviet economic system: "The economic manager who takes risks and brings in new technology or employs or makes new equipment often loses out, while the one who keeps away from innovation loses nothing"[11].

Soviet sources added to the picture of a serious, rather donnish man who believes in results, not rhetoric, and was not afraid to demand a great deal from his staff. Colleagues in the Central Committee called him a workaholic who put enormous burdens on his underlings but took care of them and was fair[12]. Walter Peinsipp, who served as Austrian Ambassador in Hungary when Andropov was the Soviet Ambassador in the 1950's remembers him saying he could not stand unreliability or lack of punctuality[13]. He usually arrives at his Kremlin office at about 9 a.m., some two hours

---

8. *Pravda*, July 7, 1983.
9. *Soviet News*, Press Department of the Soviet Embassy, London, No. 6149, November 24, 1983.
10. *Summary of World Broadcasts*, BBC, Caversham Park, SU 7267/C12, February 25, 1983.
11. *Pravda*, June 16, 1983.
12. Central Committee sources mentioned by Seweryn Bialer when interviewed by Don Larrimore, April 15, 1983.
13. Walter Peinsipp interview, May 1983.

earlier than Brezhnev did in his last few years. While head of the KGB, Andropov lived in the same high-rise, brick-built apartment block as Brezhnev, at 26 Kutuzovsky Prospekt, one of Moscow's broadest avenues, about ten minutes drive from the Kremlin across the Moscow river. Now he prefers a dacha outside Moscow. He is chauffeured to and from work in a Zil limousine, accompanied by a second car, full of armed KGB agents. While all traffic is stopped to allow the cars to pass, as it was in Brezhnev's time, they drive at a more modest speed. In his first summer as Party leader, Andropov broke with his predecessor's habit of leaving Moscow for most of July and August to enjoy the sea breezes of the Crimea. He took a shorter holiday.

While close observation of Andropov in his first year in power produced a relatively clear image of the new leader in his working environment, he continued to keep his private life obscure. It was impossible to confirm, let alone credit many of the alleged revelations about him which appeared in the Western press during 1982. Many came from sources close to the KGB and were probably meant to build up an image of Andropov as a warm, almost Western figure, perhaps even a 'closet liberal'. *The Wall Street Journal* called him "silver-haired and dapper" while *Newsweek* reported that he "relaxed with American novels"[14]. *Time* went one better, describing him as a witty conversationalist and a connoisseur of modern art[15].

Harrison Salisbury wrote in the *New York Times* that a casual visitor to Andropov's dacha nearly a decade ago found him listening to an English-language Voice of America broadcast. "This was not a 'happy accident' arranged for public relations purposes. It was a long-standing habit. He likes to get his information straight and from the source"[16]. Via his unnamed source Salisbury wrote that the dacha was a spacious stone-and-stucco mansion furnished with good paintings, including contemporary abstracts, an audio system and a first-rate tape and record collection. Among the books on the shelves were American spy stories. A story in the *Washington Post*

---

14. Edward J. Epstein, 'Andropov's Western Image', *The New Republic*, February 7, 1983.
15. Ibid.
16. Ibid.

claimed he liked jazz and "telling and listening to jokes critical of the Communist system. He considered cynics his type of people"[17].

As Ambassador in Hungary, the same article continued, he "quickly established himself as a lover of gypsy music, the more sentimental, the better. The favourite song he always asked for was a tear-jerker about a bird saying goodbye to its nest. He had a gypsy band play at parties and receptions. On the dance floor he cut a dashing figure, and he followed the pre-war protocol in asking wives of officials for turns. He is remembered as an accomplished dancer of the tango, as well as the waltz and the Hungarian csardas".

The truth of most of these unsourced stories is highly questionable, because more is known about Andropov's time in Hungary, before and during the uprising of 1956, than any other aspect of his varied career. As an ambassador he was inevitably in the public eye a great deal, coming into regular contact with Hungarians and other members of the diplomatic corps. Many of those he dealt with have spoken about him, some in detail for the first time for this book. None confirmed the picture of a dashing, fun-loving *bon viveur*, as portrayed in the stories which swept the Western press in 1982.

Miklos Vasarhelyi, who served as press spokesman and foreign affairs adviser to the Hungarian Prime Minister, Imre Nagy, in 1956 and was a journalist before that, told us that the stories of his tennis-playing and lively party-going arose from a confusion. They really applied to Andropov's boss and predecessor, Ambassador Kiselev, who went back to Moscow in 1954: "Andropov was taciturn and reserved, very disciplined and not talkative at all, not like his predecessor Kiselev, who was very much a man of the world, and had lots of contact with people. I am convinced Andropov had no friends among Hungarians whom he would have visited privately or who would have visited him"[18]. Vasarhelyi says there was nothing unusual or remarkable in his behaviour, no breath of scandal or hint of flirtation to give rise to gossip in a very gossip-conscious town.

Vasarhelyi was one of those who found Andropov's coolness disconcerting: "One never knew from his face behind his glasses,

17. Charles Fenyvesi, *Washington Post*, May 30, 1982.
18. Miklos Vasarhelyi interview, May 1983.

whom he would actually support. Andropov was a man whom no-one trusted too much"[19]. Gyorgy Marosan was a former Social Democrat who helped to arrange the merger with the Communists after the war, and was later arrested. Released from prison in March 1956, he was co-opted on to the Hungarian Politburo. He first met Andropov when they shared the same table at an official dinner and later had several, more profound, encounters. He confirms that Andropov's manner was quiet, but he had a different impression of this. To him it inspired a certain confidence: "He did not seem to be a Party apparatchik, either in appearance or the way he dressed. This was a man with whom one could say what one thought....He was willing to put analytical counter-questions to issues raised. He was cultured and pleasant"[20].

Even people who had no reason to feel well-disposed to him found it hard to be angry with him. Judit Livius's husband was Pal Maleter, the Hungarian Minister of Defence, who was arrested by the Russians in the midst of negotiations during the second Soviet military intervention. Hungarian police searched her house and confiscated all her private correspondence and papers. In March 1957 she went to the Soviet embassy to plead for her husband's release. Although Andropov claimed he could do nothing to help as it was entirely a matter for the Hungarians, she found him "polite and very gentlemanly"[21].

Andropov had clearly learnt to play the diplomatic game, concealing his personal opinions behind a facade of courtesy. Walter Peinsipp, the Austrian Ambassador, as the representative of a neutral country, had closer relations with him than the Western envoys had. Peinsipp spoke English with Andropov and found him "a man of austere mien but not stiff like so many others from the Eastern block"[22]. He found Andropov pleasant and with a sense of humour, but a man "who never betrayed his feelings or got into controversies or political disputes". He was a man who was deeply conscious of dignity, both for himself and the Soviet Union. He told Peinsipp that if people expected concessions from the Soviet Union

19. Miklos Vasarhelyi interview, May 1983.
20. Gyorgy Marosan interview, May 1983.
21. Judit Livius interview, May 1983.
22. Walter Peinsipp interview.

on any issue, they must not trumpet them afterwards as victories. He expressed cautious general support for progress. Nothing in the world was static, no regime or state, or even (he told Peinsipp this with a smile) "your church in Austria". One must reckon with changes everywhere, but make them gradually and with a clear view of one's destination. If one tried to make reforms which aimed too far too fast, events like those in Hungary were likely to occur.

Andras Hegedus, who was Deputy Prime Minister when Andropov arrived from Moscow, saw him often. He recalls one small incident which reveals Andropov's coolness and common sense[23]. On an inspection tour of oil installations at Nagykanizsa in south-west Hungary both men were soaked when oil gushed out suddenly from one of the wells. It was not clear if it was an accident or sabotage. "We had to have a change of clothes brought down from Budapest", Hegedus remembers, "and our bodyguards from the Ministry of the Interior wanted to conduct an immediate investigation to see if it was deliberate or not. I stopped it, and Andropov strongly supported me. This in itself does not say much but it was characteristic of the man that, in an era when looking for enemies was so common, he preferred to treat it as an accident".

Andropov and his family have divulged little about themselves. But the thrust of what they have said also makes the Soviet leader seem more orthodox than the early accounts published in the West. Yuri's son, Igor, told a Western reporter that his father "does not have time to indulge in art"[24]. He was no more keen on abstract painting than any other kind. Andropov himself told the publisher of *Der Spiegel* that he liked music, "particularly classical music of the traditional kind"[25]. He made no mention of jazz. His favourite piece was Beethoven's *Pathetique* Sonata, Opus 13. Among Russian composers he liked Tchaikovsky, Rimsky-Korsakov, and Prokofiev. His favourite Soviet musician was Georgi Sviridov, described by Charles Grove's *Dictionary of Music and Musicians* as a composer who specialises in setting national and patriotic texts to tuneful music. His major work is a composition of seven poems by

---

23. Andras Hegedus interview, May 1983. For more details from this interview, see Chapter 3.
24. Reuters from Madrid, February 22, 1983.
25. *Der Spiegel*, April 25, 1983.

Mayakovsky, "agitprop pieces which invoke the memory of Lenin in crude, vulgar, larger-than-life terms" according to Grove[26].

Whether Andropov's interest in music was more than a casual one is not clear. What is known is that his daughter, Irina (born around 1947), has made a career out of music and theatre. She has been Deputy Chief Editor of the magazine, *Muzikal'naya Zhizn* (*Musical Life*), since September 1982 and is married to Mikhail Filippov, an actor at the Mayakovsky Theatre in Moscow. Judging at least by Filippov's appearance, no-one could suggest she married a replica of her father. At a production of a new play by Afanasy Salynsky, called *The Rumour*, in the spring of 1983, Filippov took the part of a short, stocky and jovial entertainer. His first entrance (greeted by a frisson of whispers as people told their neighbours that this was Andropov's son-in-law) was to perform a vigorous song-and-dance number, complete with leers and winks at the audience.

Irina did some acting herself at school. One play she was in was taken off after criticism that it was too modernistic. Later, as a rather wild teenager in the mid-1960's, according to Vladimir Bukovsky, Irina is said to have been friendly with a group of young poets known as SMOG who obtained a Party printing machine on which they ran off a collection of verses called *Masterskaya*. All were children of prominent people. When the KGB discovered it, they were detained in comfortable quarters at the Lubyanka prison in Moscow before being sent back to their parents. Some parents punished their children severely. Andropov was reportedly calm. He quietly told his daughter to think of her career, warning her that he would never try to help if she got into trouble again[27].

Andropov's son, Igor (born around 1942), has had the typical career of an ambitious young member of the Party elite. At one time he was briefly interested in the theatre, like his sister. In 1964 he and Irina approached Yuri Lyubimov, the Director of Moscow's Taganka Theatre about the chances of becoming actors, but were turned down. Andropov was delighted. He thanked Lyubimov 'man to man' for rejecting them[28]. Instead, Igor joined the

---

26. *The Guardian*, April 27, 1983.
27. Vladimir Bukovsky, interviewed by Don Larrimore, March 1983.
28. Interview with Yuri Lyubimov, *The Times*, September 5, 1983.

prestigious Institute of International Relations, where he studied in the American department. The Institute trains academics, researchers, diplomats, intelligence officers, and future Central Committee specialists. Igor later transferred to the Institute of the United States and Canada which is run by Georgy Arbatov, an old associate of Andropov's. In 1982 he joined the Soviet delegation at the conference on European Security and Co-operation held in Madrid. Igor and his wife, Tanya, have two children, Konstantin, who was four when the new leader took over, and a 12-year-old girl, also called Tanya.

Andropov's wife is another Tanya, – short for Tatyana. According to a Soviet journalist, who knew Andropov well during the war when he was living in Petrozavodsk, the capital of Soviet Karelia, she had come up there from Rybinsk, the town on the Volga where Andropov began his political career[29]. The journalist denied speculation that she was of Finnish origin. Mrs Andropov has not been seen by Westerners in public for many years, although she used to attend diplomatic functions when they lived in Budapest. During the relatively relaxed and ostentatious Khrushchev period, and even in the early Brezhnev days, it was common for the Soviet media to mention that senior Soviet officials were accompanied to major functions "by their spouses". Brezhnev, Gromyko, the late Prime Minister Alexei Kosygin and other lesser figures frequently appeared with their wives. But the three Party "intellectuals" – Mikhail Suslov, Boris Ponomarev, and Andropov – were never reported as taking theirs.

Nowadays wives appear less often. One of the rare exceptions is Mrs Gromyko, who occasionally hosts visiting Foreign Ministers' wives. ("Her cover is completely blown", one Western diplomat joked.) Mrs Andropov's cover is a better-kept secret. Soviet protocol provides one occasion a year where the spouses of Politburo members are expected to fulfil a diplomatic duty. On International Women's Day in March the Politburo ladies organise a bizarre reception at the Bolshoi Theatre in Moscow for the wives of the diplomatic corps. It is an all-female affair at which the Politburo hostesses invite their lady guests for a foxtrot or waltz.

29. Rudolf Sykiäinen, Moscow correspondent of *Neuvosto-Karjala*, Petrozavodsk, interviewed on Finnish television, November 24, 1982.

Introductions are rare, except for the main hostess, and the diplomats are not usually sure who their partners are. Mrs Viktoria Brezhnev used to appear regularly at these stilted occasions, and anxious Western diplomats primed their wives in March 1983 to observe whether anyone who had been unidentified in previous years suddenly emerged as Mrs Andropov, wife of the new leader.

Alas, no Mrs Andropov appeared. Soviet protocol officials explained that she did not like formality. At the sixtieth anniversary celebrations of the Soviet Union in December 1982 a diplomat who asked whether Mrs Andropov would be coming was told she had toothache. Before Chancellor Kohl travelled with his wife to Moscow in July 1983, West German officials inquired whether Mrs Kohl would be entertained by Andropov's wife. They were informed that this would not be known until shortly before they arrived in Moscow. In the event she never appeared.

Her continual absence from public life has led to rumours that she is dead or divorced from Andropov. Western Kremlinologists, who carefully study the official condolences published in *Pravda*, have found no mention of Mrs Andropov's death in the ten years since he became a full member of the Politburo, although the Politburo has offered public sympathy on the death of the wives of Alexei Kosygin, the present Prime Minister Nikolai Tikhonov, the Defence Minister Dmitry Ustinov, and Mikhail Suslov. Igor, Andropov's son, told people on the conference circuit in Madrid in 1983 that his mother was still alive.

Andropov's health has not been good for many years. As early as 1957, when he was in his early forties, there were suggestions that he had heart problems[30]. In 1966 he disappeared from public view for over three months, after what is believed to have been a heart attack. That summer he failed to meet with his electors in his constituency at the time of the Supreme Soviet elections, an occasion which Soviet leaders rarely, if ever, miss unless they are unwell. Since then he has often gone absent for a month or more at a time. Arkady Shevchenko, who held the most senior Soviet

---

30. Walter Peinsipp remembers him saying he had heart problems. Gyorgy Marosan says he had to go to a sanatorium in March 1957, when he left Budapest. This in itself is not conclusive. In the Soviet system, officials frequently attend sanatoria for a medical check-up and general rest. After the Hungarian events, Andropov could well have needed one.

position at the United Nations secretariat until he defected in the late 1970's, has recalled staying at the same elite sanatorium as Andropov at Kislovodsk in the Caucasus in 1977. The same doctor attended both men. Shevchenko describes Andropov's ailment as "a rather serious heart condition" and says that the then head of the KGB spent almost all his time in his secluded villa away from the main sanatorium building[31].

There is some evidence that Andropov may have had an eye operation in 1980. He was not seen in public between mid-February and mid-April, and reappeared wearing dark glasses for a time. But as usual with Soviet leaders, no official medical information on Andropov has been divulged. The only medical bulletin ever published on Brezhnev, in spite of clear signs of failing health in the late 1970's and early 1980's, was the announcement of his death and its causes. In the absence of official data, the United States employs what is known as the 'ghoul squad'. This is a team of doctors operating for the CIA, and the Defence and State Departments, who try to diagnose foreign leaders on the basis of 'photographic medicine', primarily the study of film and video pictures supplemented by direct observation.

The 'ghoul squad' has been kept especially busy with Andropov, from the first day he became leader. As a new man taking over supreme power at an advanced age, would he be able to move the Soviet Union out of the apparent policy doldrums of Brezhnev's last few months? In the spring of 1983 the question seemed to become more acute amid signs that Andropov's health had taken a turn for the worse. A regular Thursday meeting of the Politburo was cancelled in mid-March. Andropov avoided public appearances in April. At the May Day festivities he was seen being helped up – some observers described it as "pushed up" – the steps of the Lenin Mausoleum by two aides, who appeared again a few weeks later when the President of Finland visited Moscow. The aides seemed almost to carry Andropov from under his elbows at one point. During the Finnish President's visit protocol officials announced that in future during state dinners the speeches would be given from a sitting position. Only for the toasts at the end would the

---

31. Arkady Shevchenko, interviewed on *Panorama*, BBC Television, November 15, 1982.

speaker and his guests stand up. Television coverage was restricted to occasions when Andropov was sitting down. When Chancellor Kohl met Andropov, the cameras were allowed into the room only after Andropov and Kohl had already taken their places at a table.

The deterioration in Andropov's health led to a new bout of speculation, including rumours that he was put regularly on a kidney dialysis machine, and had Parkinson's disease which forced his hands to tremble uncontrollably. But the 'ghoul squad' was less alarmist. In July 1983 it was reported that "American analysts say he apparently is not suffering from some of the grave maladies ascribed to him. As one analyst put it, 'We're going to have to do business with him for several years, in all likelihood'"[32]. According to the analysts the chances that Andropov would not survive another year were only one in ten. The Soviet leader was thought to have a cardiovascular disorder and a kidney problem. Another report said that

> after a major re-assessment of the Soviet leader's health US intelligence officials...have concluded that Andropov does not suffer from any major nervous diseases or cancer. They have also ruled out a serious kidney ailment requiring dialysis....A videotape study showed that Andropov's hands trembled when he used them – a common problem for older people – not when he rested them. The conclusion was the tremors did not indicate Parkinson's disease[33].

According to the report, Andropov once hinted that he had an American-made pace-maker for his heart. At a meeting with a Western delegation, Minneapolis was mentioned. Andropov tapped his chest and said he knew about Minneapolis. A firm in the city supplied a pace-maker for the former West German Chancellor Helmut Schmidt, and also sells about a dozen devices a year which are believed to be re-exported to the Soviet Union.

The understandable emphasis by ordinary Russians as well as the Western media on Andropov's period at the KGB has tended to

---

32. *Boston Globe*, July 7, 1983.
33. *Newsweek*, July 25, 1983.

obscure the fact that his career has been relatively broad in Soviet terms. By any standard he is better qualified, in experience and intelligence, than Konstantin Chernenko, who was his nearest rival in the struggle to succeed Brezhnev.

Andropov's formal education was not impressive. He left school at the age of sixteen in 1930. Between 1932 and 1936 he studied at a water transport school at Rybinsk, a middle-level technical college. He finished in 1936. He enrolled briefly in 1940 at the University of Petrozavodsk in Soviet Karelia, but had to break off when the Nazis invaded the Soviet Union the following year. After the war he signed up again and completed five courses as a part-time student, although his official biography does not state in what subjects they were. In 1951, now aged 37, he moved to Moscow and attended the Central Committee's Higher Party School, again on a part-time basis, while he worked in the Central Committee. He completed four courses but this was still not enough to obtain a university-level degree. (Until 1979 his official biographies credited him only with "incomplete higher education" but since then he has been described as having higher education[34]. The assumption must be that at some point during his KGB period he passed the requirement for a degree. Whether this was by genuine study or thanks to a ghost researcher who took the examinations for him and/or wrote a thesis is unknown. The concept of a senior member of the Politburo personally writing a university thesis is somewhat hard to believe.)

Andropov's patchy and frequently interrupted education was not unusual for rising Soviet politicians of his time. Where his career was different was in its relative breadth of experience. During the war he served as a youth leader in the Communist Party in the Karelo-Finnish Republic, an important border area. It was partly occupied by the enemy and one of Andropov's jobs was to organise the partisan struggle going on behind the lines. Although there is no evidence that he was required to show any physical courage, either by coming under fire or operating in enemy-held territory, his experience must have stamped him as one of the war-time

---

34. *Deputaty Verkhovnogo Sovieta SSR.* Sbornik, Moscow, Izvestiya, 1970 and 1979.

generation, determined not to permit the Soviet Union ever to be invaded again.

After the war he rose to become the second most important man in the Republic as Second Secretary of the Central Committee, a job in which he was expected to keep a general oversight of all aspects of political and economic life. He took a special interest in agriculture and the food-processing industry. In 1951, after a scandal which almost ended his career prematurely (see Chapter 2), he moved to Moscow to work in the Central Committee. Two years later he joined the diplomatic service and was sent to Hungary, first as Counsellor and then as Ambassador, a post in which he served for three years, including the period of the Hungarian uprising which was put down by Soviet tanks in 1956. Neither of his immediate predecessors, Khrushchev or Brezhnev, ever had such direct contact with the fragility of Soviet rule in Eastern Europe.

It was in Hungary, at least in the relatively quiet years before the Soviet intervention, that Andropov first had a chance to develop his knowledge of English among other diplomats. His English is not fluent enough to allow him to use it on formal occasions, and since he became General Secretary he has so far proved unwilling even to use a few words informally in his several encounters with English-speaking visitors. (In Karelia he had picked up a little Finnish, which helped him when he started to learn Hungarian as the two languages are related. He also understands a few words of German.)

On return from Hungary in 1957 he was given one of the most important foreign policy jobs available. He became head of the Central Committee's Department for Liaison with the Communist and Workers' Parties of the Socialist Countries, in effect supervising not just Hungary but all the Soviet Union's troublesome allies from China to Czechoslovakia. In his new post he was involved in the crucial exchanges with Mao Zedong which culminated in the split with China. He visited Hanoi three times between 1962 and 1965 as Vietnam's confrontation with the United States grew. He kept a continuing watch on Hungary as Janos Kadar, the new leader whom he had helped to select at the time of the intervention, gradually regained the confidence of the population. His job in charge of relations with the Socialist countries lasted for ten years, providing another useful store of experience for his later position as the Soviet Union's number one man.

Andropov transferred to the KGB in 1967. His colleagues appointed him partly in order to bring the vast Soviet secret police apparatus firmly under Party control but also to make it a more professional service. He succeeded on both scores. "The fifteen years he was in the KGB saw a considerable sophistication in its operations", according to William Colby, a former director of the CIA[35]. Professor Leonard Schapiro of the London School of Economics says, "In the 1930's the KGB was full of thugs. Now it has become an elite that skims the cream from the universities"[36]. Andropov took over the KGB at a time of growing intellectual, artistic, and political dissent. Pamphlets, books, and statements poured from dissidents to the West. Many were broadcast back to the Soviet Union via Western radio stations. Andropov promptly formed a new Chief Directorate in the KGB, the Fifth, to deal with internal dissent. By the time he left the KGB he had used a variety of techniques from intimidation, imprisonment, incarceration in mental hospitals, or exile to reduce the various groups of political dissidents to a handful of isolated individuals. Most of these techniques were ones which Andropov inherited, and he used them without resort to the mass terror of the Stalin era. He also expanded the overseas operations of the KGB. The gathering of scientific and technical intelligence from abroad increased enormously.

Taken together, Andropov's experience as local Party official, diplomat, Central Committee Secretary, and police chief gave him an unrivalled knowledge of the external and internal issues facing the Soviet Union. Add to that his obvious intelligence and mental energy, and it can be seen how far his qualifications exceeded those of any potential rival. But there were also flaws. He has never travelled outside the Socialist world. He has no direct experience of running a factory or collective farm. He has no real power base in the Party, having worked since 1951 only in the more "intellectual" side of the Central Committee Secretariat, i.e. foreign affairs, rather than in the organisational sections which deal with personnel and Party management.

35. William Colby, interviewed by Don Larrimore, April 1983.
36. *Time*, February 14, 1983.

He inherited a country which was beset with problems at home and abroad. The growth rate of the economy was falling. Food production, which had never been adequate under Brezhnev, was stagnant. Labour morale was low. The defence bill was threatening to eat more deeply into the national budget. While the system needed some reform, it was not going to be easy to push change past suspicious Party ideologues and lower-level officials who feared that their own jobs in the bureaucracy could be threatened. Abroad, the Soviet Union was confronted by the most hardline American administration for many years. In Western Europe every major country had a government which was more anti-Soviet than its predecessor. China was still wary of detente with Moscow. Soviet influence in the Middle East was confined to only one 'front-line' state, Syria, while Egypt, in spite of some disillusionment with the Camp David process, was showing no sign of returning to the Soviet orbit. Elsewhere among the roughly 100 countries of the Third World the Soviet Union could number its firm friends in single figures.

Faced with this daunting balance sheet Andropov made a slow but steady start. He had problems with his colleagues. He had problems with his health. He had problems with a system which is hard to change. But by the end of his first year in power it was clear that he was determined to soldier on with a programme of controlled modernisation. Before he became supreme Party leader he had proved to be a tough, intelligent, hard-working survivor, at times brutal, at times a subtle manipulator, but for the most part ready to adjust to reality. His varied background had shaped him. Could he now shape the Soviet Union?

2
Up and almost Down

Yuri Andropov was born at the railway station of Nagutskaya in the North Caucasus on June 15, 1914. His father, Vladimir, worked at the station as what Andropov's official biography calls an "employee". Whether this means he had a white-collar job or was perhaps even the station-master is unclear. At all events the station was small, probably little more than a halt on the main Moscow-Baku line, and is unmarked on most Soviet maps. Vladimir's job cannot have been well-paid, making the Andropov family essentially working-class.

The maps do mark the village of Nagutskoye, about ten miles from the railway line. The area is part of the rich farming region of Stavropol in the basin of the lower Volga, and not far from the North Caucasian health resorts. The region is one of considerable ethnic diversity but in his official biographies Andropov has always given his nationality as Russian. Rumours that his father's name was originally Andropian, suggesting that he may have been Armenian, or that his mother's maiden name was Jewish – Erinshtein – cannot be confirmed. As far as is known, Yuri was an only child. At least there has been no mention of any surviving brothers or sisters since Andropov became prominent in Soviet public life.

In the period that Andropov was growing up the economy of the Stavropol region, like that of the rest of the Soviet Union, was governed by Lenin's so-called New Economic Policy (NEP), introduced in 1921. Everything was being done to maintain the support of the peasants who were allowed to sell their farm produce for private profit on the open market. The railway line where

Andropov's father worked, and the nearby small towns with their slow industrialisation were little more than islands of incipient socialism in a sea of peasant capitalism.

Indeed, as the 1920's reached their halfway mark, Bolshevik influence in the countryside was diminishing at a rapid pace. Communist journalists sent out into the countryside were assassinated. The local 'soviets' or village councils had little influence or were dominated by the richer peasants. To those of proletarian origin, like Andropov, growing up in the countryside, it must have seemed as though the great socialist revolution was in retreat.

By the late 1920's the Soviet leadership was confronted with a dilemma. With everything geared towards favouring the peasants, the towns were subsidising the countryside. Socialist industrialisation, intended by Stalin to ensure Soviet Russia's survival in a hostile world, required that the balance had to be switched to the advantage of the towns. At the same time, in order to provide the capital for industrialisation, workers' wages had to be squeezed. The only way to do this without provoking a working-class revolt appeared to be to have the state bring down food prices. But faced with lower prices, peasants simply hoarded their products hoping that their refusal to sell would force prices up again.

This was the economic genesis of the forced collectivisation of agriculture which was launched in November 1929, just as young Yuri was about to leave school. There was a political dimension to it, too. The crisis of 1927-9 which led to all-out collectivisation took place against a background of intense international hostility to the Soviet Union. Stalin saw the urban traders (NEPmen) and the richer peasants (kulaks) as a fifth column for international capitalism. The forced collectivisation of agriculture thus had a political function in removing from Soviet society what Stalin believed to be a subversive element.

In 1930, at the age of 16, Andropov started his working life as a telegraph operator and then a cinema operator in another railway settlement at Mozdok, some 125 miles east of his home town, in the northern tip of what was then the North Ossetian autonomous oblast, now the North Ossetian Autonomous Soviet Socialist Republic. He joined the Komsomol (Young Communist League) in 1930. This period which saw the start of collectivisation and the beginning of the first five-year plan of industrialisation was known as "the socialist offensive". It became a decisive turning-point in Soviet history. The Soviet regime tried to mobilise the enthusiasm of pro-socialist elements to the maximum possible effect.

It is not known whether Yuri's father, Vladimir, was a Party member, let alone an old Bolshevik, or whether he encouraged or discouraged his son from making open cause with the Revolution. But to join the Komsomol at this time would most probably have been a result of the upsurge in socialist enthusiasm inspired by the regime. It was not simply a question of automatically signing up, and later moving into the Party's ranks out of careerism or opportunism, as it is for many Soviet young people today. In 1930 Party or Komsomol membership meant being an activist and living dangerously, particularly in the countryside where the atmosphere, especially in the lower Volga region, verged on civil war.

The regime thought collectivisation would be achieved speedily and fairly bloodlessly. It was wrong. By late February 1930 much of the countryside was literally up in arms. The Red Army was called in with increasing frequency to restore law and order, and since its ranks were filled with the sons of the better-fed peasants, unrest in the countryside soon threatened the cohesion of the Soviet armed forces. Although Stalin retreated from collectivisation in March 1930, he renewed the pace again in the autumn. That year's successful harvest convinced Stalin that forced collectivisation would work. As a result, more grain was forcibly collected from the peasants without regard to sowing requirements, let alone the peasants' own family needs. Towards the end of 1931, after a disastrous harvest, peasants were beginning to starve.

The North Caucasus had become the scene of sporadic battles between peasants and government forces by the spring of 1932. Any Komsomol member working in this environment would certainly have seen bloodshed at first hand, if not have participated in it. Enthusiasts joined the raids on peasants and participated in acts of brutality to collect the grain. People reacted differently to the experience. It confirmed some in their belief that savagery was vital and justified. Others came to believe this was a disastrous policy imposed from above by Stalin.

Whatever Andropov's position as a teen-aged Komsomol member, it is unlikely that he escaped baptism by fire. In 1932 he moved north to become a 'Volga boatman', actually a crew member on the Volga shipping lines, and settled in the important Volga port of Rybinsk in Yaroslavl oblast, north-east of Moscow. Here he attended the local water transport college. By the end of 1933, after a good harvest which beat back the famine, political stability was returning. Industry was more or less on its feet, and a period of relative calm ensued. The leadership acted less arbitrarily. Moves were made to weaken the power of the security police (OGPU), goods re-appeared in the shops, and Red Army officers, their Tsarist ranks now returned to them, were instructed to learn to dance.

Party membership had swollen in the years between 1929 and 1932 and Stalin partly attributed the growing criticism of his rule to 'alien' elements that had entered the Party. He therefore introduced a purge of Party members from 1933-4. At the beginning it was relatively mild but after the murder of the old Bolshevik, Sergei Kirov, in December 1934 and Stalin's arrests of two other senior Party men, Zinoviev and Kamenev, the purge led to the imprisonment of an increasing number of Party officials. Enrolment of new members was suspended between 1935 and 1936, and many were summarily thrown out. Thus there were two opposing trends at work at different levels of Soviet society: outside the Party life was getting less dangerous; within the Party life was getting more dangerous.

It was at exactly this time that Andropov launched out on his political career, first as Secretary of the Komsomol organisation of the Rybinsk Water Transport Technical College and soon afterwards as full-time Komsomol organiser at the Volodarsky shipyard in Rybinsk. He later became head of the Department of Political Education at the Rybinsk town Komsomol organisation. At this period the shipyards were heavily affected by the Stakhanovite movement of so-called shock work (named after the prodigious efforts of a model coal-miner) whereby workers were required to find methods of increasing their tempo of production and were paid by results. In June and July 1936 Stakhanov visited Yaroslavl, an important industrial centre in the region where Andropov was shortly to move. As a Komsomol organiser Andropov would have been pre-occupied with building a Stakhanovite movement in his own parish. Increasing tempos would undoubtedly have led to animosity among workers while galvanising some into extra efforts. Here and there workers assaulted and even killed Stakhanovites and smashed machines. Andropov would have had to learn to cope with such tensions.

The Party purges naturally produced dissent but Stalin moved to crush every symbol, real or imagined, of rebellion. In February 1937, after a wild speech to the Central Committee, he launched a terror campaign. It paralysed decision-making in all walks of life. Everyone waited for orders to act before daring to do anything. Industrial performance in 1937 was very poor. At the same time the terror provided an enormous opportunity to a rising star. One could step into dead men's shoes. Extremely rapid mobility was the order of the day. It was undoubtedly a temptation for ambitious Komsomol and Party members to denounce their superiors as a means of taking their place.

In 1937 Andropov moved to Yaroslavl as Third Secretary of the Komsomol in the Yaroslavl region. The following year his official biography says he was elected Komsomol First Secretary. A clear sign of his rapid promotion as well as the confusion created by the purges was the fact that at this time he was not yet a Party member, even though the regulations in force at the time specify that in order to be elected Secretary of an oblast Komsomol committee a person has to have had at least three years Party membership.

Yaroslavl was a microcosm of what industrialisation meant to the country as a whole. One of its factories pioneered the production of synthetic rubber. Its industry was closely tied to tyre and bus construction. It also invested heavily in hydro-electricity. Although Andropov matured in the provinces, he witnessed and presumably participated in all the major changes of his time, whether economic, social, or political, albeit at a low level. It was an era of traumatic change, the era of the belief in the machine. Andropov was in this sense the child of Stalin's revolution.

The terror also hit the Komsomol. In November 1938 Stalin used a meeting of the Central Committee of the Komsomol in Moscow to attack its leadership. The First Secretary and most of the other leaders were removed and soon afterwards arrested. At the age of 24 Andropov was perhaps too young to be affected by the purges, and perhaps he shared in the denunciation of others. At all events, he benefited from them.

In May 1940 Andropov was sent up to Petrozavodsk, the capital of the newly formed Karelo-Finnish Soviet Socialist Republic, to chair a meeting of the Republic's Komsomol organisation. This was a signal that he had already been selected by senior officials in Moscow to take over the Karelian Komsomol, about which there was considerable concern (reflected in a speech made by the Karelian Party Secretary, General Gennadi Kupriyanov, later that year). In his own speech at the Komsomol meeting Andropov complained that although many members were good shots and were ready to work and defend the country, others could not shoot or ski[1]. At the end of the meeting Andropov became First Secretary of the Republic's Komsomol.

The Republic was one of the most sensitive border regions of the country at the time, and Andropov's selection as its number one youth organiser was a significant promotion. Two months before he arrived the Soviet Union and Finland had ended a short but bloody war. "In the vast drama of the Second World War", the historian, Max Jakobson, has written, "the Soviet-Finnish conflict was merely an incident within an episode.... Were there nothing more to it, the Winter War, as it is called in Finland, would hardly stand out among the countless bloody skirmishes – brush-fire wars they would be called today – that throughout history have been fought along the edges of empires"[2]. Yet in the West the Winter War had a tremendous emotional impact as the Finns fought the Soviet Union against overwhelming odds. "The Finns", as Jakobson puts it, "defended democracy and freedom and justice, all the things the Western democracies stood for but had at the time [December 1939] little chance actually to fight for. Many a modern Byron on skis volunteered to go to the scene of the action"[3].

On the Soviet side geography was the determining factor, particularly Peter the Great's decision to build his capital city on the doorstep of Finland and the emergence of a Western capitalist

---

1. Rudolf Sykiäinen, Moscow correspondent of *Neuvosto-Karjala*, Petrozavodsk, interviewed in the Finnish paper, *Tiedonantarja*, Helsinki, December 12, 1982.
2. Max Jakobson, *The Diplomacy of the Winter War*, Cambridge, Harvard University Press, 1961, p. 4.
3. Ibid.

state which almost abutted the outskirts of Leningrad. The Winter War arose from Stalin's efforts to stave off the Nazi threat. In 1938 Stalin had become convinced that Hitler was preparing to attack Russia and that his plans included the use of Finland as his northern launching-pad. Moscow warned Finland that if German troops were allowed to operate in Finland, the Red Army would invade. It would be far better for Finland to ally itself with the Soviet Union.

The Finns resisted the Soviet argument and tried to maintain their neutrality. Soviet pressure intensified and in October 1939, after the Nazi attack on Poland, Stalin demanded that Finland lease part of its coast for thirty years to enable the Soviet Union to establish a naval base to defend the sea approaches to Leningrad. Stalin also asked to move the Soviet-Finnish frontier on the Karelian isthmus which was only twenty miles from Leningrad further north, in exchange for a larger but strategically less significant part of Soviet Karelia. The Finns wavered, and on November 30 Stalin lost patience. He sent his forces across the border and ordered bombing raids on Helsinki.

What was expected to be a knock-out punch failed. The war lasted for three and half months. In the bitter northern winter the Finns were fighting for their state's existence, knew the terrain better, and had more experience on skis. The Soviet troops suffered heavy casualties. Wave upon wave of Soviet assault troops stormed across the frozen Gulf of Vyborg (Viipuri) and were massacred on the ice. Thousands more died in the forests. Twenty-five thousand Finnish soldiers perished, while Moscow's estimates were that 48,000 Soviet troops were killed. Finnish intelligence estimates put the figure at 200,000 [4]. A peace treaty signed in Moscow in March 1940 gave Stalin most of his pre-war objectives but left a legacy of hatred in Finland. Behind Finland's official neutrality there grew a strong tendency to look for German support for revenge against the Soviet Union.

This was the background of the region to which Andropov moved in May 1940 two months after the armistice. The Karelo-Finnish Soviet Socialist Republic, where he was now the leading

---

4. Ibid., p. 273.

Komsomol official, was a new creation, formed from the merger of pre-war Soviet Karelia and a large slice of territory captured from Finland in the Winter War. Politics in the Republic were dominated by two major issues. One was the question of security and the continuing threat of a Nazi invasion of the Soviet Union through Finland. The other – unconnected to the Winter War – was the issue of relations between ethnic Russians and local nationals.

Stalin's terror had severely affected Karelia, just as it hit all minority ethnic groups, particularly those living in border regions, whom Stalin suspected of potential disloyalty. Hardly a single Finn or Karelian who was at all well known remained in the Party or Government by 1940. The purge spread to Finnish groups all over the USSR and resulted in an estimated 20,000 Finns being sent to labour camps, where thousands died. The school system was Russified and local Soviet defence forces disintegrated with the imprisonment of Finnish and Karelian officers. Only those Finnish Red commanders who had earlier been transferred to Soviet units survived and remained free. Of all the leading emigré Finns in the Soviet Union only one, Otto Kuusinen, survived. He lent his voice to condemnation of "Finnish nationalism" among Karelian Communists. A similar purge went on among other emigré Communists who were sheltering from fascism, such as Poles and Germans. Many of the workers employed in Eastern Karelia in the 1930's, mainly on forestry work and the building of a canal from Lake Onega to Belomorsk (Sorokka), were forced labourers drawn from the region's prison camps. Many were kulaks. In 1939 there were about 8,000 prisoners at Kemi near Belomorsk and 40,000 at a former monastery on the Solovetski islands in the White Sea. In 1940, when Andropov arrived in Karelia, the camps were still in operation.

After the territories which had been captured from Finland were joined to pre-war Karelia, Kuusinen was chosen as Chairman of the Supreme Soviet of the new Republic. A few survivors of the Finnish Communist Party took other positions alongside Russians. Security and defence issues dominated the life of the Republic, especially after September 1940 when German troops were granted the right of transit through Finland to and from occupied Norway. The

Nazis established a base of operations in the north of Finland, although Finland claimed she was still neutral. Some effort was made at peaceful construction in the Karelo-Finnish Republic in spite of the looming threat from the north-west. In September 1940, for example, a university was founded in Petrozavodsk (at which Andropov himself enrolled).

In June 1941 German troops attacked the Soviet Union through Poland. A few days later Finnish troops crossed the frontier and moved swiftly into the Karelo-Finnish Republic. Kuusinen called an emergency conference in July at which he laid down the Party's military and strategic priorities. A "workers'front" was to be mobilised to prevent the enemy from making use of the Karelian region for an attack on Leningrad. He emphasised that the most urgent task for the Karelian Party organisation was to build the Belomorsk-Obozersky railway to run along the shores of the White Sea and connect with the Northern railways. One of Andropov's jobs was to mobilise Komsomol groups to help to build the line. Every District and Party organisation took part in this considerable engineering feat. The extremely rapid construction of the line which was ready by October 1941, linking the vital port of Murmansk to the central heartland of the Soviet Union, was carried out, no doubt, at considerable human expense. But the nation was at war and the line later proved crucial for the military supplies to the Soviet Union from the Western allies, which arrived at Murmansk under the American Lend Lease programme.

It seems unlikely that prison labour could have been used for this construction project in the manner of the canal-building in the 1930's in Karelia. Because Stalin was afraid that the Germans might move into Karelia in force, he had ordered all the prison and labour camps to be evacuated and moved into the Russian hinterland. In fact, Stalin had overestimated the strength of the Nazis, who left it to the Finns to play the major role in invading and occupying Karelia. Nevertheless it is possible that in helping to organise the construction work Andropov may have used labour mobilisation techniques originally developed in the camps. The organiser of the construction work on the canal from the White Sea to the Baltic in the 1930's was a security official, Yakov Rappoport, who was later in charge of the hydraulic works at Rybinsk at the time that Andropov was studying water transport technology there.

The most important task in the early months of the war was, of course, the formation of partisan groups which could function behind enemy lines. Andropov's Karelian Komsomol became directly involved in military operations as part of the chain of political authority which was responsible for Soviet partisan activity. Overall command of front-line operations lay in the hands of Army General K.A. Meretskov and the Chief of the General Staff, General B.N. Pigarevich. They gave orders to Lt.-General M.A. Antonyuk who commanded the Petrozavodsk military group. But the Party under General Kupriyanov established a general staff of the partisan league in Karelia. Working with the Party the Komsomol made strenuous efforts to create the infrastructure for a local partisan league. Andropov's job was to recruit Komsomol members for partisan activity and check their reliability.

The first groups were formed in July and by mid-August fifteen partisan groups containing nearly 1,800 young people were ready for action. Young women as well as men volunteered. Many Komsomol members left to form the backbone of these newly formed youth detachments in a voluntary expression of political and patriotic fervour, but others presumably were given directives which they could not ignore. Andropov proposed that one of the three Komsomol Secretaries directly responsible to him be appointed commissar of the Vpered partisan division in July. In the year before the outbreak of war Andropov had established links with the Komsomol organisations of the Soviet field troops and the border guards, and these connections were put to good use during the summer of 1941. One of the most important immediate measures at the beginning of the war was the creation of partisan sabotage detachments, three of which were formed in Petrozavodsk.

There is no evidence that Andropov acted as a commissar to any of the partisan groups himself, or that he took part in any of their military engagements. His job was to encourage others. In the first article which he ever had published in the Soviet press, in the magazine *Smena* in 1942, he extolled the heroic deeds of the young men and women of the local Komsomol. He wrote of the eagerness of volunteers who applied to join the partisan brigades, and the disappointment of those who were rejected on health or physical fitness grounds. He mentioned the special ski battalion and the sappers who mined railway lines behind the front. He described the "extra Tuesdays" when once a week at the end of the normal working day young people at the Belomorsk timber factory would work a second shift to boost production for the war. The high point of the article was Andropov's account of how a young Karelian Komsomol member managed to approach Finnish positions, deceiving the Finnish soldiers into thinking he was one of them by speaking Finnish and then destroying them with hand-grenades. Andropov cited this as an example for all partisans to follow. Courage was not a headlong rush forward. Partisans had to "skilfully combine courage, caution, and exact calculation to achieve positive results"[5].

Throughout September 1941 Soviet troops fought to defend Petrozavodsk, and, although the partisan detachments were not meant for front-line operations, eight groups helped in the town's defence. But on September 10 the Finns cut the railway linking the Karelian front to Leningrad, and on October 2 Soviet forces had to withdraw from the capital of the Republic. The Finns gained control of a broad area, including several industrial towns, forest resources, and the fertile Aunus plain. The new power station at Syväri, which had supplied electricity to the Leningrad region before the war, was in their hands. The Finns had also cut Leningrad's other important link to the north, the canal from the White Sea to the Baltic.

After abandoning Petrozavodsk the Karelian military and political headquarters moved north to Belomorsk, a small town on the White Sea. Not only was this town strategically more secure than Petrozavodsk, but it had traditionally had a higher proportion of ethnic Russians. As before, Andropov divided his time between civilian and politico-military duties. Thousands of young people were sent to work in the forests of Karelia in harsh conditions to provide production for the front. In many enterprises the majority of workers were young people. On the initiative of the Komsomol organisation of the Belomorsk timber works it was decided that

5. Yuri Andropov, 'We will defend you, Karelian motherland!', *Smena*, Moscow, No. 23-4, published in Andropov, *Selected Speeches and Articles*, Moscow, Politizdat, 1979.

each Komsomol member would do the work of two members who had been sent to the front. Komsomol members in other factories followed this example. A high proportion of this "youth shock work" was undertaken by girls, who had never handled large saws and axes in the forests before. Andropov claimed that "the productivity of the youth brigades is growing continuously"[6] and he was praised by Party officials for organising this success.

From Belomorsk Andropov would sometimes travel up to Murmansk to help with the unloading of supplies from the Western allies. It is here that he first picked up a few words of English, as he later told a diplomat in Hungary in the 1950's. He would also visit the small village of Pudozh on a river a few miles upstream from Lake Onega. This was the site of the largest training base in Karelia for Soviet partisans, and Komsomol headquarters moved there later in the war.

Rudolf Sykiäinen, the Moscow correspondent of the Karelian Party paper *Neuvosto-Karjala*, recalls meeting Andropov for the first time in Belomorsk in March 1942. Like most officials in the border regions he was wearing military uniform, but his rank was the lowest of the low. "He had in his office a sturdy, green field telephone. Every time it rang he used to answer it by saying 'Untrained Private Andropov'"[7]. By then Andropov was married. Sykiäinen first met Andropov's wife, Tanya, in 1940 in Petrozavodsk where she was a Komsomol Secretary.

After the transfer to Belomorsk Andropov continued his work of organising groups of partisans. The area occupied by the Finns north of Lake Ladoga suited partisan operations, but the region was sparsely inhabited and the Finns put many people into concentration camps. This made it hard to conduct a conventional partisan war based on the support of a local civilian population. Soviet writers claim the partisans in Karelia carried out severe strikes against enemy forces, killing officers and men, blowing up bridges, and cutting telephone lines. Soviet partisans certainly created difficulties behind the Finnish lines and forced the Finns to withdraw men from the front for the protection of the hinterland.

6. Cited by K. Morozov, 'On the Front and in the Rear', *Neuvosto-Karjala*, June 27, 1982.
7. Rudolf Sykiäinen, interviewed on Finnish television, November 24, 1982.

But despite their activity the partisans were unable to cause sufficient losses to influence Finland's conduct of the war decisively. The Soviet claim that their partisans killed, wounded, or took prisoner over 13,500 enemy soldiers and officers in Karelia is disputed by Finnish specialists[8].

The Karelian Party leadership and the military command of the front bore joint responsibility for a partisan brigade which was sent deep into the Finnish hinterland in the summer of 1942 with the aim of cutting the railway line between Suojärvi and Petrozavodsk, destroying Finnish command posts, liberating prisoners of war, and fomenting a rebellion in the Karelian villages against the Finns. This brigade of 640 men failed to achieve any of its tasks and was almost destroyed. The partisan leadership on the Karelian front lost almost all its best people on this mission and had to recognise from the bitter experience that it was very difficult to get large partisan detachments into the enemy interior. Smaller groups were more effective.

Kuusinen showed particular interest in the effect of the ethnic divisions in Karelia on the resistance of the population. In September 1942 he visited the 71st Infantry Division and later distributed a letter to all its units in praise of its morale. This division was primarily composed of Finns, Karelians, and other minorities and was one example of how Finland's forces were sometimes fighting against kindred Finnish people on the Soviet side. For these reasons the work of Soviet military intelligence had to be harsher and more effective in Karelia than elsewhere on the various Soviet fronts. Kuusinen also studied the attitudes adopted by the inhabitants of Karelian villages which had not been evacuated before the Finnish army advanced. Kuusinen expressed the official view at a Supreme Soviet session in February 1943. Local people had helped Soviet partisans to carry out their military

---

8. The Soviet estimate is made by I.S. Yakovlev, *V. Lesakh Karelii, Sovetskiye Partizany*, Moscow, 1961, p. 708. It was based on statements made by the partisans themselves. Finnish scholars have not been able to make an exact account of the losses caused by Soviet partisans, since they were not considered to be of military significance and there were no means to carry out such a count. But in the view of a Finnish partisan expert, Colonel H. Seppälä, this Soviet figure was "entirely wrong", *Neuvosto-Partisaanit Toisessa Maailmansodassa (Soviet Partisans in the Second World War)*, Parvoo-Helsinki, 1971, p. 196.

operations and all attempts by the occupiers to sow dissension between the Karelian and Russian people had failed dismally, he claimed. The issue continued to be of major importance for the success of Soviet partisan operations and the activities of Soviet political and military intelligence.

Many of the best partisan leaders and officers operating from the Soviet side were kindred people to the Finns, or actual Finns, who possessed a good knowledge of the awkward terrain of swamp and forest, full of small lakes, and punctuated by wide rivers with marshy banks. Although the soldiers of the Finnish army traditionally considered themselves guerrillas, partisans operating from the Finnish side only rarely penetrated into the Soviet hinterland, apart from reconnaissance patrols. The Finns had gone into Eastern Karelia as liberators but they were not universally acclaimed as such. About half the people caught by the Finns in their original advance were Russians but the other half were either ethnically related to the Finns or were more distant ethnic groups. Kuusinen trusted that the Karelians would offer passive resistance to the Finnish occupiers, which some did.

Andropov was in charge of the underground information network set up behind the Finnish lines. It provided information about Finnish troop movements, the formation of new military detachments, and local attitudes in the occupied areas. One aim was to create underground district committees of the Party to work politically with local people. It was anticipated that help could be sought from the Finnish Communist Party working underground in Finland itself as well as in Finnish-occupied Karelia. This work certainly brought Andropov into close contact with Kuusinen. Andropov succeeded in creating at least the skeleton of underground district committees in Aunus and Äänisniemi, including a Komsomol Secretary in the former district. It appears, however, that Andropov's most important contact behind the Finnish lines was in Petrozavodsk itself. Andropov and Kuprianov sent F.F. Timoskainen, a Finn by nationality, who had become one of the Komsomol Secretaries of the Karelo-Finnish Republic in 1940, back to the capital to work as Secretary of the underground Party committee. There he formed several groups of colleagues who regularly sent information to Belomorsk about enemy troop

Up and almost Down

Karelia (North-West USSR) area of Andropov's activities 1940-51

numbers and movements and the political and economic situation in the town. Andropov's intelligence must have suffered a major blow when at the end of 1943 Timoskainen was arrested and sentenced to death by a Finnish military court.

Other Soviet spies of Karelian and Finnish nationality were also executed. Finnish counter-intelligence in Petrozavodsk was effective, and the success of the Soviet information network should not be exaggerated. Nor was all the resistance in Finnish-occupied Karelia connected with Andropov and other Soviet officials in Belomorsk. There were cases of independent action taken against the occupiers. It must also be understood that Andropov's network was only one part of the Soviet intelligence apparatus directed from Belomorsk and Andropov cannot be held responsible for the overall character of Soviet operations in Karelia.

Soviet spies and saboteurs, generally in civilian clothes or Finnish military uniform, were dropped by plane or sometimes sent over land or water into the areas controlled by the Finns. They had to be able to move among Finns unchallenged, which presumed perfect knowledge of Finnish and proper identity papers. In many cases these men were Karelians who spoke Finnish. They had all undergone political training. Their political function was to prepare the ground for the re-establishment of Soviet control by distributing leaflets, organising local people, recruiting partisans, and contacting and training agents. There were also Soviet attempts to conduct intelligence operations in Finland itself, but this work proved very hard. In the first three months of the war 164 Soviet agents were dropped or sent into Finland, of whom 145 were captured almost immediately. This failure rate sharply reduced the number sent into Finland, at least for the time being. In the spring of 1942 the flow picked up again.

It is difficult to evaluate the extent of security police (NKGB) operations on these cross-border missions or those of SMERSH, the special assassination squads which went in to eliminate enemy informers. It is clear that NKGB officials did operate from Belomorsk. SMERSH operations were quite separate from partisan activity on the Karelian front, and were under full and distinct control from Moscow. Such cross-border missions were intended mainly for espionage against Germany through Finland. Nikolai

Ogarkov, who later became Chief of the General Staff when Andropov was in the Politburo and is sometimes mentioned as his supporter during the succession moves against Brezhnev in 1982, was a young military engineer on the Karelian front at this time but there is no evidence that he and Andropov met or became friends.

The final Soviet offensive against the Finns saw Andropov eager and impatient to return to Petrozavodsk and start the business of reconstruction. He entered the town on June 27, 1944 with the first Soviet infantry troops, the 368th Division[9]. The main bulk of the Soviet assault force, soldiers of the Seventh and Thirty-Second Armies, arrived two days later, while N.A. Dildenkin, the Party Secretary of the town committee of Petrozavodsk, only turned up on June 30. They found parts of the town destroyed. Before evacuating on June 27, Finnish troops blew up or burnt down the public buildings and industrial works, the power station, the sawmill, the dockyard and the harbour – some 666 buildings in all. The returning Soviet troops released thousands of Petrozavodsk citizens from the local prison camps.

The Party apparatus of Petrozavodsk had worked throughout the war in Belomorsk and had effectively functioned as the Belomorsk town committee in all but name. On return to Petrozavodsk Dildenkin was soon replaced. Andropov was chosen as Second Secretary of the town committee while the post of First Secretary of Petrozavodsk as well as of the whole Karelian Party organisation was kept in the hands of Kupriyanov.

Andropov's new post in Petrozavodsk was his first official job in the Party as opposed to the Komsomol. Although he was nominally only a town official, he soon showed that he had a grasp of events outside the capital, and the authority to express criticism. At the end of 1944 he sharply attacked the Council of People's Commissars of the Republic for busying itself with minor matters instead of taking charge of the broader activities of the whole Republic[10].

---

9. Andropov's arrival time is mentioned in the memoirs of G.N. Kupriyanov, *Ot Barentsego Morya do Ladogi (From the Barent Sea to Ladoga)*, Leningrad, Lenizdat, 1972, p. 351. The later arrival of the Seventh and Thirty-Second Armies is related in S.P. Platonov, *Taistelut Suomen Rintamalla 1941-4 (The Battles on the Finnish Front 1941-4)*, Kirjayhtymä, Helsinki, 1976, p. 200. This account was originally published in the Soviet Union.
10. Rudolf Sykiäinen, *Tiedonantarja*, December 12, 1982.

One of these broader issues which led to a dispute between Finland and the Allied Control Commission (set up on Finnish soil to supervise the Finnish armistice, and dominated by Soviet representatives) concerned the Soviet charge of espionage levelled against Finland. Soviet officials made persistent enquiries in 1944 about the whereabouts of intelligence archives which they believed the Finns had built up and then removed from the occupied regions of Karelia. Finnish radio intelligence had been of a very high standard. During the war Soviet messages and signals were caught and decoded and the information was used to assist Finnish partisans. Soviet messages from Murmansk were also passed on to the Germans.

Of more immediate relevance to Soviet Karelia after the war was the issue of Soviet nationals in Karelia who had possibly served Finnish intelligence during the occupation. It is unlikely that Andropov remained uninvolved in the security operation which the Soviet authorities mounted in order to weed out people who had not acted as "faithful patriots" and those who could actually be accused of treason. At the beginning of 1944 the population of the occupied areas consisted of 41,875 people ethnically related to the Finns, and 41,510 people from other nationalities, primarily Russians. Some 15,000 Russians had been confined in Finnish camps. The Finns had given intelligence training to some prisoners of war and sent them over the border into Soviet-controlled territory. The results had been poor and few of these small patrols returned. This activity and the identity of those trained for it strongly interested the Control Commission. Soviet officials also demanded a list of people who had been enroled as informers in Karelia and of civilians who had had contacts with German military officials as well as an explanation of the espionage schools.

Under the terms of the armistice of September 1944 Finland was obliged to give up all prisoners of war and interned civilians to the allies (which meant to the USSR). Large numbers of East Karelians and other non-Russian minorities had moved to Finland during the war. After the armistice they all had to be returned and Control Commission officials were tireless in ensuring that this happened. In performing this task the Soviet authorities had some help from the the Finnish security police, Valpo, which was reorganised in 1945. Its deputy chief, Aimo Aaltonen, was chairman of the newly established Finnish Communist Party and, according to one estimate, between 45 and 60 per cent of Valpo's staff were Communists, as was the Finnish Minister of the Interior, Yrjö Leino, who had married Kuusinen's daughter.

Among the displaced people in Finland were 330 orphans who had been taken into the care of Finnish foster parents or Finnish children's homes. In spite of efforts by the Finnish Foreign Minister to persuade the Control Commission to make an exception, its deputy chairman, Lt.-General Savonenkov insisted that all these children except those less than a year old had to be returned.

A large number of Karelian prisoners of war had moved into the Finnish Army in which they formed their own detachment, the Heimo (kindred) battalion. It had already been despatched to northern Finland to expel German troops when the Control Commission demanded that the entire battalion be given over to the Soviet Union. This unfortunate group was loaded into a train and sent directly to the USSR, where most of its people presumably ended up in Soviet camps, the usual fate of returning prisoners of war. The extradition order also covered the 'Ostbattalion' made up of troops from the Ingrian minority which the Germans had assigned to the Finnish front in Karelia. Most of these men managed to escape and according to the Soviet Union over 1,200 of them were still missing in 1946-7.

The Soviet Union was also obliged to repatriate people. At the end of the war approximately 6,500 Finns were missing. Of these 1,252 were returned at the end of November 1944. The Russians provided a list of some 400 who had died in Soviet camps, but in spite of Finnish efforts to discover how many Finns were still imprisoned the fate of about 4,000 people remained unresolved. At the end of 1945 Soviet officials denied all knowledge of the missing group.

Under the terms of the armistice Finland was obliged to arrest and try Finnish officials deemed guilty of war crimes in East Karelia, such as the Finnish military comander of Petrozavodsk and the commandants of the concentration camps in the region. Few of these men were imprisoned, nor did Finland return many of the 300

Soviet citizens described by Moscow as war criminals who had remained in Finland.

The tension and bitterness caused by the war and the early post-war disputes gradually abated. Finland remained a Western capitalist democracy but developed close economic links with the Soviet Union. It became the only non-Communist European country to sign a friendship treaty with Moscow. Andropov retained a special interest in Soviet-Finnish relations because of his years in Karelia and it was no accident that in his brief remarks at the Kremlin reception celebrating the sixtieth anniversary of the Soviet Union in December 1982 Andropov singled out Finland by name although a hundred foreign delegations were present. The first foreign head of state he invited to Moscow after succeeding Brezhnev was the President of Finland, Mauno Koivisto.

One change in the Party administration of Soviet Karelia after the war was the absence of Otto Kuusinen. He left for Moscow at the end of 1943 or the beginning of 1944 and entrusted the care of Karelian affairs to Kupriyanov while he worked in the Supreme Soviet of the USSR and remained nominally President of the Karelo-Finnish Republic. But Kuusinen continued to write actively about Karelian affairs in Party newspapers and kept a close watch over the Republic. It seems likely that Andropov impressed him and became a kind of Kuusinen protégé – a move which later proved valuable to Andropov.

An important task in which Andropov was involved in the immediate post-armistice period was the resettlement of civilians who had been evacuated into Central Russia to escape the Finnish occupation. Of the roughly half a million evacuees who left Karelia as the Finnish Army advanced, some 220,000 had been relocated by the Soviet authorities in the Eastern part of the republic. It was relatively easy to move them back to their homes. Less easy was the question of the others. Local officials in the provinces to which they had moved were reluctant to release them because this would inevitably affect production plans. The war with Germany was still on and all industrial enterprises were obliged to fulfil orders for the front.

Another priority issue, in which Andropov was certainly engaged, was improving the political education of workers in the areas won back from Finland, in which the population "had come under the influence of lying Fascist propaganda for a long time"[11]. Party members were instructed to "enhance the militant, offensive, and concrete character of propaganda and agitation"[12] in these regions, where an ideological as well as a security campaign was being waged. At the plenary meeting of the Karelian Communist Party in 1945 it was observed that the Party had carried out significant work "for the mobilisation of Communists for the reconstruction of the economy and the liquidation of the after-effects of the Fascist occupation"[13].

Andropov became Second Secretary of the Central Committee of the Republic in January 1947, making him its second most powerful man. He was still only 32. Petrozavodsk was a town of simple wooden houses with only a few stone buildings in the centre. But the Onega tractor factory was operating again as well as a new paper and cellulose factory at Kondopoga, which provided newsprint for *Pravda* and other Soviet newspapers. At least once, several years later, a strike took place at the Onega factory but it ended soon after the two strike leaders were arrested. There were rumours at the same time of a violent conflict involving the deaths of soldiers and workers at Kondopoga. Nevertheless, by 1950 Kupriyanov could claim that the industrial output of the Karelian Republic had increased five times in as many years. This was an appreciable achievement. When he presented the town of Petrozavodsk with the Order of the Red Banner of Labour in 1978 Andropov recalled the post-war period, when "the beautiful, new capital of Karelia rose from the ashes literally before our eyes"[14]. Agriculture appears to have been more troublesome. The Party rapidly collectivised farms in the areas captured from Finland. Without being specific Kupriyanov later praised Andropov for resolving difficult problems in agriculture.

It is hard to judge the relations between Andropov and Kupriyanov, his nominal boss. Kupriyanov published the first

11. *Ocherki Istorii Karelskoi Organizatsii KPSS*, Petrozavodsk, Izdatelstvo Kareliya, 1974, p. 365.
12. Ibid.
13. Ibid., p. 364.
14. Yuri Andropov, 'A High Award for Labour and Courage in Battle', speech in Petrozavodsk. August 5, 1978, in Andropov, *Andropov, Selected Speeches and Writings*, Oxford, Pergamon, 1983, p. 193.

volume of his memoirs in 1972 when Andropov was already head of the KGB and a candidate member of the Politburo. It was hardly likely that he would have been able or willing to say anything critical of him. "Andropov quickly acclimatised himself to Karelia....It was easy to work and pleasant to chat with him. In matters great and small he found something new and always infused a new spirit into any undertaking",[15] Kupriyanov wrote.

At one point he appears to have held Andropov's career back, evidently because he valued him as a useful colleague. At the end of 1943 a senior official of the Komsomol in Moscow proposed that Andropov be made First Secretary of the Komsomol in the Ukraine[16]. This would have been a significant promotion. The Ukraine was the second largest republic in European Russia, and heavily populated. It was still partly occupied by the Nazis although the Soviet armies had liberated the capital city, Kiev. To have taken over the entire organisation of youth work in the Ukraine would have given Andropov enormous experience for his subsequent career. But Kupriyanov opposed the transfer, and wrote to Moscow saying that he wanted Andropov to stay. His wishes prevailed.

If Andropov was unlucky to miss this promotion, he could hardly have complained of bad luck some six years later when the Party organisation of the Karelo-Finnish Republic came under fierce criticism from the Central Committee in Moscow. Kupriyanov was dismissed and arrested, but Andropov, the second most important figure in the Republic, managed to survive unscathed. He must have used some fast footwork to emerge with his reputation in Moscow apparently unharmed.

Andropov later admitted that he had been afraid he would also be arrested. "Every day I expected to be arrested", he told the dissident economist, Viktor Krasin, in 1973 during a discussion of Stalinism[17]. "I was the Second Secretary of the Karelo-Finnish Republic. They had arrested the First Secretary and I expected they would take me too. But the crisis passed". The episode was the most dangerous

---

15. Kupriyanov, *From the Barent Sea*, pp. 243-4.
16. Ibid.
17. Viktor Krasin, *Sud (Trial)*, New York, Chalidze Publications, 1983. More details from Krasin's extraordinary encounter with Andropov are discussed in Chapter 5.

Up and almost Down

period in Andropov's career and, in other circumstances, could have brought it to a sudden stop.

The crisis broke in January 1950 after a team of Central Committee inspectors from Moscow had conducted an investigation into allegations of mismanagement and inefficiency in the Republic's affairs. Andropov was somehow able to convince the inspectors that his responsibility was minor although he did feel the need to take some of the blame later at a conference of the Petrozavodsk Party organisation held on February 13 and 14 and described in the Karelian Party newspaper, *Leninskoe Znamya*[18]. In a speech opening the conference, Andropov acknowledged that one of the main faults discovered by the Central Committee was "the low level of criticism and self-criticism"[19]. At meetings of the republican Central Committee Kupriyanov had attacked other speakers and given inaccurate replies, preventing them from criticising the local Party leadership. The leadership had failed to act on complaints made in workers' letters or take heed of other signs of shortcomings in the running of Government departments. It was only thanks to intervention by the Central Committee in Moscow that punishment had been meted out to officials guilty of massive misappropriations in the Ministry of Fisheries as well as to two other officials who had covered up the embezzlement of state funds and allowed a man to be victimised after trying to publicise the misdemeanours of the director of the Belomorsk fish processing plant.

It was a blistering indictment by the Central Committee in Moscow and Andropov's name cropped up in it. Instead of solving problems in a principled, Bolshevik manner, the Central Committee said, the republican Party leadership had gone along with Kupriyanov as though they were all one family. Kupriyanov had created an atmosphere of fawning and servility and the other Party Secretaries, – Andropov, Tsvetkov, Vakulkin, and Chernepova – had succumbed to it[20]. Hardly a single aspect of the Party's administration escaped criticism. Faults had been discovered in ideological work, in the editing of the Party newspapers, and in

---
18. *Leninskoe Znamya*, Petrozavodsk, February 17, 1950.
19. Ibid.
20. Ibid.

handling local languages and culture. In future the Party must take workers' complaints seriously, improve the region's economic management, and ensure a better supply of food and other goods for the population.

Andropov apologised twice as he read the Central Committee's report. After mentioning the republican Party leadership's failure to act on the signs of shortcomings in the food industry and meat and milk production, "Andropov acknowledged that he was to blame since he had had responsibility for these areas"[21]. Later he said that the leadership's greatest mistake had been the fact that "we Secretaries had cut ourselves off from the Party membership, ignored members' views, violated inner-Party democracy, and flouted the rights of other Communists".

Andropov's report provoked what the local newspaper called a lively discussion. The irony that Andropov had been entrusted with the task of reading the report was not lost on some speakers. Comrade Kupriyanov had made many serious errors but "Where were the other Secretaries at the time – comrades Andropov, Tsvetkov, and Vakulkin?" asked one speaker from the floor. "Why did they play up to the selfishness of this officious bureaucrat and not take issue with his non-Party style of leadership?" Another speaker thought it "abnormal that Party Secretaries, like comrades Andropov, Tsvetkov, Vakulkin and the other local leaders, cut themselves off from the masses and do not attend workers' meetings or know how factory workers live". "Comrade Andropov was not equal to his tasks and responded in an unprincipled way by adopting the non-Party practice of suppressing criticism", said a third speaker.

Another speaker, named in the local newspaper account simply as Comrade Klishko, expressed his anger at Andropov and his colleagues with an outburst of sarcasm:

> Some leading officials behave like the lieutenant's widow. They flagellate themselves and think this counts as self-criticism. This is what happened with you, comrades Andropov, Vakulkin, and Tsvetkov. 'We overlooked what was

---

21. *Leninskoe Znamya*, Petrozavodsk, February 17, 1950.

happening.' 'We didn't see.' What do you want? A health certificate from the Party saying you temporarily lost your political vision? No. It's not that they didn't see. They didn't want to see, because they're afraid of genuine self-criticism and criticism[22].

The debate stirred by the Central Committee's investigation reverberated through the local Party for months. On February 25 and 26 another conference of the Petrozavodsk Party branch was held. In May the republican Central Committee discussed defects in the work of the Komsomol. Articles appeared in the press analysing the problems raised.

How Andropov escaped dismissal remains a mystery. His connection with Kuusinen, whose star was on the ascendant in Moscow, may have been the decisive factor. Kuusinen was to be appointed to the Presidium (the then equivalent of the Politburo) in 1952. Another ally was the man chosen by senior officials in Moscow to succeed Kupriyanov and become Andropov's new boss. This was Alexander Kondakov, who had worked in various posts in the regional Party apparatus in Yaroslavl from 1937 to 1940, when Andropov was there. In fact Kondakov did not last long. He resigned in September 1950 because of serious illness. His place was taken by Alexander Yegorov who had also worked with Andropov in Yaroslavl as head of the department of agitation and propaganda.

Andropov's public reprimand at the time of Kupriyanov's downfall was the first and last blemish in a career which was to take him to supreme power. In July 1951 he left Karelia after being selected to work in the Central Committee apparatus in Moscow. His latest official biography stresses the importance of this move, stating that it was "by decision of the Central Committee of the Communist Party of the Soviet Union"[23], a phrase which usually means that the Politburo itself had approved the appointment. In the Central Committee he was first an inspector, then head of an unidentified department, probably – to judge from his speeches at the time – the Party Organs Department, which deals with Party

---

22. Ibid.
23. *Pravda*, November 13, 1982.

membership and supervises new applications. After two years he was transferred to the Ministry of Foreign Affairs to become head of the Fourth European Department, dealing with Czechoslovakia and Poland. Thus began his close connection with the Soviet Union's Eastern European empire, a link that would soon take him abroad as a diplomat and test his skills at the centre of a major international crisis.

3

Their Man in Hungary

For a brief period in the autumn of 1956 Hungary almost broke out of the Soviet Union's tight control of Eastern Europe. No country had come so close to achieving independence since Yugoslavia's Marshal Tito defied Stalin in 1948. For three turbulent weeks Hungary was a stage for massive street demonstrations, armed revolt, a collapse of Communist Party rule, and two Soviet military interventions, the second of which caused more bloodshed than any event in Europe since the end of the Second World War.

The Hungarian uprising was a reaction to a decade of increasingly unpopular Soviet rule, marked by wavering policies whose only common feature was that Hungarians felt they were treated like a colony. The imprisonment of non-Communist politicians in 1947, the removal and execution of several leading Communists in 1949, forced collectivisation of agriculture, and a programme of rapid industrialisation which imposed heavy production norms on miners and factory workers, caused resentment and bitterness. In 1953 Stalin's death produced a sudden relaxation under a new Soviet-supported Prime Minister, Imre Nagy, who announced a series of reforms, but a year and a half later the pendulum swung again and he was removed from power. Then in 1956 the new Soviet strongman, Nikita Khrushchev, made a fierce attack on Stalin's legacy in a speech in Moscow, apparently signalling a new chance for liberalisation.

Backed by pressure from workers and students, reformists within the Hungarian Communist Party tried to take charge and ensure that this time the liberalisation would not be reversed. Demands for an end to Stalinism took shape on the streets, placing Moscow in a situation where it risked losing control. No longer could the Kremlin simply impose policies on clients within a local Communist Party. In the first place the Party itself was split into different factions, not all of which were prepared to obey the Russians. Secondly, the Kremlin also had to deal with people who were ready to use demonstrations and strikes as a tactic for change. In response, Moscow began to consider a military 'solution'. Soviet tanks were deployed in the streets of Budapest, not initially in order to crush the demonstrations, but as an unmistakeable warning.

Few occasions in the unfolding crisis were more tense than the morning of November 1. Imre Nagy, back in power as Hungarian Prime Minister, was in his office in the Parliament building on the south bank of the Danube, anxiously conferring with colleagues over the latest reports of Soviet troop movements. On the previous day Soviet tanks which surrounded the Parliament, the Ministry of Defence and other public buildings had withdrawn and begun a gradual retreat from Budapest. Jubilant crowds watched as Russian diplomats and army officers embarked on the Danube river boat. But during the night disturbing reports started to come in. Soviet anti-aircraft and field artillery units were spotted digging in on the outskirts of the Hungarian capital. Other accounts told of new Soviet tanks pouring across the Soviet border from the Ukraine and taking up positions along main roads in eastern Hungary. A worried Nagy sent for the Soviet Ambassador to demand an explanation.

The Kremlin's man in Budapest at the time was a tall, 42-year-old called Yuri Vladimirovich Andropov. He had been sent to Budapest three years earlier from the Foreign Ministry in Moscow. Although he began as the number two man in the Embassy with the rank of Counsellor, he replaced the then Soviet Ambassador Kiselev within a few months, a promotion which was assumed by Hungarian officials to have been planned by Andropov's superiors in Moscow from the start. In three years in Budapest Andropov had made a good impression on most of the Hungarian officials and Western diplomats, with whom he came into contact. His behaviour was different from that of other Soviet personnel. George Heltai, Nagy's foreign policy adviser, remembers the scene on that morning of November 1:

I was sitting in the big anteroom of Imre Nagy's office talking with somebody. Many people came to see Nagy and I had to talk to them. I looked up and among some four or five other people in the room there was Andropov, alone. Nobody noticed him, nobody even knew him. There were some secretaries working. They didn't even look at him. And I thought: 'But this is the Soviet Ambassador!' No fanfare. Just a modest, greyish man. Stooped. He was heavier than he is now[1].

Heltai's impression of a quiet, controlled man, with an undemonstrative manner, says much about Andropov's character. Where another person might have betrayed some signs of excitement or embarrassment at a time of crisis, Andropov remained cool. He was to show the same self-discipline several times during those eventful days.

To be the senior Soviet official in a confrontation as intense as the Hungarian uprising must have been an enormously important experience in Andropov's life. He came through it with his reputation in Moscow enhanced, for he was promoted only six months later to become head of the Central Committee department dealing with all the Socialist countries.

Several questions arise over Andropov's role in the Hungarian events. What attitude did he take toward the internal Hungarian debate over reform, and which individuals within the Party leadership did he support in the pre-crisis period? What advice did he give the Kremlin and was it heeded? What role did he perform after the first outbreaks of fighting on October 23 1956? Was he aware during his negotiations with Hungarian Party leaders that a second Soviet intervention was imminent? Was he therefore acting in good faith, or simply playing for time? Did he in general play a minor role during the uprising, taking detailed instructions from Moscow, or was he an important decision-maker?

Although Andropov's Hungarian period is clearer than the rest of his career, he has never spoken publicly about it. Much therefore rests on deduction from indirect or circumstantial evidence and not

---

1. George Heltai, interviewed by Don Larrimore, March 1983.

every detail about his role can be answered unequivocally. Nevertheless, in spite of these limitations, interviews with those who remember him provide a strong picture of an efficient and undogmatic professional operator who was able to control his emotions and understood the value of cautious reform. In no sense was he a liberal but he tried to maintain Soviet power with a minimum of bloodshed.

The Hungarian who probably saw most of Andropov in the early stage of his Budapest career was Andras Hegedus. A 31-year-old Party functionary who was made first deputy to the Prime Minister, Imre Nagy, in 1953 with special responsibility for agriculture. Hegedus found himself spending a good deal of time with Andropov who arrived in Budapest that September. Stalin's death in March 1953 had launched a movement for change in Moscow and throughout Eastern Europe. The new Kremlin leadership soon saw that Hungary was one of their most difficult satellites and in June the entire Hungarian leadership was summoned to Moscow and told to reform itself. In July Imre Nagy took over from the old Stalinist Matyas Rakosi as Prime Minister, with Andras Hegedus as his deputy. Andropov's appointment to Hungary two months later was apparently designed to give the Kremlin an intelligent inspector and overlord on the spot in Budapest at a time of potential change and uncertainty.

Hegedus used to travel round the countryside with Andropov looking at agriculture and visiting co-operative farms. He was impressed with his Soviet colleague's willingness to learn about Hungarian society at first hand. This was different from most Russians who acted as though they knew the country already. "In the Ministry of Agriculture" Hegedus says now "I knew many Soviet advisors and specialists. They were well-intentioned but had some sort of profesional haughtiness, a sense of superiority which prevented them from becoming acquainted with the reality of Hungary. Andropov didn't come as though he knew Hungary already. He came because he wanted to get to know it. He was open to social problems, interested, and not dogmatic"[2]. As a symbol of that, the new Soviet diplomat set out to learn Hungarian. By the

2. Andras Hegedus interview, May 1983.

time he became Ambassador a few months after arriving in Budapest he could understand it and later even spoke it, though not fluently.

Hegedus found Andropov to be generally an advocate of caution: he was "not an aggressive Communist functionary". He recalls one occasion at a village co-operative, where the members were poor peasants who felt strongly opposed to the richer peasants in the village. They complained to the two men about the richer peasants but Andropov warned them that nothing immediate could be done. Agriculture was one of the key issues in Hungary, of course. Unlike Czechoslovakia or East Germany, post-war Hungary was still largely an agrarian country. Some three million Hungarians were landless farm labourers or owners of small plots unable to support a family. In 1945 a land reform act expropriated the large estates and redistributed them to peasants who were encouraged, but not forced, to join co-operatives. A general election in that year resulted in 57 per cent of the votes going to the Smallholders' Party and roughly 17 per cent each to the Social Democrats and Communists. In 1946 at Soviet instigation these two parties joined a fourth party, the National Peasant Party, to form a left-wing alliance which pressed for the total collectivisation of agriculture and attempted to break the power of the Smallholders' Party. Over the next six years collectivisation went ahead rapidly. The result was a fall in agricultural production, a collapse of incentives for individual farmers, and the destruction of much farm machinery by disgruntled peasants. The New Course, which was launched shortly before Andropov arrived in Budapest, was designed to reverse the trend towards collectivisation. Individual members of co-operatives who wanted to return to private farming were to be allowed to do so. Co-operatives could be liquidated if a majority of members wanted this.

Although Hegedus frequently saw Andropov and shared many of his political views, they rarely discussed their private feelings. Partly, this was a result of Andropov's natural reserve. But it was also a function of the policy, observed by all Soviet diplomats, of keeping their official and their social lives separate. The two men's families never met. Even when Hegedus and Andropov visited the Party's weekend house at Lake Balaton, this remained an official occasion. As Hegedus describes it now, any functionary, even an ambassador, had little freedom in his personal life.

> It is inconceivable that Andropov would have discussed his own career or career expectations with me, just as I would not have discussed my own career expectations with anyone at that time. These issues and the course of one's life were decided so thoroughly along the various steps in the Party hierarchy, up to and including Moscow, that it hardly could have become a subject for conversation. It is perfectly natural that Andropov could not have shown me, or wanted to show his real relationship with or real opinion of Stalin, Molotov, or Suslov[3].

Between Stalin's death and October 1956 Hungarian politics were marked by a series of forward and backward lurches around the question of reform. One set of issues concerned the future of the economy, the degree of independence to be given to the peasantry, and the amount of investment devoted to heavy industry as opposed to consumer goods. Another question was the pace and scope of political de-Stalinisation, that is, how far to go in releasing and rehabilitating the people who had been imprisoned or executed in the late 1940's for allegedly working as Western or Titoist agents. Had these debates been allowed to resolve themselves in a vacuum, Hungary might have maintained some political stability. Instead, they were conditioned by the ebb and flow of the post-Stalin debate and power struggle in Moscow itself. Hungary had to stay in tune with what its masters in Moscow were saying and doing.

These debates over issues were also continually distorted by political tensions within the Hungarian Party and its different leadership factions, each of which tried to appeal to supporters in Moscow. One crude division was caused by the different war-time experience of the men involved. A significant group had spent the war as emigrés in the Soviet Union. They included Matyas Rakosi, the Party leader who was in charge during the Stalin period, Erno Gero, and Imre Nagy. A second group of Communists had spent the war in the underground or Nazi prisons. These were the so-

---

3. Andras Hegedus interview, May 1983.

called National Communists, men like Janos Kadar and Laszlo Rajk, whose links to the Soviet Union tended to be less strong. A generation younger than both these groups was made up of young men who had been part of the war-time resistance movement and adopted Communist views during the liberation struggle or the immediate post-war period. Some, like Hegedus, fitted easily into the apparatus and remained there throughout the 1956 events. Others formed the core of Party journalists, low-level functionaries, and intellectuals who later coalesced behind Nagy and saw him as the vehicle for a major liberalisation of the system.

As Moscow's chief permanent representative in Hungary, Andropov kept in contact with the various factions. His office was connected to a special internal telephone system which linked up all the offices of the leading power centres in Budapest from the Party Secretary to the Prime Minister. His job was to evaluate the opinions and the political strengths of the different groups. Of course the Kremlin had other sources of information and points of contact. Rakosi used to fly regularly to Moscow to see Khrushchev, and at moments of crisis the Kremlin would send its own senior figures to Budapest.

One such occasion was July 1956 when Rakosi called a Central Committee meeting in the hope of finding a political justification for the arrest of some four hundred of his opponents. Ever since Imre Nagy's appointment as Prime Minister, Rakosi had fought a tenacious rear-guard action to preserve his position and resist reform. He managed to retain his post as First Secretary of the Party even when Nagy became Prime Minister and in 1955 he succeeded in having Nagy criticised by the Central Committee as a 'rightist' and expelled from all his Party posts. But after Khrushchev's relaunching of de-Stalinisation with his attack on the dead dictator in February 1956, Rakosi's position came under new threat. In July, as pressure for reform mounted within the Party, and the first street demonstrations took place, Anastas Mikoyan, the Soviet Deputy Prime Minister, hastened to Budapest to attend the Central Committee meeting.

The meeting ended with Rakosi's removal "for health reasons" (he was spirited off in a Soviet plane to Moscow for "treatment") but his successor was not Nagy but Rakosi's deputy, Gero, a man whose public reputation was hardly more acceptable than that of Rakosi. The surprise was the promotion to the number two position in the Party of Janos Kadar, who had been imprisoned in the Stalinist period on charges of nationalism, espionage, and treason, and only been released two years earlier.

Hegedus believes that Andropov played an important role in giving the Kremlin the advice which led to these changes. In the struggle between Rakosi and Nagy which had dominated the first year and a half of his time in Hungary, Andropov had taken a middle position, though somewhat closer to Rakosi than Nagy. In this he was following Gero whose arguments had considerable influence in shaping Andropov's opinions, according to Hegedus:

> I think that Andropov was really a reformer but in the struggle for power that was going on between Rakosi and Nagy, he was closer to Rakosi than Nagy. This was not so much to Rakosi's credit whom, as far as I saw, Andropov did not particularly respect, but because of Gero who had very great influence in Party circles in Moscow. Gero was anti-Nagy. At the same time without Andropov the amount of re-habilitation of persecuted Party officials would not have taken on the dimensions that they did. There was nothing comparable in other countries"[4].

Although Nagy was a Communist who had spent the war in Moscow, the Kremlin did not trust him. His political views were 'revisionist'[5]. In his extensive writings he argued that the concepts of class struggle and proletarian dictatorship were out-dated and should be replaced by efforts at class collaboration and democratic co-operation. The Communist Party should exercise more patience and consideration towards the intelligentsia, the petty bourgeoisie, and the peasants. Gradualism and progressive reforms rather than a revolutionary transformation were the right methods for moving a society towards socialism. In addition, Nagy was a nationalist. He believed that each country should find its own national road to

---

4. Andras Hegedus interview, May 1983.
5. Ibid.

socialism rather than slavishly follow the Soviet model. Indeed he went further. Even before the crisis of October 1956 he had talked of Hungary becoming neutral between East and West. With the benefit of hindsight the danger of this line of thinking now seems painfully obvious. The Kremlin has never willingly allowed a country which it defines as being on the road to socialism to become non-aligned. But at the time the idea may not have seemed so risky. In 1955 the Soviet Union had accepted Yugoslavia's independence (seven years after the event) and agreed to recognise the neutrality of Austria and withdraw its troops.

Any chance that Nagy's views could seriously have found favour in Moscow was remote. The only possibility might have been if the Kremlin had realised the depth of popular alienation with the regime. At that point a figure like Nagy might have seemed to offer a last chance to preserve Communist rule short of the use of force, since he might have commanded greater popular support than a more orthodox figure. (Later in the crisis the Kremlin considered this option.) But in July 1956 Andropov was not aware that the mood of the country was already one of massive disillusionment with the Party. His position was that of what one might call an enlightened colonialist. He was not an out-and-out hardliner committed to Rakosi, but he favoured making only the smallest possible change in the prevailing system. Not in touch with the feelings of groups outside the ranks of the Party, his advice was that the crisis could be controlled by adjustments in the leadership rather than a broadening of the system.

The one original feature in his approach was his support for Kadar's promotion. Hegedus sees this as essentially Andropov's doing. The idea of a victim of the Stalinist terror who had been wrongfully imprisoned in the 1940's becoming the second highest figure in the Party hierarchy was at that time unprecedented. It was to happen a few months later in Poland with Wladyslaw Gomulka (though not at Soviet behest) and again after the Soviet invasion of Czechoslovakia with Gustav Husak, but Hungary provided the first case. Since Andropov was the only Soviet figure who had had any contact with Kadar in the two years since he had emerged from prison, it can safely be assumed that it was his advice which led to Kadar's promotion. Indeed, one of Kadar's potential advantages over both Rakosi and Gero was precisely the fact that he had no Moscow past. His record of being victimised in the Stalinist purges also gave him a 'national' identity which neither Rakosi nor Gero had. In advancing Kadar, Andropov may therefore have been grooming him as a potential successor to Gero if that should prove necessary. This can only be speculation but it would not be unreasonable for an intelligent political operator such as Andropov to imagine that Kadar could one day satisfy the two essential criteria for preserving orthodox Party control in Hungary – loyalty to Moscow combined with a degree of national appeal.

Whether this was in Andropov's mind or not, events soon overtook the original intentions behind the July Party changes. Elections of non-Communists to the presidium of the Writers' Association, massive demonstrations in the street for the ceremonial reburial of Laszlo Rajk, another victim of the Stalinist purges, and a growing wave of student protests, created a mood of nationalism which gained strength from similar calls for total de-Stalinisation in nearby Poland. On October 23 crowds tore down the statue of Stalin in Budapest and fighting broke out at the radio station against the Hungarian police. The Government called on Soviet troops and tanks. Who proposed this approach to the Russians is still a matter of dispute, but it is known that the Party and Government leaders who assembled in the heavily guarded Central Committee building included Gero, Kadar, Hegedus, and Nagy, who at that time held no official post. They all went along with the decision which was passed by telephone to the Russians. The meeting also decided to appoint Nagy as Prime Minister in the hope that his popularity could be used to appeal to the crowds for calm.

The crisis was the most dramatic which the Kremlin had yet had to face in Eastern Europe, and Mikoyan was promptly sent back to Budapest, this time with Mikhail Suslov, the Central Committee Secretary in charge of relations with the Socialist countries. At 2 p.m. on October 24 troops outside the beleaguered Central Committee building on Academy Street had the improbable experience of seeing a Soviet tank hatch opening up and two of the Kremlin's most distinguished figures clambering out. For the next seven days Mikoyan and Suslov remained in Budapest desperately trying to find a way to restore control. It was a formidable task since the advent of their troops on October 24 only provoked the Hungarian crowds into a new upsurge of nationalism and caused severe demoralisation inside the Hungarian army.

Miklos Vasarhelyi, Nagy's press spokesman, recalls that throughout these days while sporadic fighting continued in the streets Andropov used to travel, as Mikoyan and Suslov also did, only in Soviet armoured cars or tanks. There is no basis for stories that he sometimes used to go on foot as a show of courage, or that the Kremlin hoped he would be kidnapped or killed in order to provide a justification for military intervention.

Andropov's role in this period was subsidiary. The military decisions were taken by Soviet commanders while the political negotiations were in the hands of Mikoyan and Suslov. For the next week Andropov was overshadowed although Hegedus reports that he continued to play a key part as an adviser since he was by then Moscow's best expert on Hungary. He also remained a champion of Kadar, and it was presumably partly his influence that led to Gero's replacement by Kadar as First Secretary on October 25, the day after Suslov and Mikoyan arrived. Andropov's only reported action during their stay was his request to Hegedus to obtain Nagy's signature on a typed copy of a piece of paper[6]. It read "On behalf of the Cabinet of the Hungarian People's Republic, I request the Government of the Soviet Union to send Soviet troops to Budapest to put down the disturbances that have taken place in Budapest, restore order quickly, and create conditions favourable to peaceful and constructive work." To counter international criticism, the Russians wanted official retroactive confirmation of the hasty telephone request which had been made on the evening of October 23. Nagy refused to sign the paper, so Hegedus signed it instead.

Fighting went on in the capital while Mikoyan and Suslov attempted to find a political solution. Many Hungarians lost their lives and scores of Soviet tanks were destroyed. In the rest of the country the level of violence was lower. The Soviet troops acted with restraint and most of the crowd confrontations were against the headquarters of the hated Hungarian security police, the AVH (Allamvedelmi Hatosag). Many of them were lynched by angry

---

6. David Irving, *Uprising*, London, Hodder and Stoughton, 1981, p. 364.

demonstrators. On October 29, after an uneasy ceasefire had been established, Mikoyan and Suslov appeared to concede defeat. It was announced that Soviet troops would pull out of Budapest and were ready to leave Hungary altogether. Two days later the two Soviet negotiators gave Nagy a copy of a declaration on Soviet relations with other Socialist countries which seemed to promise Soviet respect for Hungary's right to choose its own form of socialism.

By then the Russians were already thinking seriously of removing Nagy. In the afternoon of October 31 in the Central Committee headquarters Mikoyan talked to Kadar about the chances of reviving the Communist Party under a new name. In Moscow on the same day Khrushchev was meeting his colleagues in the Politburo to discuss the crisis. Mikoyan and Suslov flew out of Hungary that evening to join their colleagues in the Kremlin. Khrushchev later told the Yugoslavs that the Politburo concluded that day that outright Soviet military intervention was the only way to stop what they considered to be counter-revolution in Hungary. But a few more days were still needed [7]. The Kremlin had to consult the other Socialist countries, and the army had to make its preparations. Khrushchev discussed his plans with a high-level delegation from China which was in Moscow and then on November 1 departed on a strange whistle-stop tour of Eastern Europe. He saw the Poles in Brest on the Soviet border, the Romanians and Czechs in Bucharest, the Bulgarians in Sofia, and finally arrived at Tito's private island of Brioni on the evening of November 2. There Khrushchev explained that Soviet military preparations were going ahead well. In two days all resistance in Hungary would be crushed. The British and French attack on Egypt provided a favourable moment since Western criticism would be muted. "They are bogged down in Egypt and we are stuck in Hungary"[8].

After Mikoyan and Suslov had returned to Moscow Andropov was the senior Soviet political figure in Hungary. The Soviet army commanders of course were there as well as the head of the KGB, General Ivan Serov. According to Gyorgy Marosan, a member of the Hungarian Politburo at the time, Andropov held the strings,

---

7. Veljko Micunovic, *Moscow Diary*, tr. David Floyd, New York Doubleday, 1980, p. 133.
8. Ibid.

and even Serov relied on his information. He reported to Khrushchev and Malenkov every hour and knew exactly where they were on their flight round Eastern Europe to consult Moscow's allies. Every evening he would meet the ambassadors of the other Socialist countries to brief them. Andropov had an important part to perform. His job comprised two extremely delicate functions. One was to play for time and to try to prevent Hungarian resistance mounting in advance of the projected Soviet intervention. The other was, in Marosan's phrase, "to act as a puppet-master, getting all the people into the right place and then select the right ones for the situation"[9]. In particular this meant persuading Kadar and his colleague Ferenc Munnich to accept the necessity of the intervention and agree to form a new administration in its aftermath.

To judge from his behaviour Andropov decided to handle the first of his two tasks by adopting the ultimate in diplomatic modesty and restraint. The unobtrusive impression he made when he waited in Nagy's outer office on the morning of November 1 was mentioned at the beginning of the chapter. This in itself was not an artificial pose since it fitted with what Hungarians had already seen of his style as Ambassador long before the crisis. When Nagy challenged him about the reports of Soviet troop movements, Andropov replied "I don't know. I have no idea. I'll have to ask"[10]. He returned to the Soviet Embassy and was back in Nagy's office two hours later. The arrival of the new troops was "quite normal". The Soviet Union had promised to withdraw its troops and would do so, but their withdrawal had to be safeguarded. The new troops were police troops whose job it was to cover the withdrawal of the main forces who were demoralised after several days in Hungary.

Andropov's explanation was far-fetched. It did not convince the Hungarians and it is impossible to imagine that he could have believed it himself. It is barely conceivable that as the senior Soviet diplomat in Budapest and in constant contact with Khrushchev he would not have been told that the leadership in Moscow was planning a military intervention. He must have been lying. This in itself is hardly unprecedented for a diplomat, and the relevant fact is that he carried it off on the whole coolly and without visible

9. Gyorgy Marosan interview, May 1983.
10. Ibid.

embarrassment. On the phone to Nagy several times during the day, he repeatedly claimed that the new troops were securing the withdrawal of the old ones, that he knew nothing more and that he could only tell Nagy what his government had told him.

Only twice did he show any emotion. When Nagy told him in the afternoon that the Hungarian Government intended to proclaim the country's neutrality and withdraw from the Warsaw Pact, Andropov said he did not agree. But, he added, he would immediately inform the Politburo[11]. Later that evening at about 6 p.m. Andropov returned to the parliament building for a meeting of the Hungarian Government. Nagy said the country was in a trap. The new Soviet troops were within a hundred miles of the capital and had occupied the most important strategic points and airfields in the country. Andropov asked permission to speak. He said he represented the opinion of his government which was trying to help Hungary defend itself against a counter-revolution. At this point Kadar jumped up in dismay, and according to Heltai who was present, shouted "Counter-revolution! There is no counter-revolution! It is your troops who are moving into our cities that are creating a counter-revolution. You know that I am a Communist. I was brought up by the Party. But my only duty now is to go into the street with my pistol and shoot at your tanks"[12]. Andropov lost his composure for the first time, Heltai recalls. "He was deeply impressed. It was not an angry reddishness. It was something else. Perhaps for the first time in his whole life he had met a real Communist".

In spite of his outburst, Kadar seems to have been impressed by the Soviet determination to intervene. He changed his mind about resistance. That evening, with the agreement of Nagy, he broadcast a radio appeal to the nation denouncing the despotism of the Rakosi period and announcing the formation of a new Party. But in implicit acceptance that there was the danger of a counter-revolution which had to be dealt with if a Soviet intervention was to be forestalled, he warned that "a grave and alarming danger exists that foreign armed intervention may allot to our country the tragic fate of Korea....We must eliminate the nests of counter-revolution

11. Gyorgy Marosan interview, May 1983.
12. George Heltai interview, May 1983.

and reaction"[13]. This presumably was Andropov's argument too. By threatening a Soviet intervention, he was trying to urge the Hungarians to put their own Communist house in order.

Shortly after his broadcast Kadar and Munnich were at the Soviet embassy. Some confusion surrounds the manner of their arrival there[14]. According to one account they drove there together but another version, based on the recollections of his chauffeur, maintains that Kadar met Munnich in the street and was virtually pushed into the back seat of Munnich's car and driven off. If the implication is that Kadar was kidnapped and then forced to change his opinion, it does not square fully with Kadar's broadcast where he already appeared to have accepted the Soviet argument. At all events, Kadar left the embassy the following morning and was flown to Uzhgorod in the Ukraine where he waited for the outcome of the Soviet invasion. Whether Kadar was persuaded by the force of argument, by threats, or the promise of the rewards of power, is still unclear. Andropov had fulfilled his second function. He had delivered a pliant Kadar and his colleague Munnich into Soviet safe-keeping. Miklos Vasarhelyi is convinced that it was "Andropov who persuaded Kadar to go over to the Soviet viewpoint"[15].

Khrushchev was still not sure which of the two men to put at the head of the new post-invasion government. He preferred Munnich, who was twenty-six years older than Kadar, and an old Communist who had taken part in the Russian revolution. He had a background in intelligence work, had fought with the Red Army in the war and then served as Hungarian Ambassador in Moscow. During his visit to Tito in Brioni Khrushchev discussed the issue with the Yugoslavs who advised him that Kadar was likely to be more acceptable to Hungarians because he had been in prison during the Rakosi period. This was also Andropov's view. Khrushchev accepted it, and when the Soviet troops brought the two men back to Budapest Kadar was the new leader and Munnich his deputy.

With the two men safely in Soviet hands on the evening of November 1, Andropov continued to play for time and to try to find

---

13. David Irving, *Uprising*, p. 473.
14. William Shawcross, *Crime and Compromise: Janos Kadar and the Politics of Hungary since the Revolution*, London, Weidenfeld and Nicholson, 1974, p. 85.
15. *New York Times*, December 29, 1982.

influential allies among the Hungarian elite. A main aim was to neutralise the Hungarian forces, the Hungarian National Guard. On November 2 he telephoned Nagy claiming that Hungarian "hooligans" were surrounding the Soviet embassy. If the Hungarian Government was not in a position to protect a foreign diplomatic mission, he would have to call in Soviet troops to protect it. Nagy despatched the newly appointed head of the National Guard, General Bela Kiraly, to see Andropov. Kiraly was an officer who had switched to the Russian side in 1944. He became a Communist after the war and was imprisoned for five years during the Stalinist purges. He remembers his visit to the Soviet embassy well. He was allowed to bring only one person, his interpreter, with him. Andropov received him in the hall with the entire embassy staff drawn up to be introduced to him. Andropov was "well-dressed and tremendously polite".…."My impression is that he was measuring up the man who was in command of the Hungarian troops which would meet the Soviet attack. Just as he had measured up Kadar, he might even have been thinking 'Probably this man is someone with whom we can make a deal'"[16], Kiraly says. After the intervention Kiraly did receive phone calls from other generals urging him to announce a ceasefire.

As they went up the embassy's baroque staircase, Andropov stopped and told Kiraly, "You know, General, that the Soviet government and the Soviet people are the warmest friends of the Hungarians". Kiraly replied sarcastically "I know". To himself he thought that Andropov was like some kind of boa constrictor ready to swallow its prey. "Here was this man Andropov", he says bitterly now, "who clearly understood what was going on, yet he pretended until the last moment to me and the Prime Minister and others that everything was business as usual. Even pirates before they attack a ship hoist a black flag. He was absolutely calculating"[17].

As they entered his office, Andropov told Kiraly to forget this "business of the embassy being under siege". Nagy and his people had probably misunderstood him. In fact there was no Hungarian crowd outside the building. But as Kiraly left, he noted that,

16. Bela Kiraly, interviewed on *Panorama*, BBC Television, November 15, 1982.
17. Ibid.

contrary to normal practice, there was not a single uniformed policeman or soldier in the embassy. Kiraly took this as a sign that the Russians were indeed afraid that the building might eventually be overrun. It would be easier to escape in civilian clothes.

That afternoon Andropov passed a memorandum to Nagy suggesting that the two governments start a high-level negotiation on the withdrawal of Soviet troops from Hungary. This too was a device to gain time and lull the potential resistance. At 10 a.m. the next morning, while Andropov was in Nagy's office, the Soviet military delegation came in. They handed over a ten-page document listing the conditions under which the Soviet troops would leave. The next round of talks would be held at the Soviet military headquarters at Tököl outside Budapest. The device of starting negotiations worked, since while they were underway General Pal Maleter, the Hungarian Minister of Defence, stood by the orders which he had given to his forces that no steps should be taken against the Soviet troops unless they attacked. On the evening of November 3 General Kiraly even issued an order for all Hungarian tanks to be returned to barracks[18]. The result was that when the Russians did attack in the early hours of November 4 with a massive assault on Budapest and Hungary's other main cities, the only resistance came from unorganised workers, students, and ordinary citizens.

General Maleter was arrested by the head of the KGB, General Serov, as he took part in the second round of talks at Tököl. Nagy was caught off-balance. When General Kiraly telephoned him at dawn to tell him of the Soviet attack, Nagy still could not believe it. Ever anxious to keep up his calming role, Andropov had already arrived at Nagy's office. Nagy told Kiraly on the phone that Andropov was with him, "and is trying to contact Moscow for instructions. He is of the opinion that someone has made a tragic mistake, and he is trying to stop the slaughter"[19]. As Kiraly pleaded for permission to open fire and issue a call for resistance, Nagy refused. "Up to the last minute," Kiraly concludes, "Imre Nagy

---

18. David Irving, *Uprising*, p. 501.
19. Bela Kiraly, 'From Death to Revolution', *Dissent*, New York, November–December, 1966, p. 721.

believed that he was not witnessing an act of infamy, but an unintentional disaster".

Andropov could feel well pleased. He had helped to split the Hungarian leadership and persuade Kadar to join the Soviet side. His advice that Kadar would make the best new leader had been accepted by Khrushchev. His attentive consultations with Nagy and his repeated visits to Nagy's office had lulled the Prime Minister and his military commanders into taking no defensive action until it was too late. It was a consummate diplomatic performance. He could also argue that he had saved lives by ensuring a one-sided Soviet victory. The final estimates contained in a confidential report made by the Hungarian Central Statistical Office at the end of 1956 were that 1,945 died in Budapest and 557 outside[20].

Andropov also took care that his fellow diplomats were well looked after. Walter Peinsipp, the former Austrian Ambassador in Budapest, recalls a typical wry comment from Andropov when he discussed the convoys of embassy personnel and foreigners who were driving out of Hungary to Austria during the fighting. The Austrian Ambassador's car flew its official banner, a one-headed eagle carrying a sickle in its right hand and hammer in its left above a broken chain, a concoction of the post-war Austrian republic which was meant to symbolise farmers, workers, and liberty. Andropov told the Ambassador to be careful of the rebels. "If they see a hammer and sickle, they may think you are us"[21].

After the invasion, Andropov's role declined. Most of the key decisions were taken by the Soviet military commanders. Since they and Serov's security police had the prime responsibility for ensuring order, this also involved them in political decisions. For example, Kadar's suggestion of a coalition government was vetoed by the Soviet military[22]. It also seems unlikely that Andropov had a special role in enticing Nagy out of the Yugoslav embassy where he had taken asylum. Vasarhelyi argues that this was a decision which would have been taken by the Soviet Politburo on the advice of their military and intelligence chiefs. Nagy was arrested after

---

20. David Irving, *Uprising*, p. 547.
21. Walter Peinsipp interview, May 1983.
22. Bill Lomax, *Hungary 1956*, London, Allison and Busby, 1976, p. 174.

leaving the embassy and executed the following year. The abduction of Nagy was only one incident in a catalogue of repression in which all the various centres of resistance were systematically smashed. The workers' councils were broken and the organisations of students and intellectuals had to disband. Tens of thousands of Hungarians were imprisoned. Although Andropov did not carry the prime responsibility for these acts, he clearly was consulted on many of them. When he became head of the KGB a decade later, his experience in Hungary must have been valuable to him.

In March 1957 Andropov returned to Moscow. The trials and executions of scores of Hungarians who had taken part in the uprising took place after his departure. The irony was that fifteen years later the regime which he had helped to install had become the most popular government in Soviet-controlled Eastern Europe.

4
Ten Years in the Central Committee

Andropov's tour of duty as Soviet Ambassador in Hungary evidently satisfied the Kremlin. On recall to Moscow from Budapest he was promoted to become head of a new department in the Central Committee, responsible for relations with the Communist Parties of the other Socialist countries. This was a key job, covering not only the Soviet Union's vital front-yard in Eastern Europe, but also China, North Korea, and North Vietnam. In the Soviet system, since the Party is more powerful than the government, the job was at least as important as being a deputy foreign minister.

Andropov was to spend the next ten years in that post, rising slowly but surely up the ranks of the Party. In 1962 he became a Secretary of the Central Committee, joining the Secretariat, the second most influential body in the Soviet Union. The Politburo is the main decision-making body, but the Secretariat plays a vital role in the policy process, formulating issues and options and preparing briefing papers for the Politburo.

The Secretariat itself is serviced by some twenty specialised departments with a permanent staff of about a thousand. In the foreign policy sphere the most powerful is, the International Department. Originally it controlled the relations of the Communist Party of the Soviet Union (CPSU) with ruling and non-ruling Communist Parties all over the world. In 1957 it split. One part, which retained the title International Department, kept responsibility for the CPSU's relations with non-ruling Parties and national liberation movements. A new department, known as the Department for Liaison with the Communist and Workers' Parties of the

Socialist Countries (abbreviated here to Liaison Department) was to supervise relations with the ruling Parties of Eastern Europe and Asia. Its first head was Yuri Andropov.

The decision to restructure the International Department and increase its staff appears to have been taken as a result of the crises in Poland and Hungary in 1956, which convinced the Soviet leadership that relations with Eastern Europe were badly in need of repair. While the Polish crisis of 1956 was not as severe as Hungary's, it had also been brought about by strong popular demands for reform, a crisis within the Party, and street demonstrations. In one episode at Poznan Polish troops had shot and killed striking workers. Like Janos Kadar in Hungary, the new Polish leader, Wladyslaw Gomulka was a 'national Communist' who had spent time in prison under Stalin. The difference was that he did not come to power as a result of intervention by Soviet tanks.

Andropov's decade as head of the Liaison Department was overshadowed by the growing conflict with China – which may also have persuaded the Kremlin that it needed more expert advice. At first, the disagreements between the Soviet Union and China were muted and both sides made studious attempts to conceal them behind a facade of unity. As the arguments became more bitter, they became more open, until they threatened to split the entire world communist movement.

At the same time the Soviet Union's relations with Eastern Europe were going through an uneasy phase. One of the first moves of the post-Stalin leadership had been to mend its fences with Yugoslavia, which had been expelled from the socialist camp by Stalin in 1948. The Soviet rapprochement with Tito acted as a signal and spur, as did the gradual unfolding of the Sino-Soviet split, to centrifugal forces in Eastern Europe and the rest of the world communist movement. Trying to strike a new balance with Eastern Europe, Andropov – under Khrushchev's leadership – ran Soviet policy towards the area on a relatively light rein while also striving to prevent the quarrel with China from leading to an open break. It was to prove an impossible task.

Andropov was a relatively junior member of the Soviet decision-making apparatus in the early years of his new job. Not only was he subordinate to Suslov, the Central Committee Secretary who supervised inter-Party relations but also to Khrushchev, who showed a strong tendency to run his own foreign policy, often in a highly idiosyncratic way. Khrushchev frequently conducted personal diplomacy without consulting his colleagues or considering the recommendations of advisers such as Andropov and the Liaison Department. (This was one of the reasons for his eventual downfall.)

After Andropov's election to membership of the Secretariat in November 1962 his activities became more visible and were reported more often in the Soviet media. But he made relatively few public pronouncements during the period from 1957 to 1967. His role was that of behind-the-scenes adviser and, in some cases, negotiator. As might be expected, his speeches and articles stayed close to the Party line of the moment, whatever it happened to be. But there were detectable nuances which suggested that he was among the Soviet officials who showed a certain degree of tolerance towards divergences within the world communist movement.

His personal connections were significant. Some of his associates were people who can only be described in a Soviet political context as reformist, or progressive. In the great debate over re-Stalinisation which took place in the mid-to-late 1960's, Andropov's contacts were firmly in the camp of those who called for greater democratisation of Soviet society. Both the historian Roy Medvedev[1] and the dissident Vladimir Bukovsky[2] describe the decade that Andropov spent in the Central Committee apparatus as a formative period in his political career and a time when he made many of the contacts which he has kept to this day and which helped to shape his opinions. In Medvedev's words, "Andropov proved himself to be an energetic and intellectually capable man, not at all inclined to dogmatism". He was not a routine bureaucrat but rather "a professional politician with undoubtedly long-term political ambitions....He introduced into the Central Committee apparatus a substantial number of young intellectuals: philosophers, Sinologists, economists, people who had already started a successful

1. *La Repubblica*, January 4, 1983.
2. Vladimir Bukovsky, interviewed by Don Larrimore, March 1983.

career. At that time I knew some of those people well, and they greatly esteemed Andropov's political and managerial skills"[3].

As to Andropov's own patrons, the picture is unclear. As Ambassador in Hungary he presumably caught the eye of Mikoyan and Suslov, who were sent to Budapest at the height of the crisis. Either or both could have recommended his transfer to a more responsible post in Moscow. Certainly, it is highly unlikely that Andropov would have been promoted had either opposed the move. On the contrary, Andropov must have owed much of his advancement in this ten-year period to the support, if not the patronage, of Suslov, who had overall responsibility for inter-Party relations and who became the chief architect of the Soviet Union's China policy. If Suslov and Andropov had not seen broadly eye to eye, Andropov would not have lasted in the job (nor would he have made the transfer to the KGB in 1967, had Suslov been against it).

Nevertheless the two men had some differences of emphasis on specific issues. Andropov took a milder line on China than Suslov, who was particularly virulent once the row between the two countries became public. Andropov was consistently less alarmist than Suslov, and seemed not to agree with Suslov's determination to expel the Chinese from the socialist camp after 1963. Andropov also seems to have differed with Suslov on the issue of re-Stalinisation. Andropov opposed a return to more repressive measures of control over the Soviet population. Suslov, though he initially supported Khrushchev's de-Stalinisation campaign, seems later to have felt the process had gone far enough. But as Suslov's lieutenant in foreign policy, Andropov could not have stayed for ten years in the Liaison Department, let alone gained promotion to the Secretariat, if he and Suslov had had fundamental disagreements.

They were intelligent men involved in the making and execution of policy in highly sensitive and complex areas, and were bound to differ from time to time. But as specialists in the same field, arguing sometimes against other interest groups in the

---

3. *La Repubblica*, January 4, 1983.

policy-making process such as economic managers or the military, Suslov and Andropov presumably put their differences behind them and presented a common front in defence of their own interests.

Indeed, the concept of 'turf' seems to be one key to understanding Andropov's attitudes in this period. It helps to explain not only why some of his statements differed from Suslov's but also why what he was saying at that time occasionally contradicts what he has been saying more recently. As head of the Liaison Department Andropov's attitudes must have been determined by the adage that 'where you stand depends on where you sit'. His main concern would have been to protect his turf, minimising his department's problems while maximising the influence it wielded. Seen in this light, Andropov's concern to keep Eastern Europe happy by moving away from exploitative forms of control which could provoke rebellion and resentment would go along with his concern not to see China leave the socialist community, since that would lead to a loss of influence for his department. Later, when the disruptive pull of the conflict with China became so great that it threatened to undermine the Soviet Union's relations with its Eastern European neighbours, Andropov had less incentive to block the harder line against China for which Suslov, with his wider responsibilities for the whole world communist movement, had been pressing for some time.

Andropov's occasional differences with Suslov make it clear that he was never Suslov's protégé or mouthpiece. Indeed throughout his career, he was never any one man's man. The only person to whom he ever seems to have been seriously indebted politically was the colourful Finnish Communist, Otto Kuusinen who probably helped him to escape from serious trouble in 1950 (as described in Chapter 2). In June 1957, shortly after Andropov's return to Moscow, Khrushchev narrowly survived an attempt to unseat him as Party leader. The failure of the "anti-Party Group", as Khrushchev dubbed his opponents, led to a shake-up in the apparatus. Kuusinen returned to full membership of the Secretariat and the Presidium (as the Politburo was known at the time). His return cannot have failed to help Andropov. One other putative patron was Alexander Panyushkin, who was head of the Central

Committee's Department for Foreign Cadres, and is said to have recommended Andropov to head the Liaison Department[4].

In his new job Andropov's first assignment was to work on a new Soviet attempt to restore good relations with Yugoslavia. The break with Tito in 1948 had been bitter, but Khrushchev managed to surmount it two years after Stalin's death when he visited Belgrade in 1955 and apologised for the Soviet Union's earlier policy. The hopes aroused then were set back a year later with the Soviet Union's armed intervention in Hungary and Imre Nagy's escape to asylum in the Yugoslav embassy in Budapest. While Tito was seriously concerned about a possible counter-revolution in Hungary, he had advised the Kremlin to deal with the situation more cautiously. Nagy's departure from the Yugoslav embassy under an apparent safe-conduct and his immediate arrest was the last straw.

Suslov had played a major role in Stalin's original break with Tito and so he was not the best man to be closely involved in the new attempt at reconciliation which began soon after Andropov became head of the Liaison Department. Tito and Khrushchev met in Bucharest in August 1957. The Soviet side included Mikoyan, Ponomarev (the head of the International Department), Kuusinen and Andropov. The Yugoslav side included Kardelj and the Ambassador in Moscow, Veljko Micunovic. Both sides considered the meeting a success, though, as Micunovic reported in his diary, for different reasons: "To the Russians it appeared that they had again drawn Yugoslavia closer to the Soviet camp. To the Yugoslavs, on the other hand, it appeared as a reaffirmation that they were a factor in the situation when it came to the internal political struggle in the Soviet Union...and that Khrushchev would now put the policy of de-Stalinisation into practice with greater determination"[5]. Though Micunovic judged Soviet-Yugoslav relations to be on the upgrade again, he added that "this latest normalisation will probably not be the last nor will the conflict which preceded it"[6].

---

4. Ernst Volkman and Vladimir Sakharov, 'Yuri Andropov: the Spy who Came in from the Cold', *Penthouse*, March 1983.
5. Veljko Micunovic, *Moscow Diary*, tr. David Floyd, New York, Doubleday, 1980, p. 289.
6. Ibid.

Within a few months Yugoslavia was balking at adding her signature to the declaration which the Kremlin was preparing for the upcoming world conference of Communist Parties to be held in Moscow in November, 1957. Shortly before the meeting Ponomarev and Andropov went to Belgrade to try to persuade Tito to sign. They failed. He felt the Kremlin was trying to use the conference as an occasion to re-assert its claim to a dominant role in the world communist movement. Yugoslavia insisted on the independence and equality of each Socialist country and Party.

The conference also came close to provoking a public row with China. Sino-Soviet differences had begun to re-emerge in 1956, although the interests of the Soviet and Chinese Parties had never been identical and disputes between them date back at least to the mid-1920's. There was a logic to the development of their disagreements which suggested that the split was more or less inevitable from the beginning. Indeed, the normal state of relations between them has been one of suspicion and tension, a kind of Cold War. The period of relative harmony between 1953 and 1956 was a rare time of detente[7].

The new differences dated back to the Twentieth Congress of the CPSU in 1956 at which, in a secret speech, Khrushchev denounced Stalin's terror and the harmful consequences of the personality cult. In an open speech to the Congress, moreover, he announced a number of fundamental revisions of Soviet policy which were in the long run even more significant than what he had said in the secret speech. He stated that the Leninist theory of the inevitability of war between socialism and imperialism was no longer applicable in the era of nuclear weapons; that certain countries might make the revolutionary transition from capitalism to socialism by peaceful, even parliamentary means; and that it was up to each individual Party to decide on its own 'national road' to socialism.

These policy revisions pleased a number of Communist Parties, but Mao Zedong was appalled at Khrushchev's treatment of Stalin and profoundly angered by the fact that Khrushchev had made his pronouncements without any consultation with other Parties. In particular, Mao could not accept Khrushchev's assertion that war

7. For a fuller discussion of this point see Jonathan Steele, *World Power: Soviet Foreign Policy under Brezhnev and Andropov*, London, Michael Joseph, 1983, p. 133.

between capitalism and socialism was no longer essential for the world-wide triumph of socialism. Mao advocated a more assertive and revolutionary course of action, with more emphasis on helping wars of national liberation in the Third World. The Soviet leaders did not agree with the Chinese analysis of the world balance of power. They were more frightened of the danger of provoking a nuclear war between East and West – which they thought would be likely if the Communist countries followed assertive policies in the Third World – and they considered China's attitude to be dangerous, adventuristic, and irresponsible[8].

At first the Chinese went along with the Soviet line for the sake of maintaining a public appearance of unity. Mao attended the world conference of Communist Parties in Moscow in November, 1957 and signed the declaration even though it repeated that war was no longer inevitable. This was the only international meeting of Communists which he attended. Andropov was also there, though the Soviet media reveal no more than his protocol duties, such as escorting fraternal delegations, including the Chinese, on their arrival and departure.

The following years saw an intensification of the Sino-Soviet dispute, focused round two words, 'revisionism' and 'dogmatism'. Both were first used by Lenin as terms of abuse against political opponents. 'Dogmatism' describes an over-literal interpretation of Marxist theory, an unthinking insistence on the letter of Marx's texts and an inability to change with the times or adapt to new circumstances. 'Revisionism' implies too loose an interpretation of Marxist-Leninist ideas, watering down their revolutionary essence, in particular the concept of the dictatorship of the proletariat. The declaration signed at the end of the 1957 conference condemned both dogmatism and revisionism as dangerous trends in the communist movement. As a concession to Mao, revisionism was described as "the main danger at present", though the fact that the declaration represented a compromise could be seen from its statement that "dogmatism and sectarianism can also be the main

---

8. The following books contain useful discussions of the Sino-Soviet dispute: Edward Crankshaw, *The New Cold War: Moscow v. Peking*, Harmondsworth, Penguin, 1963; John Gittings, *Survey of the Sino-Soviet Dispute*, London, Oxford University Press, 1968; Gerald Segal, *The China Factor: Peking and the Superpowers*, London, Croom Helm, 1982.

danger at different phases of development in one Party or another"⁹.

In 1958 the Chinese launched a new economic policy, the so-called Great Leap Forward, which marked China's dissatisfaction not only with the Soviet model of development but also with the amount of Soviet economic aid. Khrushchev expressed doubts about the Great Leap from the beginning. On the surface unity was preserved and Andropov was, therefore, dutifully toeing the Soviet line when he wrote glowingly about the Great Leap Forward in *Pravda* in April 1959. The new policy, he assured his readers, "promises that China will outstrip the advanced capitalist countries, in particular England, in industrial production within the next fifteen years"[10]. Although he warned that acccount must be taken of national differences among Socialist states, he echoed Khrushchev's confident assertion that "the transition to communism of all the socialist countries in the near future is becoming ever more feasible". (Since those optimistic days both the Brezhnev and Andropov leaderships have stated that the transition to communism will not take years but generations. Andropov's wistful remark at the Central Committee meeting on June 15, 1983 that "the past two decades have enriched our idea of the world of socialism, and shown more vividly how diverse and complex it is....This is only natural, even if it seemed to us at one time that it would be more uniform"[11] seems to have been made with his earlier, more optimistic statement in mind.)

Khrushchev's decision to improve Soviet relations with the United States angered Mao. When it was announced in August 1959 that Khrushchev would visit the USA to confer with President Eisenhower, the Chinese concluded that the Soviet Union had rejected their warning against the "naive amateurishness of those who imagine that it is possible to lie down with imperialist lions"[12]. Khrushchev, on the other hand, saw his visit to the USA as a turning-point in Soviet history, public recognition that the USSR now ranked alongside the USA as a major power. He also wanted a

---

9. Cited in Jonathan Steele, *Eastern Europe since Stalin*, London, David and Charles, 1974, p. 91.
10. *Pravda*, April 24, 1959.
11. Ibid., June 16, 1983.
12. Peter Calvocoressi, *World Politics since 1945*, 3 edn, London, Longman, 1977, p. 68.

rapprochement with the United States because he saw the possibility of nuclear war as a real danger, to be avoided at all costs. The Chinese professed to see the United States as a "paper tiger".

Khrushchev went on to China immediately after his triumphant tour of the United States in September 1959. Andropov was a member of the Soviet delegation which preceded Khrushchev to Peking for talks with Mao. Khrushchev arrived directly from the United States and the Chinese felt he was throwing his policies of peaceful co-existence in their faces. The visit must have produced bitter discussions, for it had the almost unparalleled consequence of failing to produce a communique.

Whatever Andropov's personal feelings about the Chinese, at this stage he must have been eager to preserve peace and unity within his own domain, that is, the ruling Communist Parties which included the Chinese and the East Europeans. But the Sino-Soviet quarrel was beginning to disrupt Moscow's relations with Eastern Europe as well as the rest of the world communist movement. Khrushchev's handling of the dispute, and his insistence on enlisting other Parties' support, disturbed a number of ruling and non-ruling Party leaders who found themselves forced to take sides. This was disruptive to the whole movement. Moscow and Peking by this time had diametrically opposed views on world issues and relations between Communist Parties. The stage was rapidly approaching when compromise was no longer possible.

The CPSU found itself caught in the crossfire between the criticisms of the Yugoslavs on the right and the Chinese on the left. The Soviet leaders claimed to be holding the middle ground of Marxist-Leninist orthodoxy between these two extremes, assigning the charge of 'revisionism' to heresies of the right and 'dogmatism' to the Chinese. In May 1960 Andropov was co-author with Ponomarev and Fedor Konstantinov of an article in which they denounced Yugoslavia's domestic and foreign policies as "revisionist"[13].

In June 1960 the Sino-Soviet split burst out publicly at the congress of the Romanian Communist Party in Bucharest, and it dominated the world conference of eighty-one Parties held five

---

13. *Kommunist*, Moscow, No. 8, May 1960, pp. 24–8.

months later in Moscow. Andropov was active at both gatherings. Ponomarev and Andropov accompanied Khrushchev to Bucharest. The aim was to use the congress for preliminary discussions before the world conference planned for November. On the eve of the Bucharest meeting Ponomarev and Andropov circulated a "letter of information" among the other delegates, setting out the Soviet view of China's ideological errors. Ponomarev lobbied the ruling Party delegations and Andropov the non-ruling ones. They did their work well, for at a private meeting convened by the Soviet delegations Party leaders from all over the world denounced the Chinese positions – as they had heard them interpreted by Ponomarev and Andropov. Only the Albanians spoke in support of China. After the Chinese had retaliated with strong criticism of Moscow, Khrushchev launched a violent tirade in which he accused Mao in personal terms of being "an ultra-leftist, ultra-dogmatist, indeed a left revisionist...oblivious of any interests other than his own"[14].

The CPSU Central Committee (of which, it is important to note, Andropov was not yet a member, in spite of his responsible post) met in July 1960 and decided that, if the world communist conference did not resolve the dispute, an open breach would be declared. Though Andropov did not have a voice or vote in the decision, it is hard to imagine that he would have advised so drastic a step at this stage. It was in his interest to maintain his department's control over Sino-Soviet relations, which would have been lost if ties were cut. But he was still relatively junior. When bilateral talks – which turned out to be angry and unproductive – were held in Moscow in September 1960, the delegations were led respectively by Ponomarev and Deng Xiaoping. There is no record of Andropov's presence.

By now the battle of words was being matched by concrete actions. In August 1960 Khrushchev cut back on trade and withdrew all Soviet technicians from China, a typically impulsive and rash move. It was almost a repetition of Stalin's harsh actions against Yugoslavia in 1948. When the world conference of Communist Parties convened in November, there was little chance

---

14. Edward Crankshaw, *The New Cold War*, pp. 98, 104.

that it could repair the damage. All the old disagreements between Peking and Moscow were aired in the course of closed debates: the question of war and peace, the possibility of a peaceful transition from capitalism to socialism, revisionism versus dogmatism. A compromise statement was worked out but satisfied neither side. The Kremlin had a considerable majority of support, but not an overwhelming one, and the concluding statement merely repeated the assertion of the 1957 conference that dogmatism and sectarianism "might at some stage" become the main danger. China was not expelled.

The Albanian Party leader, Enver Hoxha, used the conference to make a fierce personal attack on Khrushchev, accusing him of trickery and stupidity. From then on the Albanians became for the Kremlin a symbol of the dispute with China, as the Yugoslavs were for the Chinese. Andropov was sent on a trouble-shooting mission to Albania in February 1961. He represented the Soviet Union at the congress of the Albanian Party of Labour in Tirana, but his attempt to bring China's main ally back into the Soviet camp was unsuccessful. Criticism of Stalin, who was still revered by the Chinese and Albanians, was reaching a height in Moscow. The Twenty-Second Congress of the CPSU, held in October 1961, was the most outspokenly anti-Stalinist that the CPSU has ever held. It culminated in the removal of Stalin's embalmed body from the mausoleum in Red Square.

It was at this congress that Andropov received the honour of being elected to full membership in the Central Committee. A few weeks later he published an article in *Pravda* in which he condemned the Albanians for the cult of personality of Enver Hoxha, the Party leader, and Mehmet Shehu, the Prime Minister, and for supporting Stalin's personality cult[15]. This was a coded way of attacking the Chinese and Mao's personality cult, but Andropov also took the opportunity to say something else that was perhaps more interesting. He attacked Vyacheslav Molotov, one of Stalin's most loyal lieutenants. A number of other speakers at the congress had criticised Molotov and other members of the "anti-Party Group" for opposing de-Stalinisation. The polemics, of course, had

---

15. Ibid., pp. 104–6.

little to do with Molotov, who had been in disgrace for several years. They were really part of the confrontation going on not only in the Soviet leadership but throughout Soviet society between those pressing for greater liberalisation and those who wanted to reverse the process. Andropov used Molotov as a whipping-boy, charging him with "juggling Stalinist formulas" and offending Eastern Europeans by trampling on "their socialist patriotism, the love of each people for its homeland"[16].

One analyst has suggested that Andropov was expressing reluctance to press for too much political and economic integration within the Socialist block[17]. It is certainly true that Khrushchev was preparing a proposal for a supranational central planning system for Eastern Europe with powers to direct investment in individual countries in the region. Andropov may have disagreed with it. The plan had to be abandoned after strong Romanian objections. It has been assumed here that Andropov wanted to run Eastern Europe on a light rein not merely because he realised after his own experience in Hungary that exploitative Stalinist methods were no longer productive, but also because he wished to avoid conflict within his own area. If this is correct, then Andropov's position of December 1961 makes political sense. (In 1983, as General Secretary, Andropov has argued for greater integration within Eastern Europe's trading block, the Council for Mutual Economic Assistance, Comecon, though not on the same lines as Khrushchev's 1962 proposal[18]. The Romanians are still uneasy, as are the Hungarians.)

The dispute with China was still worsening. In a speech in February 1962 Suslov implied that dogmatism, personified by China, had replaced revisionism as the main danger to the unity of the world communist movement. "Dogmatism", he said, "is the most dangerous form of the isolation of theory from practice"[19]. Andropov echoed Suslov's lead in future pronouncements. He was elected a delegate to the Council of the Union, one of two chambers of the USSR Supreme Soviet (theoretically the chief legislative

---

16. *Pravda*, December 2, 1961.
17. Sidney Ploss, in *Problems of Communism*, September–October, 1982, p. 47.
18. See Andropov's speech to the Central Committee, *Pravda*, June 16, 1983.
19. *Pravda*, February 4, 1962.

authority, or parliament) in March 1962. At a session of the Supreme Soviet a month later he was elected a member of its International Affairs Committee. Since the committee chairman was Suslov, the two men must have been on good terms at this stage. Otherwise Suslov would surely have been able to block his appointment.

Several Soviet actions irritated China in 1962. Moscow observed a studied neutrality in the border war between China and India. In August it announced that it had given a positive reply to an American proposal on non-proliferation of nuclear weapons, in effect confirming that the Soviet Union would not co-operate with China on nuclear technology. The Kremlin made another effort to improve relations with Yugoslavia, long the focus of Chinese taunts of 'revisionism'. Andropov accompanied the new Soviet President, Leonid Brezhnev, on a visit to Yugoslavia in September. In October Khrushchev's conduct of the Cuban missile crisis infuriated Mao.

The Cuban crisis also caused disquiet in the Kremlin. A number of conservatives took the opportunity to assert their advantage and push forward on the issue of re-Stalinisation. Opposition to Khrushchev's liberalisation began to gather strength. In November Andropov was one of four men elected to the Central Committee Secretariat, bringing the numbers up to twelve. All four new members were younger Party technocrats from the Central Committee apparatus, and their promotion appears to have been intended by Khrushchev to strengthen his position. If so, this would be further confirmation of Andropov's role as a supporter of de-Stalinisation against the conservatives.

As a Secretary, Andropov would have attended the Secretariat's weekly meetings and had a far greater say in the foreign policy-making process. He also began to play a more important part in official engagements. He acted as the leader of a CPSU delegation for the first time in January 1963 when he visited Hanoi and was received by Ho Chi Minh. He also attended a wide range of public functions in the spheres of art and literature, and took part in military celebrations – an indication that he had attained a greater degree of authority and prestige in the leadership.

The signing of the Nuclear Test Ban Treaty by the Soviet Union, the United States, and the United Kingdom in August 1963 led to a new round of polemics with China. Since 1962 Mao had been asking for a new world conference of Communist Parties to thrash out their differences. Initially the Soviet Union blocked the proposal but by late 1963 the Kremlin changed its mind. Suslov had decided to use the conference to isolate China once and for all. The time had come to expel them, he argued. Throughout this period Suslov was the main protagonist in the ideological conflict with China, editing all communications sent to the Chinese by the CPSU. A new set of talks between Chinese and Soviet Party delegations opened in Moscow on July 5, 1963. Suslov led the Soviet side, which included Ponomarev and Andropov. Deng Xiaoping headed the Chinese team. After two weeks the talks were adjourned indefinitely without any agreement. The Russians now felt closer to Yugoslavia. From August 20 to September 4 Andropov accompanied Khrushchev to Yugoslavia – ostensibly on holiday. Khrushchev was determined to go ahead with the visit, even though it was likely to lead to a further deterioration in relations with China.

Variations between Suslov's and Andropov's approaches to China can be seen clearly at this time. Suslov made the main speech at a meeting of the Central Committee in February 1964. In it he publicly launched his controversial effort to convene a world conference of Communist Parties to isolate the Chinese, and predicted a serious and "prolonged" struggle with Peking. His speech was the most comprehensive and outspoken attack on the Chinese ever made for public consumption. Publication was in fact delayed for two months until April 3. Thus when Andropov was chosen for the signal honour of delivering the keynote speech at the Kremlin celebrations of Lenin's birthday on April 22, his speech was significant, not only because it was his most important public address so far and an unmistakable sign of his growing influence as a member of the Secretariat, but also because of the different nuances of his approach to the Chinese question from that of Suslov[20].

Andropov took a more conciliatory line. He described the dispute in pointedly less stark and permanent terms. While denouncing the divisive activities of the Chinese, he referred to Sino-Soviet

20. *Pravda*, April 23, 1964.

differences as "temporary" (in contrast to Suslov's "prolonged") and insisted that they could and would be overcome. He sidestepped the issue of the world communist conference, mocking the notion that Moscow wanted to expel China from the movement and stressing that the CPSU "has regarded and still regards" the People's Republic of China as a socialist state[21]. Andropov also emphasised the Soviet fear of war and hinted at the Kremlin's apprehension lest China drag it into war with the United States. Andropov ridiculed Mao's claim that "in the event of a major world crisis" the USSR would be bound to stand by China if China became involved in hostilities with another power. On this point Andropov appeared to be giving a signal to the United States. This was a tendency repeated in the 1970's when Andropov again seemed somewhat more vocal than other Soviet leaders in supporting detente and an improvement of relations with the United States.

Andropov was otherwise careful in his Lenin Anniversary speech to stick to the prevailing line. He denounced both "petty-bourgeois reformism" and "petty-bourgeois revolutionism" (that is, revisionism and dogmatism), coming down hardest against "dogmatic, sectarian positions" and ridiculing those who "seek to intimidate others with the scarecrow of revisionism". The Marxist-Leninist Parties, he said, "defeated revisionism ideologically and politically some years ago. Now, the left-wing opportunism and nationalism of the Chinese leaders are increasingly coming to the fore as a serious danger to the world communist movement".

Andropov again avoided the issue of Chinese expulsion when he led the Soviet delegation to East Berlin in September 1964 for centenary celebrations of the founding of the First International. He stressed in his speech that despite the danger presented by China's divisive activities "the world communist movement will successfully overcome the present differences of opinion among individual Parties"[22]. He called for a united front, suggesting that whatever differences Parties might have over tactics they should remain together on their larger strategic goal, the defeat of imperialism. The speech reflected Andropov's unwillingness to rock

21. Ibid.
22. Yuri Andropov, *Selected Speeches and Articles*, Moscow, Politizdat, 1979, pp. 91–107.

the boat unduly by forcing Parties to choose sides, thus complicating life for his department.

The speech also reflected something of Andropov's approach to Eastern Europe during his decade as head of the Liaison Department. Not only is he credited with having tolerated the introduction of successful economic reforms in Hungary but his junior officials are also reported to have reacted calmly to the growth of 'revisionist' ideas in Czechoslovakia in the early and mid-1960's. At that time intellectuals in the Czechoslovak Academy of Sciences and the Party itself were cautiously developing a wide range of reformist views. They eventually concluded that Czechoslovakia needed to allow different interest groups to operate politically. The country should import Western technology on a large scale and institute a radical economic reform. Czechoslovak officials who had contact with Andropov's department were warned not to carry this thinking too far. Nevertheless under Andropov's direction the Liaison Department did not panic at the new ideas coming from Czechoslovakia. It was only after Dubcek came to power in 1968 and reformist ideas began to win widespread support in the Party and the media in Czechoslovakia that the Kremlin stepped in. By then Andropov had left the Liaison Department for the KGB.

Khrushchev's removal from power in October 1964 led to a new Kremlin attempt to achieve a reconciliation with China. Many mistakes had contributed to Khrushchev's downfall. What seems to have annoyed his colleagues most of all were his idiosyncratic ways, his 'hare-brained schemes' for changes in agriculture and industry, his arbitrariness, his impetuosity, and his failure to consult with others. The humiliation suffered by the Soviet Union over the Cuban missile crisis when Moscow was forced into an embarrassing retreat was a factor, as was Khrushchev's hint of a possible deal with West Germany at the expense of the East.

Soviet relations with China, however, were not a major factor. Although the new leadership in the Kremlin as well as the Chinese thought that Khrushchev's departure at least provided the occasion for a new start, the depth of the conflict between the two sides was too great. Brezhnev and his colleagues delayed plans for a new world conference of Communist Parties and halted anti-Chinese propaganda for a while. Zhou Enlai came to Moscow for the anniversary of the October Revolution. The Russians proposed a summit meeting with Mao and offered to resume scientific and cultural co-operation and trade. But this was not enough to change Mao's mind. The most dramatic symbol of the problem had come by coincidence on the day that Khrushchev was ousted. China exploded its first atomic bomb. This was proof, if any were needed, that China was a great power, and that, unless the Kremlin recognised it as such and treated it with parity, there could be no lasting basis for Sino-Soviet relations. A new issue had also come up – the escalating United States involvement in Vietnam. Andropov accompanied the Soviet Prime Minister, Alexei Kosygin, to Hanoi and Peking in February 1965 in an attempt to create a united front in defence of North Vietnam but the talks failed. This was the last serious effort to find a *modus vivendi* between the Soviet Union and China for more than ten years. From then on the relationship deteriorated, and by the end of 1965 the Kremlin had embarked on a massive military escalation of its troop strengths on their common frontier. China's Cultural Revolution also began to absorb the Chinese leadership's energies and reduced the chances of any moves on the diplomatic front.

Khrushchev's downfall had no impact on Andropov's position in the hierarchy. Although he was identified as a supporter of de-Stalinisation, he was never close enough to Khrushchev to be endangered by the plot against him. Andropov had also always been careful to keep himself one step removed from any direct association with the creative intelligentsia which was pressing hardest for liberalisation. Andropov's contacts with intellectuals were confined to the progressive wing of the Party and to people whose loyalty to the system could not seriously be called into question. They were intelligent technocrats, journalists, and academics working in political science or foreign policy rather than 'liberals'. In respecting their opinions and making use of their advice Andropov was unusual. Most other Party leaders who, like him, had not enjoyed the advantage of an advanced education, showed the suspicion of intellectuals which is common among self-made men.

Andropov was different, but not unique. His use of expert consultants in his Liaison Department was one of the innovations he picked up from his old mentor, Otto Kuusinen. When Kuusinen returned to the Secretariat in 1957 he put together a small private staff of advisers who reported purely to him. Kuusinen was an old Bolshevik with a long career of service to the Party, described by one Western analyst as "a reformist, non-dogmatic ideologist who served as a counterpoint to the more conservative Suslov"[23]. As the first head of his group of consultants Kuusinen appointed a 30-year-old intellectual, Fedor Burlatsky. Burlatsky has been one of the Soviet Establishment's leading thinkers ever since, often in the role of a gadfly. But his outspoken advocacy of democratisation has also frequently brought him into trouble. He is credited with having invented the definition of the Soviet Union as a "state of the whole people", a term which Khrushchev picked up, implying that class contradictions had faded away and that the internal, political management of Soviet society could therefore relax. He was also the first writer to use the phrase "developed socialism" in print. This was another key concept which rationalised the Soviet Union's potential for moving away from Stalinism and a system of terror.

When Andropov inherited the group of consultants on Kuusinen's death in May 1964, he did not keep Burlatsky long. Burlatsky moved to become a political commentator on *Pravda*. Whether this counted as a promotion or whether Andropov thought that Burlatsky was too risky an adviser to have on his staff is not clear. At all events, he appointed in his place Georgy Arbatov who, like Burlatsky, had been working on Kuusinen's staff since 1957. Arbatov was a strong advocate of US-Soviet detente in the early and mid-1950's. Shortly before Andropov moved to the KGB in 1967, Arbatov became the first head of the newly created Institute of the USA (later re-named Institute of the USA and Canada), a think-tank set up to analyse American politics. Arbatov still heads the institute (where Andropov's son, Igor, was once employed).

The last head of the group of consultants was Alexander Bovin, a huge, roly-poly man with a sharp mind, whom Andropov appointed to his Liaison Department staff in 1963 before giving him Arbatov's post four years later. Bovin accompanied Andropov to East Berlin

---

23. Jerry Hough, 'The KGB Boss might make a Reform-minded Liberal', *International Herald Tribune*, May 31, 1983.

in 1964 and to Peking in 1965. Other intellectuals who worked with Andropov at this time were L.P. Delyusin, a former *Pravda* correspondent in Peking (now Director of the China Department at the Institute of Oriental Studies) who was well-known for his optimistic assessments of the potential for change in China[24], and the economist Oleg Bogomolov (now Director of the Institute of the Economics of the World Socialist System) who has recently advocated the introduction into the Soviet economic system of those reforms which have proved their worth in Eastern Europe[25].

These men all had a reformist and undogmatic cast of mind. As consultants they helped to prepare papers, draft policy, and assist with their boss's ideological writings. It is primarily through them that Andropov had links with other progressives. Zhores Medvedev reports that Andropov took an interest in the row over the Stalinist geneticist, T.D. Lysenko, who was still dominant in 1963 and 1964[26]. Lysenko's theories cast a blight over large parts of Soviet scientific research, and Andropov was said to be against him in spite of the favour Lysenko still enjoyed with Khrushchev. Andropov had to mediate between the Soviet and Czechoslovak leaderships when the Czech Academy of Sciences wanted to reopen a museum for Gregor Mendel, one of the targets of Lysenko's criticism. Medvedev also credits Andropov with recommending the promotion of a talented and independent-minded journalist, Alexei Rumyantsev, from being Editor of the international journal, *Problems of Peace and Socialism* to become Chief Editor of *Pravda* after Khrushchev's downfall[27].

But Andropov was careful not to go too far out on a limb. He did not prevent Rumyantsev's dismissal in September 1965 after Rumyantsev wrote an unusually liberal article on "the Party and the Intelligentsia" with the assistance of another progressive journalist, Yuri Karyakin, who was a friend of the writer, Alexander Solzhenitsyn. Solzhenitsyn has described how Karyakin saved a copy of his novel, *The First Circle*, from destruction by the KGB[28].

24. *The Guardian*, March 22, 1983.
25. *Pravda*, November 23, 1982.
26. Zhores Medvedev, *Andropov*, Oxford, Basil Blackwell, 1983.
27. Ibid., p. 47.
28. Alexander Solzhenitsyn, *The Oak and the Calf*, London, Collins and Harvill Press, 1980, p. 102.

Medvedev, who was himself active in these progressive circles at the time, reports one other clue to Andropov's links with these groups. In February 1966 a prominent journalist, Semyon Rostovsky (better known as Ernst Henry), wrote an appeal against re-Stalinisation, which he addressed to the Twenty-Third Congress of the CPSU. Several prominent figures from the arts and sciences signed it, including the ballerina Maya Piisetskaya, the nuclear physicist Andrei Sakharov, the former diplomat and Ambassador in London Ivan Maisky, the scientist Pyotr Kapitsa, and the mathematician Igor Tamm. According to Medvedev,

> Henry had no difficulty in persuading people to sign the letter since he claimed to be taking the step on behalf of influential anti-Stalinist Central Committee members whose position at the congress would be strengthened if the major figures of Soviet art and science expressed themselves against re-Stalinisation. Andropov was one of the 'unofficial sponsors' claimed by Ernst Henry, and junior employees in his department tried, in a discreet way, to confirm this.[29]

The appeal had only a limited effect in restraining the return to tougher controls on intellectuals. Later in the year Moscow's intellectual community was shocked by the heavy sentences passed on two writers, Andrei Sinyavsky and Yuli Daniel. Liberal magazines like *Novy Mir* and *Yunnost* came under pressure. Solzhenitsyn began to realise that no more of his works were ever likely to be published in the Soviet Union. The increasing pressures began to turn more and more intellectuals into potential, and later active, dissidents as their hopes for permanent liberalisation faded.

Andropov's link with these intellectuals had been tenous at most. Clearly there were contacts between the creative intelligentsia and the progressive wing of the Central Committee apparatus with its various institutes and think-tanks. Marriage, family ties, and professional association obviously meant that people from the different tendencies knew each other as friends or acquaintances.

---

29. Zhores Medvedev, *Andropov*, p. 52.

Many were children of Stalin's labour camp victims or had suffered themselves.

Andropov ensured that he remained aloof from the most outspoken or critical of them. If one can speak of a political continuum stretching from the reformist edge of the Central Committee to the angry non-Party writers like Solzhenitsyn, Andropov kept himself well to the Party end of it. The irony was that in his next job he would have a great deal to do with those unhappy intellectuals.

5
Crushing Dissent 1967-82

Andropov's appointment as head of the Committee for State Security (Komitet Gosudarstvennoi Bezopastnosti – KGB) in May 1967 was not at first sight a promotion. As a Secretary of the Central Committee he was higher in rank than the chairman of the KGB, however important the KGB's role clearly is. Now suddenly at the age of 53 he appeared to be stepping sideways.

In fact Andropov may well have welcomed the change. Since China's break with the Soviet Union, his Liaison Department in the Central Committee had lost a major part of its responsibilities. Its other main component, Eastern Europe, was quiet in the mid-1960's and Andropov could have imagined that the KGB job, at a time when internal dissent was on the increase, would provide a more interesting challenge, as well as giving him useful new experience.

What is certain is that the switch to the KGB did not mean he was in any way in disfavour. Rather, it resulted from the continuing manoeuvrings in the Kremlin since Khrushchev's overthrow, in particular Brezhnev's determination to undermine Alexander Shelepin, the principal rival he had to deal with since taking over as First Party Secretary in October 1964. Shelepin was a young Party official from the Ukraine whom Khrushchev had appointed KGB chairman in 1958. Three years later he was promoted to become the Secretary of the Central Committee with responsibility for the police, the KGB, and the Committee of State and Party Control, and his KGB job was given to another young Ukrainian, Vladimir Semichastny.

With Khrushchev out, Brezhnev wanted to remove Shelepin and Semichastny as well, and in the spring of 1967 he succeeded. In

May, while Shelepin was absent from the Politburo for an appendix operation, his protégé, Semichastny, was sacked from the KGB. The following month it was Shelepin's turn. He was ousted from the Secretariat and given the – in Kremlin terms – unimportant job of chairman of the trade unions.

Why was Andropov chosen to succeed Semichastny? At its most negative, almost anyone could have done better than Semichastny. Even before he became head of the KGB he had been notorious for crude remarks made about the writer Boris Pasternak after *Doctor Zhivago* was published abroad – "even a pig does not shit where it eats"[1]. In 1966 he had mishandled the trial of the writers, Andrei Sinyavsky and Yuli Daniel, which had turned into a widely-publicised international event causing great damage to the Soviet image. In March 1967 he was embarrased by the defection of Svetlana Alliluyeva, only daughter of Stalin, who approached the American Embassy in New Delhi for asylum. She had been allowed to leave the Soviet Union a few months earlier to take her late husband's ashes to his native India for burial. Not only had the KGB blundered in approving her trip but its surveillance experts had let her elude them. After a six-week stay at secluded spots in Switzerland while the KGB vainly sought to find her, Svetlana flew to New York on April 21 and announced she was "seeking the self-expression that was denied me for so long in Russia". She also said she planned to write a book about her life in the Soviet Union, an alarming prospect for the already enraged Politburo[2].

It can hardly be imagined, of course, that Semichastny would have taken the decision on his own to try Sinyavsky and Daniel and allow Svetlana to go abroad. He must have required Shelepin's approval, and probably that of the Politburo as a whole. But he and Shelepin became convenient scapegoats for the damage which ensued. At some point after Khrushcehv's overthrow Brezhnev was bound to want to put his own man into a job as sensitive as the KGB.

The KGB is the largest police and security apparatus in the world, with a staff of perhaps half a million employees. It is

1. Zhores Medvedev, *Andropov*, Oxford, Basil Blackwell, 1983, p. 55.
2. *Facts on File*, New York, 1967.

responsible for the Soviet Union's espionage and intelligence operations abroad. It has its own force of uniformed border guards, and it also looks after domestic security with a vast network of paid agents and part-time informers who keep watch on Party members and ordinary citizens alike.

The choice of Andropov to replace Semichastny was a clear sign that Brezhnev felt confident of his loyalty. He had no ties to Shelepin. He was a senior Party figure who could be relied upon to maintain the KGB under tight Party control and not try to turn it into a private empire, as Stalin's police chief, Beria, had done. He was an intelligent man with some understanding of the issues involved. In Karelia he had had to deal with the difficult security problems of re-incorporating enemy-occupied territory into Soviet control, giving him experience of police and intelligence work. In Hungary he had been associated with similar tasks, although not in a directly supervisory role. As for foreign affairs in general, he had acquired considerable experience during his ten years in the Central Committee.

A month after his shift to the KGB, Andropov was awarded with a seat on the Politburo as a non-voting or candidate member, a sign that his move out of the Secretariat of the Central Committee was not intended as a demotion. It left him answerable to Brezhnev and the rest of the Politburo. With Shelepin's removal, the Administrative Organs Department of the Central Committee which oversees the KGB came under Brezhnev's control as First Party Secretary[3]. Andropov signalled early on in his KGB post that he understood the role required of him. In a keynote speech for the fiftieth anniversary of the security organs on December 20, 1967 Andropov stressed that they had no right to forget the times when "political adventurists" tried to wrench the state security bodies out of Party control[4]. Party control had now been firmly re-established, he declared. On the question of dissidents, Andropov emphasised the KGB's role "in convincing and educating those who commit politically harmful actions".

---

3. In 1968 Nikolai Savinkin, First Deputy Head of the Administrative Organs Department was promoted to head it. Savinkin served with Brezhnev in the Red Army in the Transbaikal region in 1935-6.
4. *Pravda*, December 21, 1967.

The speech put Andropov on the moderate side of the debate in the Politburo over how to handle the apparently growing problem of political opposition. His appointment was cautiously welcomed even in dissident circles as "a victory for enlightenment", according to one experienced Western observer[5].

This was going a bit too far. Marxist-Leninist ideology, as practised in the Soviet Union, contains a strong element of paternalism, in which people who do not accept Party policy are often assumed to be acting out of some individual failing – false consciousness, out-dated pre-revolutionary thinking, or even some psychological delusion. As they grow up to be Soviet citizens, individuals are supposed to be cured of any tendency towards these failings by the combined effect of exposure to the Pioneer and Komsomol organisations, the education system and the officially-controlled media. If they still persist, then the first line of resort is discussion and persuasion. Only at a later stage do sanctions and punishment come in. Andropov is one of those who believes in at least giving the first line of resort a try. This hardly makes him a liberal, merely a paternalist. There seems to be no place in his way of thinking for the notion that other people's value systems may be as legitimate as his own. His use of intellectuals in his time as a Secretary of the Central Committee grew out of his interest in having intelligent and sophisticated advice, provided it remained within his terms of reference.

Ten years after taking over the KGB he made another important speech on security issues, this time on the occasion of the centenary of the birth of Felix Dzerzhinksy, the founder of the Cheka, the forerunner of the KGB. "Some Western figures invite us to explain what they think is an embarrassing question", he said,

> Why are there 'dissidents' in the USSR after sixty years of Soviet government? This question is embarrassing only at first glance. It would be unrealistic to imagine that among the Soviet population of over 250 million there are no individuals thinking differently from the vast majority on some specific issues. We know from statements by Marx and Engels and

---

5. Edward Crankshaw, *The Observer*, May 21, 1967.

from real life that the moulding of the new man requires much time and effort, even more than is taken by deep-going socio-economic transformations. Moreover, the moulding of the new man in the socialist countries is taking place not in a vacuum but in conditions of a stiffening ideological and political struggle in the international arena. Comparing the sixty-year record of the new life with the thousand-year-old tradition of private ownership psychology and morals, one need not be surprised to discover occasionally in Soviet society individuals who are at odds with the collectivist principles of socialism. Such individuals, however, are dwindling in number and we have every reason to regard this as a great success.

Was it not conclusive evidence of the unity of Soviet society that practically 100 per cent of the electorate voted for Party policy?, he went on.

But this does not mean that developed socialist society is guaranteed against the appearance of individuals whose actions are incompatible with either the legal or moral norms of Soviet society. The reasons for this are various: political or ideological delusions, religious fanaticism, nationalistic obsessions, resentment caused by personal offence or lack of success which is interpreted as other people's failure to appreciate one's abilities, and even in some cases mental imbalance.... In Soviet society, deluded individuals are helped through persuasion to correct their mistakes. Different measures are required when some of the so-called dissidents commit acts infringing Soviet laws[6].

The continuum which runs from "persuasion" to "different measures" has been well described by Peter Reddaway, one of the West's leading experts on Soviet dissent. The first issue for the authorities is to see whether the grievances are, in their eyes, legitimate and manageable.

---

6. *Pravda*, September 10, 1967.

Crushing Dissent 1967-82

Where discontent appears, the first line of defence is the officials most directly involved – those at the work place or, one level higher, in the local soviet. These are repeatedly enjoined by the regime to deal promptly and fairly with citizens' legitimate grievances. Clearly the leaders of an authoritarian system have an even stronger incentive than those of a pluralistic one to see grievances settled on a bilateral basis between individual and officials. In this way the illegitimate (under authoritarian rule) and potentially dangerous development of aggrieved individuals forming groups can be averted[7].

If the officials fail to satisfy the complainant, and his or her protest takes on a faintly political hue, the KGB steps in from the office it has in every work-place. At first its approach is that of the stern but friendly uncle. But if the protester persists, it escalates by stages to a mixture of cajoling and threats, then to demotion and dismissal from work, sometimes to physical attacks, then to formal warnings, arrest, pressure for a recantation in court, then to imprisonment, exile or psychiatric internment with, sometimes, vilification in the press and, finally further pressure to recant during imprisonment. If the dissenter fails to reform, he or she is subject on release to severe restrictions on his movements and place of residence, or is re-sentenced on some pretext before the term expires.

Reddaway says that under Andropov, at least until 1979, the KGB's standing orders included the instruction to avoid making political arrests, if at all possible. Numerous dissident sources show the pattern of escalation mentioned above, and some report KGB officials as describing the resort to arrest as evidence of their own failure. There seems no reason to doubt the truth of these statements, he says[8]. Arrests risk creating martyrs and undesirable publicity.

---

7. Peter Reddaway, 'Policy towards Dissent since Krushchev', in *Authority, Power and Policy in the USSR*, ed. T.H. Rigby, Archie Brown and Peter Reddaway, London, Macmillan, 1980. p. 160.
8. Ibid., p. 161.

While this system of gradual escalation was designed as the ideal code of KGB conduct, in practice it worked out considerably less tidily. KGB tactics chopped and changed, depending on the determination of the dissidents, the amount of foreign interest in the general issue and particular cases, the climate of East-West relations as a whole, and differences of view within the Politburo.

When Andropov took over the KGB, it was already clear that Kremlin policy on the dissident issue was uncertain. Khrushchev had made a major break with Stalinist policy by releasing almost ten million political detainees from prisons and camps[9]. But in the later stages of his rule Khrushchev had started campaigns against religion and "bourgeois nationalism", moves which provoked considerable opposition. At the same time the limits he set to de-Stalinisation caused discontent among intellectuals and old Bolsheviks. They were grateful for Khrushchev's practical measures and for his denunciation of the dead dictator but they wanted to prevent any repetition of the Stalinist past by means of a thorough and continuing examination of its deeper causes.

After Khrushchev's removal, the new leadership halted all arrests for a period of almost nine months. Crude anti-religious propaganda stopped and almost half the nearly 200 Baptists in captivity were released. Delegations of Crimean Tatars, representing a people who had been deported from their traditional homeland by Stalin and now wanted to return, were received by high Party officials in Moscow.

In September 1965 the trend was partly reversed with the confiscation of an archive from the writer Alexander Solzhenitsyn and the arrest of Sinyavsky and Daniel. Tougher laws were brought in against religious dissidents. In February 1966 the KGB revived a practice which had been common in the pre-war period, the despatch of troublesome citizens into exile abroad. Valery Tarsis had won attention by having an exposé of psychiatric abuse, *Ward 7*, published in the West. The stir caused by the book made it awkward for the KGB to arrest him. Tarsis exploited his fame and apparent immunity by developing a practice, unprecedented for a dissident, of holding press conferences for Western reporters in his

---

9. Peter Reddaway in *Authority, Power and Policy in the USSR*, p. 160.

Moscow apartment. A few months later he was allowed to make a trip abroad, but promptly had his citizenship rescinded to prevent him from returning. In January 1967 there was an increase in the arrests of intellectuals, though care was taken to select either young and unestablished figures or people outside Moscow with little access to Western correspondents.

It is important to stress that nearly all the methods which the KGB was to use during the fifteen years that Andropov was its head were devised before he got there. The use of psychiatric hospitals, forced emigration or expulsion, and a careful effort to avoid Western publicity, if at all possible, were already being practised before May 1967. Any suggestion that Andropov was unusually inventive in finding new methods is therefore wide of the mark. Even the decision to avoid political trials in the future, whenever possible, after the fiasco of the Sinyavsky-Daniel experience was already prepared by the time Andropov took over. The two writers had been prosecuted under Article 70 of the Criminal Code which covers "anti-Soviet agitation and propaganda". The prosecution had to prove that the accused "*intended*" to weaken or undermine Soviet power or to engage in dangerous crimes against the state by distributing, preparing, or accumulating slanderous, anti-Soviet literature. Defendants could argue that they had no such intent. To avoid this difficulty, the Supreme Soviet at the end of 1966 adopted an amendment, Article 190-1 of the Criminal Code, which made the mere distribution in oral, hand-written, or printed form of any false information about the Soviet state a punishable offence. While removing the issue of intent, even this wording still left some vagueness, particularly over the definition of the word "*false*". Dissidents who simply reported information about the arrest or persecution of their friends and colleagues were able to argue that none of it was false. As Zhores Medvedev has written, "Article 190-1 did not put an end to dissent. On the contrary, it had the effect of making dissent more efficient, by making it concentrate on facts, figures, and verifiable information, rather than on rumour or generalities"[10].

Andropov's contribution at the KGB was not that he radically altered previous methods of handling dissent. Rather it was that he

---

10. Zhores Medvedev, *Andropov*, p. 73.

operated the system somewhat more smoothly than his predecessor. He also developed a few new techniques. As part of the drive to pressurise dissidents short of arrest, the KGB under Andropov would sometimes draft them into the army, block university entrance, blacklist them for foreign trips, and force new graduates to take jobs in remote and unpleasant parts of the country. There were suggestions, though they remain unproven, that after 1976 the KGB began to resort to political murders in a few cases. In an interview with a Norwegian journalist in October 1976, Academician Andrei Sakharov mentioned five dissidents who died in mysterious circumstances[11].

The KGB also extended the existing concept of committing dissidents to psychiatric hospitals, and made much more use of forced emigration. Both methods avoided putting dissidents on trial. The expulsion of the writer Valery Tarsis in February 1966 had been in a sense an experiment. Once abroad, Tarsis had gradually faded out of the limelight and the Kremlin may have felt the experiment had succeeded.

Psychiatric incarceration was a particularly vicious technique. The human rights organisation, Amnesty International, said in March 1983 that 313 people were known to have been forcibly confined to Soviet psychiatric hospitals since 1969, although the real total was thought to be much higher[12]. An explanatory annex to a European Parliament resolution passed in May 1983 called it "the darkest side of the Soviet authorities' treatment of political dissenters....Dissidents are made aware that confinement to a mental hospital is the KGB's ultimate weapon and that once confined, although perfectly sane, they will be treated with drugs that cause damage to health as well as intense pain"[13].

It is important, however, not to exaggerate the KGB's role or Andropov's position as an independent decision-maker on the issue of dissidents. It is, for example, the Ministry of Internal Affairs (MVD) and not the KGB which runs the Soviet Union's vast

11. *A Chronicle of Current Events*, London, Amnesty International, No. 44.
12. Amnesty International, *Political Abuse of Psychiatry in the USSR*, London, Amnesty International, March 1983.
13. European Parliament Document. 1-1364/82, May 11, 1983.

network of camps, prisons, and psychiatric hospitals. Andropov was not directly responsible for the appalling conditions in them. Although the KGB operates some prisons for interrogating pre-trial detainees such as Lefortovo in Moscow, it is primarily a security and police apparatus and not a penal empire. It is also clear that major decisions affecting dissidents would have been taken by the Politburo as a whole, or, if time was short or the matter was not considered important enough, after consultation with Brezhnev. Andropov was not an independent agent. The decision in early 1971 to open the doors to massive Jewish emigration must have been taken by the Politburo. Similarly, the precedent-setting decision to swap a Soviet political prisoner, Vladimir Bukovsky, for a foreign detainee, the Chilean Communist Party leader, Luis Corvalan, in 1976 cannot have been made by Andropov alone.

Although Andropov was aware of the departmental concerns of his KGB professional staff, he remained primarily a Party man throughout his KGB period. When dissent issues were discussed in the Politburo, Andropov continued to see them in the broad perspective of Kremlin strategy (the repercussions on foreign policy etc.) rather than in the narrower context of the KGB, which can safely be assumed to have tended to push for a hard line. As proof of Andropov's Party orientation, one can cite the generally moderate line of the KGB during his fifteen-year rule in spite of the pressures from inside the organisation for something tougher. Andropov drafted local Party people into the organisation at all levels except the lowest, a policy which the professionals resented. Finally, there is the evidence of the support and approval which he gained from Brezhnev for his stewardship of the KGB. His promotion to full voting membership of the Politburo in 1973 was followed by his selection as the keynote speaker for the traditional Lenin Anniversary meeting in April 1976, the first time since at least 1961 that this had been delivered by someone who was not a Party Secretary. His speech was very 'Party-orientated'. He made no mention of dissidence, as an exclusively KGB-minded man might have done. In fact he talked about protecting Soviet citizens from "callousness and incivility, red tape and arrogance on the part of certain officials". He came out strongly in favour of detente, even pointing out that detente meant a widening of cultural ties, and more contact with the world outside the Soviet Union[14]. (The fact that the Soviet Union did not subsequently honour its detente commitments is not the issue here. A KGB chief who was less of a generalist than Andropov would have been less likely even to make the rhetorical point.)

Four months after the Lenin speech Brezhnev had Andropov promoted, along with the head of the MVD, the Minister of Internal Affairs, Nikolai Shchelokov, to become an Army General. In August 1979 Brezhnev gave Andropov the Order of the October Revolution, paying him a glowing tribute for being "an extremely honest and selfless worker; a creatively minded person; and a skilled organiser, demanding of yourself and others; and first and foremost a convinced Communist"[15]. Obviously satisfied that Andropov had run the KGB as an adjunct of the Party, Brezhnev went on to declare "Our Party considers it an important principle that this keen weapon for the defence of the state's and people's security against the intrigues of the enemy should be in clean and unimpeachable hands"[16].

While maintaining tight Party control and containing pressures from within the KGB for a harder line, Andropov ensured that he preserved departmental support. He persuaded the Politburo to increase the power and influence of the KGB apparatus. Its top officials had the same access to privileged foreign luxuries and special shops as senior Party functionaries. The KGB's pride was enhanced by a media campaign glamourising its image. Films and television dramas showed heroic secret agents using superior brainpower and skill to outwit the CIA. He also used the KGB in campaigns against corruption, the best-known being the replacement of the Party and Government leaderships in Azerbaijan in 1969 and in Georgia in 1972. Zhores Medvedev argues that while the KGB received bad publicity abroad, its activity had the opposite effect within the Party and Government structure, where Andropov

---

14. *Pravda*, April 23, 1976.
15. Ibid., August 23, 1976.
16. Ibid. Brezhnev's tribute to Shchelokov looked somewhat hollow three years later, when Shchelekov was removed as Minister of Internal Affairs amid allegations that he and his wife had speculated in the buying and selling of gold, silver, furs, and other luxury goods.

"acquired the reputation of being a strong but just man, the guardian of the system"[17].

Some dissidents have reported that Andropov took a personal hand in interrogations. Alexander Ginzburg says that when he was being questioned by the KGB in 1967, shortly after Andropov's appointment, the new KGB chief once came in and sat listening for about ten minutes but did not speak. As a man in a new job, it is quite plausible that Andropov would want to see how his men were operating. At that time also, according to Ginzburg, Andropov took a great interest in the interrogations of prisoners under investigation for large-scale corruption. He would tell prisoners (which the ordinary KGB interrogator was not empowered to do) that if they co-operated they might escape execution. Ginzburg says he knows this from such prisoners who were in nearby cells to his. Some were shot anyway in spite of confessing[18].

A more extraordinary story is told by Nikolai Scharegin. He lived in a displaced persons' camp after the war and came to Britain as a boy. Not yet a British citizen, he went back to the Soviet Union on a business trip in 1968 and was arrested for alleged espionage. During his interrogation, he says, "the door opened and Andropov walked in. Everybody jumped to greet him, but he waved his hand and said 'Please continue, comrades'. The same question was being asked over and over again. I refused to answer and was a bit annoyed. Then Andropov said to them 'I don't see anybody taking notes'. Everybody grabbed some papers, pencil, pen, and started to scribble...asking the same question again." Later Andropov looked at Scharegin's British travel document, and told his KGB officials that although the papers were British Scharegin was born in Russia and they should deal with him according to their custom and pleasure. Bringing the document close to Scharegin's face, Andropov then said in English "Queen will not declare war because of you and we shall deal with you according to our pleasure". Then he left the room[19].

Unfortunately, both these stories depend on the memory of a single individual, and in neither of them is there absolute proof that

---

17. Zhores Medvedev, *Andropov*, p. 64.
18. Alexander Ginzburg, interviewed by Elizabeth Teague, April 29, 1983.
19. Nikolai Scharegin, interviewed on *Panorama*, BBC Television, November 15, 1982.

the man thought to be Andropov was in fact he, and not some other KGB official. Viktor Krasin, a dissident who was tried in 1973, has a particularly vivid recollection of a meeting with Andropov, in which the chairman of the KGB introduced himself by name[20]. Krasin and his friend Pyotr Yakir were two of the best-known and most active dissidents in Moscow in the early 1970's. Yakir's apartment was always full of human rights activists and Western reporters frequently dropped in. In June 1972 Yakir was arrested. Krasin followed him to prison three months later.

In line with its usual practice, the KGB tried to make the two men confess so that they could organise a show trial. As Krasin describes it in his short memoir of the interrogation, the KGB had not been able to break the dissident movement by means of repression alone. Instead, it hoped to discredit and demoralise it by finding some leading members who would co-operate with the authorities and turn against their friends. The KGB's choice fell on Yakir and Krasin, two men who were especially vulnerable to psychological pressure because they came from families with a long history of persecution in labour camps, and had – in Krasin's view – not yet escaped from the terror of being sent back to prison. Yakir had an extra weakness. He was an alcoholic, and it did not take the KGB long to break him. Krasin held out a few months longer. He was told that his case was in the hands of Andropov himself. If he did not co-operate, he would be shot. If he did, he would be dealt with leniently.

Eventually Krasin also gave in, and in August 1973 their trial opened in Moscow. Both men admitted having taken part in anti-Soviet activities for which they apologised. On the eve of the trial they were told by their KGB interrogators that they would get three-year prison sentences followed by three years of internal exile, but these would later be commuted. On the day after the trial Krasin was in Lefortovo prison in Moscow when a KGB lieutenant came into his cell and told him "Hurry up. The chairman of the KGB wants to see you". The prison governor Colonel Petrenko took him to his office. "Behind the table stood a tall heavy-set man in glasses. He told Petrenko to go. We were left alone. 'I am

---

20. Viktor Krasin, *Sud (Trial)*, New York, Chalidze Publications, 1983, p. 72.

Andropov, chairman of the KGB', he said as he reached out his hand. I shook it. 'I recognise you from your photograph'. He asked me to sit down and the conversation began"[21].

Andropov told him his prison sentence would be reduced on appeal, and only the internal exile would remain. He would be allowed to spend this in a town close to Moscow, and after eight months he would be pardoned and could return to Moscow. They could not be pardoned immediately because the trial had received considerable publicity, but the results of the appeal would not be published. Then Andropov raised the subject of Stalinism, asking Krasin whether he really believed that Stalinism was being revived in the Soviet Union, as he had written in a number of dissident articles. When Krasin replied that there was some evidence for it, Andropov said "Nonsense. No-one will permit any return to Stalinism. We all remember what it was like under Stalin. The leadership is very firm on this." He recalled that he too had been afraid of being arrested during the Stalin period.

Andropov moved on to the main point of the meeting. He suggested that Krasin and Yakir attend a special press conference for Western reporters at which they would repeat the confessions made at their trial. This was a new KGB idea, and presumably Andropov's own. A press conference at which they faced tough questioning would have a far greater impact both on the Western press and the Moscow dissident community than the trial. Krasin agreed, after obtaining a promise from Andropov that he would consider early release for a dissident friend who was being held in a psychiatric hospital. Andropov's plan worked, and the Krasin-Yakir press conference achieved exactly what he had hoped. One American reporter who attended it said his stomach

> went to jelly as soon as I saw them....I was summoned, with the entire Moscow press corps, to the press conference at which Yakir and Krasin appeared, but without forewarning of the purpose of the session. The auditorium at the House of Journalists was packed when suddenly the two of them walked on to the stage and took seats behind a long table. At once we

21. Ibid., p. 73.

all realised what was about to happen....Not a show trial like those that Stalin staged but a show press conference.[22]

Andropov's reported encounters with Ginzburg, Scharegin, and Krasin were exceptional. In general he kept himself in the background during his time at the KGB. It is in fact remarkable that in the mass of articles, memoirs, and testimonies of hundreds of dissidents during Andropov's fifteen years as head of the KGB there are so few details of substance about his work.

The only authenticated case of Andropov appearing before a group of dissidents was early in his KGB career. On July 20, 1967 some twenty representatives of the Crimean Tatars were received in the Kremlin. It was not the first time that they had been able to see high Soviet Party officials during the decade since Khrushchev had listed their deportation from their homeland during the war as one of Stalin's crimes. Aishe Seitmuratova, who now lives in the United States, remembers the occasion in 1967:

> We were led into a hall. There was a large table covered with a cloth. On the table were notepads for everyone. Behind the large table there were smaller tables with people already seated at them. Suddenly the door opened and a group of men entered the room. We did not know who they were as we only recognised Georgadze, the Secretary of the Presidium of the Supreme Soviet of the USSR. They all took their places and one rather sporty, young-looking man of about fifty stood up and introduced the others: 'This is Georgadze, you know him; this is the Minister of Internal Affairs, Shchelokov, this is the Procurator-General, Rudenko, and I am Andropov, Yuri Vladimirovich'.
>
> When we realised who was receiving us – prior to this we had no idea who would be receiving us and had not worked out any plan of action – we delegated one of our representatives to say 'In what capacity are you receiving us: as 'punitive organs' receiving criminals? If so, we refuse to speak with you'. Then Andropov stood up and said 'All of us are members of

22. Robert Kaiser, *Russia*, New York, Atheneum, 1976, pp. 439–40.

the Government and deputies of the Supreme Soviet and we are receiving you in this capacity as well as on the instructions of the Politburo'[23].

The delegation then explained their grievances, speaking for more than three hours. At the end Andropov reportedly stood up and promised to report their views to the Politburo, which, he said, was unanimously agreed that they should be rehabilitated but was divided over whether they should be permitted to return to the Crimea. Seitmuratova recalls that Andropov then said "I cannot give you further details even if you were to take hold of me like this", as he grabbed the front of his collar. "I've said all I have been instructed to say. What you have told me I shall pass on. I understood you perfectly: you won't settle for anything less than the Crimea". The group replied in unison: "Yes! The Crimea!"

"When the meeting drew to an end", Seitmuratova remembers, "Andropov said: 'Forgive me, comrades, I am not your host. We are the guests of Comrade Georgadze and he has not even offered tea'". Georgadze looked embarrassed. At another point during the talks Andropov said: "You understand, I am always being given questions connected with the nationalities problem to deal with. I am already considered a specialist on these matters. I also had to resolve the Hungarian problem". At this point the delegation replied with one voice: "We are not Hungarians. We are Crimean Tatars and citizens of the USSR. Crimea is within the USSR, not beyond its borders".

Says Seitmuratova:

All in all, Andropov was relaxed throughout the meeting. He did not threaten; on the contrary, it was pleasant to talk to him. He did not conceal anything, but then, he did not say any more than he had to....When we said our nation was being slandered in the Soviet press, he told us to draw up a list of the publications which had referred to our people disrespectfully. He also added that we should return to Uzbekistan and a decree would soon be published announcing the rehabilitation

---

23. Aishe Seitmuratova, interviewed by Don Larrimore, April 20, 1983.

of the Crimean Tatars. Sure enough, on September 5 the decree was passed by the presidium of the Supreme Soviet and on September 9 it was published. It did not appear in the all-Union press, however. Only in the Uzbek papers.[24]

As they were leaving, Seitmuratova told Andropov she wanted to give him one small example of discrimination. For three years she had sat the entrance examination for the Institute of History of the Academy of Sciences. "I obtain excellent marks but am rejected. Now I am about to sit the examination for a fourth time, having sampled prison and your 'sanatorium'. And I will show you convincing proof that discrimination exists'. He came up to me and said, 'Aishe, we are all Soviet people'. I replied 'That's just it. I'm regarded as Soviet, yet at the same time not Soviet'. As he was going out, I was the only one he shook hands with". The following day she went to the Institute and the secretary told her a phone call had come from the Central Committee asking for her documents. In September she sat the examinations and was accepted into the Institute of History of the Uzbek Academy of Sciences.

The decree rehabilitating the Crimean Tatars did not satisfy them since it referred to "the Tatars formerly resident in the Crimea". It gave them no right to return to their homeland as a group. It only said that members of Tatar families were entitled to settle anywhere in the Soviet Union in accordance with the existing legislation on employment and the passport regulations. In practice this gave the authorities the power to deny individuals permission to settle where they wanted. Whatever Andropov's own views may have been, the Politburo majority was obviously against full repatriation.

If his encounter with the Crimean Tatars seemed to portray Andropov as a relative moderate, this fitted with the general impression of the rest of his policy at the time. During his first nine months in power as KGB chief until February 1968 he reduced political arrests to a low level and avoided any that might cause publicity abroad. In December 1967 the Politburo was even considering whether to permit the publication of Solzhenitsyn's

---

24. Aishe Seitmuratova, interviewed by Don Larrimore, April 20, 1983.

Cancer Ward[25]. But a number of dissidents already in detention – Bukovsky, Galanskov, and Ginzburg – were given severe sentences.

This stop-go policy provoked the growth of a loosely organised alliance of human rights activists, including scientists, writers, Crimean Tatars, Jews, Ukrainians, and reformers within the Russian Orthodox Church. Meanwhile, in 1968 the Prague Spring encouraged the dissidents and worried the authorities, especially as Western interest in the issue of dissidence showed no sign of abating. Dissidents' appeals were increasingly getting back into the Soviet Union thanks to foreign broadcasting stations. The KGB response was systematic but cautious. Pressure and intimidation of one kind or another was applied to the roughly 1,000 people who had signed petitions or appeals. About three-quarters gave up.

The invasion of Czechoslovakia on August 21, 1968, prompted a small group of leading dissenters to demonstrate in Red Square. This was too much for the Politburo, and in an effort to discourage future demonstrations, the KGB put five of them on trial. The Politburo also decided to re-impose the jamming of foreign broadcasts by those stations which had been freed of it by Khrushchev.

After 'normalising' the situation in Czechoslovakia the following spring the Politburo resolved on a new crackdown at home. The level of political arrests rose again, and Solzhenitsyn (all chance of having *Cancer Ward* published in the Soviet Union now abandoned) was expelled from the Writers' Union. And, as a sign that Andropov now realised that the issue of dissidence was going to be a long-term and serious phenomenon, in 1969 he created a special Fifth Main Directorate in the KGB to co-ordinate its anti-dissident measures more efficiently.

The year 1970 saw the explosion of the Jewish emigration question. The Six-Day War in 1967 had led to a significant increase in ethnic and Zionist consciousness among Soviet Jews. Emboldened by the rise in the human rights movement and encouraged by foreign lobbies to press their cases for emigration hard, hundreds of Jews applied to leave the Soviet Union. For the most part the authorities refused. This led to the formation of underground

---

25. Alexander Solzhenitsyn, *The Oak and the Calf*, London, Collins and Harvill Press, 1980, p. 363.

groups and a plan to hijack a plane. The KGB arrested the would-be hijackers but the first trial at which two received death sentences led to a massive storm abroad. It coincided with a campaign for clemency for some Basque nationalists sentenced to death in Franco's Spain. The comparison was highly embarrassing for the Kremlin and the Politburo quickly arranged to have the sentences commuted.

Detente between the Soviet Union and the West was now beginning to move into high gear, and the Politburo realised that its strategy towards dissidents could not be totally divorced from foreign policy considerations. As Reddaway puts it,

> the Politburo had little choice but to yield. The other options must have been unacceptable. To put thousands of Jews into camps was impossible for reasons of foreign and economic policy, given the strength of the American Jewish lobby. But to tolerate the status quo in which Jews were, with virtual impunity, providing an example of militancy to other oppressed groups in various cities at the same time that anti-Soviet publicity was building up abroad and even forcing Western Communist Parties to become critical of Soviet intransigence, was also impossible[26].

On the eve of the Twenty-Fourth Congress of the Soviet Communist Party the Politburo unlocked the gates. For the next eight years Jews poured out, reaching a total of 200,000 by 1979. Although many individuals were denied exit visas (the so-called refuseniks), and most were immediately sacked from their jobs and had to wait some time before receiving their permission to leave, the overall number who were able to go was staggering. Mass emigration on this scale was a radical shift in Kremlin policy, and it was applied not just to Jews, but to Germans, Armenians, and other dissidents.

Reddaway argues that the experience of the 1960's and 1970's shows that the most important single variable in determining Soviet emigration policy was the level of militancy and resourcefulness of a

---

26. Peter Reddaway, *Authority, Power and Policy*, pp. 170-1.

President Yuri Andropov (SIPA Rex Features)

Top: Andropov and Brezhnev (SIPA Rex Features)
Above: Brezhnev's funeral, November 1982 (Novosti Press Agency)

Второй съезд Коммунистической парт[ии]

Прения по отчетному докладу
Речь тов. Ю. В. АНДРОПОВА
(Секретарь Центрального Комитета КП(б) Карело-Финской ССР)

Above: Leninskoe Znamya (Petrozavodsk), 29 April 1949, showing Andropov as a Secretary of the Karelo-Finnish Communist Party (Library of Congress)

Left: Finnish Communist Party leader Otto Kuusinen, Andropov's early mentor (Camera Press)

Top: Hungary 1956: Soviet tanks in Budapest (Popperfoto)

Above: Khrushchev (left) and Hungarian Communist Party leader Janos Kadar signing a joint statement in Budapest 1964. Andropov is standing second left (Camera Press)

Top: Soviet delegation at the Hungarian Heroes Monument, April 1964 (forefront, Khrushchev, second row left, Andropov) (Camera Press)

Above: Andropov standing between Chairman Mao (centre) and Zhou Enlai, Peking 1965 (Novosti Press Agency)

"We will think together, plan together, move together."

The winner

Above: Warsaw Pact summit, Prague, January 1983. Left to right: Janos Kadar (Hungary). Todor Zhivkov (Bulgaria), Yuri Andropov, Gustav Husak (Czechoslovakia), Erich Honecker (GDR), Nicolae Ceausescu (Romania) and Wojciech Jaruzelski (Poland) (Popperfoto)

Right: Andropov's son Igor, member of the Soviet delegation to the European Security Conference in Madrid, February 1983 (Agencia EFE)

Ailing Andropov during the visit of the Finnish President Mauno Koivisto, June 1983 (Associated Press)

group's lobbying, protest, and circulation of *samizdat* (underground) material. Next most important was the level of its foreign and domestic support[27]. The same can be said of Soviet policy towards dissidents as a whole. One should also add a third variable – the overall climate of East-West relations. The hardline strategy towards the Soviet Union adopted by the Carter Administration in its last two years, and by the Reagan Administration from the outset, left the Kremlin with nothing to lose. Whatever the reason for Washington's shift in policy (Carter put it down to the invasion of Afghanistan, while for Reagan and his team it was an ideological reversion to the containment strategy of the First Cold War), the revived Western policy of diplomatic, economic, and political cold-shouldering and sanctions against the Soviet Union reduced the Politburo's incentive to take Western public opinion into account. After a peak of 51,330 in 1979, Jewish emigration dropped to 9,447 in 1981 and to 2,692 in 1982. German emigration dropped by 80 per cent from a peak of 9,626 in 1976 to only 1,958 in 1982. As for the rate of political arrests as a whole, it rose in the first year of Andropov's rule as General Secretary.

Detente had not of course meant that Soviet dissidents were safe from persecution. With its argument that detente involved "an intensification of the ideological struggle" the Politburo made it clear that it reserved the right to stamp out dissidence. But in spite of this rhetoric its line was generally cautious. One proof of that was the relatively low number of known arrests, about 100 a year during the 1970's. The combined total of political and religious detainees in the Soviet Union's various prisons and camps was estimated by Amnesty International to be 10,000 in the mid-1970's[28]. This figure was a tiny fraction of the number held in Stalin's time. It was also low in comparison with the numbers held on non-political charges. There were reports that in one anti-corruption sweep in Georgia in 1972, 25,000 people were arrrested[29].

Other signs of caution were the relative toleration shown between 1974 and 1976 towards the *samizdat*, *Chronicle of Current Events*,

27. Ibid., p. 171.
28. Amnesty International, *Prisoners of Conscience in the USSR: Their Treatment and Conditions*, London, Amnesty International, 1975, p. 53.
29. Peter Reddaway, in *Religion in Communist Lands*, Keston College Kent, No. 4–5, 1975, p. 15.

which listed as much information on dissident activity as its Moscow compilers were able to gather, and the lifting of jamming of the BBC, the Voice of America, and Deutsche Welle in 1973. (The Munich-based Radio Liberty with its heavy coverage of sensitive domestic issues broadcast in fifteen languages of the Soviet Union continued to be jammed.) On the negative side was the expulsion of Solzhenitsyn in February 1974, though even this was a milder sanction than imprisonment would have been. The Politburo's hope was that once abroad Solzhenitsyn would cease to be attractive to Western public opinion. (His prolific publishing energy and the amount of uncompleted material he still had abroad made that Kremlin hope over-optimistic.)

The residence regulations were tightened to make it possible to prevent released prisoners from settling in or near big cities. The 'parasitism' law against people who fail to seek work was strengthened to make it easier to convict dissidents dismissed from their jobs. Legal controls over duplicators and printing-presses were tightened. Dissidents who were not in the so-called mainstream, such as less-well-known Lithuanians, Armenians, Georgians, Baptists, Pentecostalists, young Orthodox intellectuals, and a newer category of dissenters – 'alternative culture' groups – were arrested. At the same time better-known people who were in psychiatric hospitals and were the subject of foreign protests, such as the mathematician Leonid Plyushch or the Ukrainian nationalist Valentin Moroz, were freed. Sakharov was left unarrested even though the Politburo had been angered by the award of the Nobel Peace Prize to him and by his untiring activity in publicising dissident cases.

After the Helsinki conference on security and co-operation in Europe in 1975 a number of groups sprang up to monitor Soviet compliance – non-compliance, as it turned out mainly to be. For the first six months they were able to operate without significant problems but then the KGB stepped in to stop them. In a speech to KGB staff on March 24, 1976 Andropov accused Western intelligence services of supporting dissidents:

> The special services of imperialist countries subsidise the activity of anti-Soviet radio stations and various emigré

centres. They organise the despatch of anti-Soviet literature into the USSR. In their attempts to undermine the socio-political and ideological unity of the Soviet people they attempt to sow national discord among the peoples of the Soviet Union. They use the weapon of Zionism. They profiteer from the situation with regard to religious freedom, and make heroes out of renegades of various kinds. We must curtail these subversive onslaughts decisively[30].

In fact the KGB only took half-measures. Eleven people were arrested in the first ten months of 1977 before the official review conference on Helsinki compliance opened in Belgrade – not enough to stop the unofficial groups.

President Carter's emphasis on human rights irritated the Politburo enormously, and as a result Soviet policy towards mainstream dissent continued to waver. Heavy sentences were imposed on some members of the Helsinki groups, such as Yuri Orlov, Alexander Ginzburg, and Anatoly Shcharansky, in spite of strong Western protests. But a year later Ginzburg was swapped with four other dissidents for two convicted Soviet spies held in the United States.

The atmosphere changed in the second half of 1979 as East-West relations plummeted after a row in the United States Senate over the presence of a Soviet combat brigade in Cuba, the NATO decision to install new land-based medium-range missiles in Western Europe in response to the presence of Soviet SS20 missiles, and the Soviet invasion of Afghanistan. As the West imposed sanctions on the Soviet Union, the Politburo felt it had little left to lose. In early 1980 Sakharov was banished to Gorky, a city from which foreigners are barred, thus cutting his access to the Western media. In the months preceding the 1980 Olympics, before the expected influx of foreign journalists and other visitors, the KGB made many arrests. Hardliners in the KGB probably welcomed the Western boycott campaign because it reduced the number of foreign visitors and provided an excuse to clamp down at home. As

30. Yuri Andropov, *Selected Speeches and Articles*, Moscow, Politizdat, 1979, pp. 252–3.

relations continued to worsen under Reagan, the KGB's activity against dissidents continued to increase.

By 1982, when Andropov was beginning to manoeuvre actively for the succession to Brezhnev, the dissident groups and movements were weaker than they had been for more than a decade. How far he had been taking his own initiatives during all that time rather than consulting the Politburo to obtain their approval is impossible to say. Presumably as he developed experience in the job and seniority in the Politburo he must have become more independent. At all events, he could plausibly argue that his stewardship of the KGB for fifteen years had been a success. While dissent had not been eliminated, particularly among Lithuanian Catholics and other religious groups, he had largely broken the back of the main movements in Moscow and reduced their contact with Western reporters. Admittedly, detente with the West had collapsed and the Kremlin was no longer getting advantages from it. But Andropov could claim – and his argument was shared by the rest of the Politburo – that detente had not been destroyed because of the KGB's stop-go campaigns against dissent. On the contrary, as the Kremlin saw it, detente had broken down for other reasons, mainly connected with internal American politics. As a result, the Kremlin had been able to scrape at least one benefit from the ruins. It took off its kid gloves and dealt the dissidents the blows it had long wanted to.

6

Spymaster

The atmosphere in the Green Room of the Kremlin was stiff and formal as Vice-President George Bush arrived for a private chat with the new Soviet Party leader shortly after Brezhnev's funeral. Bush, who had been Director of the CIA from 1976 to 1977, tried to break the ice with a touch of humour. "I feel I already know you, since we served in similar positions"[1], he quipped. Andropov watched his American visitor intently but made no response.

It was the first time ever that a former head of the CIA had met a former head of the KGB. But while Bush had only held the CIA job for a year, Andropov's command of the KGB had lasted fifteen years, longer than any of his predecessors. In that time he expanded the KGB into a world-wide arm of Soviet foreign policy, gathering espionage and pushing propaganda in almost every major country of the world. He also improved the quality of the KGB's staff and the style of its work.

During the Andropov era the KGB's foreign directorate moved from the ochre-coloured neo-Renaissance headquarters in Dzerzhinsky Square in the centre of Moscow to a large, crescent-shaped office building on the outskirts. The switch was symbolic of the change in the KGB's foreign operations from an outfit of crude and ideologically motivated hardliners to a sophisticated intelligence organisation, able to attract some of the brightest Soviet graduates with its image of patriotism, glamour, privilege and prestige.

When Andropov took over the KGB in 1967 its reputation was low. First there was the disaster of Stalin's daughter's defection.

---

1. *Time*, February 14, 1983.

Then in March and April 1967 Western counter-intelligence agents broke up an elaborate KGB network in Austria, Belgium, Cyprus, Greece, and Italy which had spied on NATO installations. Semichastny's men, their covers as diplomats, journalists, and Aeroflot officials blown, were expelled from Rome, Nicosia, and Brussels.

In spite of such operational flops and being on the wrong side in Kremlin manoeuvrings after the overthrow of Khrushchev, Semichastny was spared the harsh fate of some of his KGB predecessors. On May 19 he was sacked and sent off to pasture as First Deputy Prime Minister of the Ukraine.

Andropov took over, obviously expected by his colleagues to pull the KGB into shape abroad as well as at home. His first few months of overseeing the KGB's foreign operations were hardly more successful than Semichastny's final months in office, with another spate of expulsions and a damaging defection when a Soviet Air Force officer, Lt. Vasily Epatko crash-landed his MiG-17 in West Germany and asked for asylum. Even worse was the defection in October 1967 of a KGB colonel, Yevgeny Runge, in West Berlin, something Andropov could have prevented. Runge was a so-called illegal, whose cover was his apparently successful job as a salesman for vending machines. He was not a spy masquerading as a legally accredited diplomat or journalist. One of his jobs was to 'control' an East German agent who had married a secretary in the West German foreign ministry. She obtained a total of 2,900 documents for KGB headquarters. In fact Moscow Centre found the operation so successful that it became suspicious. Recalled to discuss the case and for a Black Sea holiday, Runge found KGB officials reluctant to allow his wife and young son to return with him to West Germany. By then he had decided to defect, but not if his family were hostages in the Soviet Union. As a senior officer he appealed directly to Andropov, claiming that his cover would be blown if he returned to West Germany without his family. Andropov, new to the job, was convinced and sent the Runges off to the West. There they promptly defected[2].

It was a bad start for Andropov but as time went on he tightened

---

2. *The New York Times*, November 11, 1967.

up the organisation which he had inherited. In the fifteen years he ran the KGB, few of his officers defected. One who did was Stanislav Levchenko, a KGB major, who was working as a Soviet journalist in Japan and disclosed his real job to American officials in 1979. Another KGB major, Vladimir Kuzichkin, who had worked for the organisation in Afghanistan and Iran, turned up in British hands in 1982. Other defectors were Alexei Myagkov, who had worked in East Germany and Oleg Lyalin, who switched sides in London in 1971.

It is from men like these, as well as from Soviet spies who are caught, that much of the outside world's knowledge of KGB operations comes. Western intelligence agencies also have their own undisclosable (and uncheckable) sources. On the basis of this varied flow of information, Andropov's Western counterparts tend to give him high marks for efficiency, though they are naturally less willing to say how successful his KGB has been. "Within a couple of years of Andropov's taking over of the KGB", says one former Soviet affairs specialist in Washington who had close links with the CIA, "one began to see a more sophisticated service, a process of change and maturing which had probably commenced earlier. But now it was accelerated. Now there was the 'new KGB man', better trained linguistically, with more specialist knowledge, Westernised in dress, etc. And there was a change in methodology"[3]. According to this source, the KGB was given advice on Western management techniques by Kim Philby, who worked for the Soviet Union inside the British Foreign Office for many years before fleeing to Moscow in 1963.

William Colby, who directed the CIA between 1973 and 1976, says Andropov "is reputed to have upgraded the intelligence level of the ordinary KGB officer abroad....There was an increasing number of Soviets who wear decent clothes, sip Scotch whisky, and engage in very good discussions with foreigners, realising that much useful intelligence doesn't have to be gotten by spying, the way the old KGB used to think....Previously, unless you got it by spying, it couldn't be true"[4].

---

3. Former Soviet affairs specialist in Washington, interviewed by Don Larrimore, April 6, 1983.
4. William Colby, interviewed by Don Larrimore, April 1, 1983.

Colby sees the growing sophistication of Soviet studies of America, such as the expansion of the Institute of the USA and Canada, which is directed by Georgy Arbatov, a long-time associate of Andropov, as part of the improvement of the whole Soviet intelligence-gathering process. Says Colby: "I like to think that what it really amounts to is copying the American experience, because the unique thing about American intelligence was its central core of scholars. Back in World War Two we saw that the really fundamental element of intelligence is this idea of bringing all the information to the centre and analysing it"[5].

The defector Levchenko, who never personally met Andropov, describes him as a grey eminence, who would see departing station chiefs as they left Moscow for their assignments abroad, but who otherwise hardly ever appeared. His style was to have his deputies out front, while he devoted himself to policy and planning. He only became involved in major operations[6].

KGB activities abroad can be classified roughly into three areas – the Socialist countries, NATO, and the Third World. In Eastern Europe the KGB has a powerful intelligence-gathering and security system which works closely with the local regimes in times of political crisis in order to preserve Party control. In NATO the KGB runs a traditional campaign to obtain military and political secrets, the classic stuff of espionage, including details about new weapons systems, war plans, and political thinking. Under Andropov this was enlarged with the addition of a new area, an attempt to gain access to Western technological secrets, especially in the late 1970's and early 1980's, when legal Soviet access dried up after the Carter and Reagan Administrations tightened the embargoes on the sale and delivery of high-technology items to the Soviet Union. In the Third World its work is varied. Efforts are made to influence public opinion on international issues towards support for Moscow rather than Washington, often through the use of planted newspaper articles and forgeries of documents. Like its CIA rival, the KGB attempts to bribe or blackmail local politicians, journalists, and trade union and student leaders. It also maintains links

---

5. William Colby, interviewed by Don Larrimore, April 1, 1983.
6. *Der Spiegel*, No. 7, 1983.

with opposition movements. A prime function is the creation of ties to certain guerrilla movements.

THE SOCIALIST COUNTRIES

Shortly before he was appointed to head the KGB in May 1967 Andropov made two visits to Czechoslovakia. As Secretary of the Central Committee in charge of the Socialist countries it was natural that he should accompany Brezhnev. The first in February 1967 was one of the routine official visits which the Soviet Party leader made to each of his Eastern European clients. The second, two months later, was for an international conference of Communist leaders in Karlovy Vary. Although discussion of reform was already gathering strength among Czechoslovak writers and some Party intellectuals, it was not yet apparent that Czechoslovakia would soon produce a crisis threatening the whole basis of Communist rule in the region.

But during the summer criticism of the hardline Czechoslovak Party leader, Antonin Novotny, began to grow both within the Party and outside. As opposition mounted, Andropov and the rest of the Soviet leadership decided to let Novotny fall – just as they had done with the unpopular Hungarian leader, Matyas Rakosi, in Hungary in 1956. As an intelligent moderniser Andropov realised that a change at the top was overdue. Brezhnev travelled to Prague again in December 1967, this time without Andropov, to tell Novotny that he would not support him against his Party critics. A month later, Novotny was replaced as Party leader by the relatively unknown Slovak Party Secretary, Alexander Dubcek.

Originally the change was seen as largely cosmetic. But within weeks there were developments unthinkable for a faithful Soviet ally. Censorship was relaxed, the security police with their Soviet advisers at every level came under open criticism for their illegal practices in the past, and demands grew for the rehabilitation of the victims of the political trials of the 1950's. Dubcek's appointment sparked off a belated process of de-Stalinisation in which Party reformers, liberal journalists, and most of the intelligentsia eagerly joined.

With his experience of Hungary in 1956 and his ten-year stint since then in charge of Eastern Europe, Andropov was clearly going to be a key figure in the crisis. But whereas in 1956 he had been an Ambassador, representing the Soviet point of view 'up front', his job in 1968 required him to play a different role. His department, the KGB, was responsible for trying to resist what the Kremlin considered to be dangerously radical ideas by a mixture of threats, false rumours, and provocations.

Among the most sensitive issues re-opened by the Czechoslovak reformers was the death of Jan Masaryk, the former Foreign Minister whose body was found beneath a window in 1948. Popular demands grew for elucidation of the Soviet security police's role and a new investigation into what had officially been described as suicide, but which many people suspected was murder. This was clearly a direct cause for KGB concern and Andropov sought to discourage an inquiry. A blistering attack by the Soviet news agency Tass described the issue as a piece of "enemy propaganda" which was "false from start to finish"[7]. This piece of intimidation failed and the Czechoslovak Party went ahead with its investigation not only into the Masaryk case but also the whole issue of the 1950's purges and Soviet involvement in them. Another KGB effort that spring and summer was the circulation of stories that hidden arms dumps had been found near the German-Czechoslovak border, proof – it was claimed – that the West was planning to invade Czechoslovakia or provoke a counter-revolution. This clumsy deception also failed. The Czechoslovak Interior Minister, Josef Pavel, summed up the consensus when he said, after investigating the reports, that "the hidden arms were a provocation aimed at dramatising the situation"[8]. Dirty tricks continued throughout the summer with a campaign of anonymous leaflets and threatening letters against Party reformers and liberal writers.

When the Kremlin decided to invade Czechoslovakia in August, Andropov was a candidate member of the Politburo and had no vote. But his view would certainly have been listened to, though it was not necessarily decisive. His experience of Eastern Europe was

---

7. Cited in Ladislav Bittman, *The Deception Game*, Syracuse, New York, Syracuse University Research Corporation, 1982, p. 188.
8. Ibid., p. 195.

greater than that of most of his colleagues. What he thought about the wisdom of invading an allied country cannot be known for certain, but the balance of probability is that he was against it. The efforts he had made on the Politburo's instructions to threaten and provoke the Czechoslovaks had backfired and must have left him with a new awareness of the strength of the reform movement. Although he cannot have liked this, as a realist he must have known that a more subtle, long-term approach was needed if the reforms were to be effectively controlled. When the Politburo sat down to discuss a possible invasion, he must also have been aware that no proper plans had been made for a new Czechoslovak leadership to take over after the invasion. At least this had been done in Hungary in 1956. He had had a hand in it.

The job in Prague was left to the Soviet Ambassador, Stepan Chervonenko. He bungled it, as well as the key task of engineering a formal signed invitation from senior Czechoslovak leaders to be broadcast or transmitted to Moscow, which could create a legal cover for the entry of the Soviet and other Warsaw Pact troops. The official Czechoslovak media never transmitted such a document although the Kremlin later said its troops had been invited by an important group of Party officials. (They were all well-known hardliners, and included several members of the subsequent post-Dubcek leadership.) More evidence of clumsiness and Soviet indecision came once the invasion was underway. The original plan was to arrest Dubcek and the other leading reformers and replace them by a more orthodox team, but this was changed after the invasion. Dubcek and most of the rest of the leadership were detained and taken to Moscow, and then reinstated during President Svoboda's negotiations with Brezhnev in the Kremlin.

Some observers have noted a divergence between the way *Pravda* and *Izvestia* reported the invasion and the way it was handled in *Trud*, the Soviet trade union newspaper – suggesting differences of opinion in Moscow. *Trud* hinted strongly that the invasion had been received with rather less enthusiasm than the other Soviet papers claimed[9]. Zdenek Mlynar, a Secretary of the Czechoslovak Communist Party who went with Svoboda to Moscow for the

---

9. Philip Windsor and Adam Roberts, *Czechoslovakia 1968*, London, Chatto and Windus, 1969, pp. 67–8.

negotiations after the invasion (and who now lives in Austria), said in an interview for this book

> We all presumed that somehow Andropov did not belong to those who were supporting the invasion, more like being against it. As far as we had any information we believed it to be along these lines: the KGB believed that Dubcek and his people would themselves be forced to take a lot of unpopular measures, especially after the Party Congress (which was to take place in September 1968) and the leadership would have to act firmly against radical demands for change.[10]

Jiri Valenta, a leading authority on the history of the invasion, believes the KGB was itself divided. There were narrow departmental reasons both for and against the invasion, though the anti-invasion ones were slightly stronger.

> I really think that Andropov, like several of the Soviet leaders whom I call 'centrists' couldn't make up his mind. There were certain features of the Prague spring he despised – particularly the investigation of KGB activities in the 1950's. I think, actually, one of the reasons why the invasion happened was the report which was going to be published a week later on KGB involvement in Jan Masaryk's death and the Rudolf Slansky trial. It was very dangerous to the KGB mission in Czechoslovakia but also in all Eastern Europe, exposing the KGB agents within the Czechoslovak and East European governments. So he certainly didn't like that. He probably would have sided with those who argued this had to be stopped.
> On the other hand, he knew the invasion would hurt the organisational mission of the KGB abroad, particularly the gathering of foreign information in Western Europe where the Czechoslovak intelligence service was extremely important, better than the East Germans. And that happened...many

---

10. Zdenek Mylnar interview, May 5, 1983.

devoted agents who were Czechoslovak patriots defected in the wake of the invasion – exactly what Andropov was afraid of – and brought with them dozens of names of Czechoslovak agents working for the Soviet Union....I think Andropov sat on a pyramid of different subgroups within the KGB, and his view reflected those different interests and pressures. I don't think he was really very enthusiastic about the invasion.[11]

Once the decision was taken to invade, the KGB had to play its professional part in carrying it out. During the night of August 20-1 some 200,000 troops of the Soviet Union, Bulgaria, East Germany, Hungary and Poland swept across Czechoslovakia's borders in a four-pronged armoured invasion. The Czechoslovak leadership asked the population not to resist. Prague was occupied in an airborne operation. Special KGB detachments were airlifted in to seize key Party, government, and communications facilities. KGB officers worked with Soviet troops in arresting Dubcek, Smrkovsky, and other reformers. A KGB contingent took over the Ministry of the Interior and the Czechoslovak intelligence services. According to some Western intelligence sources, Andropov may personally have flown to Prague to oversee the operation. The KGB's propaganda apparatus moved into action in a big way. A previously unknown broadcasting station, calling itself Radio Vltava after the river which runs through Prague, started beaming attacks on "counter-revolutionaries". It was based in East Germany and staffed by KGB specialists. Soviet helicopters dropped leaflets on Prague and other cities spelling out Moscow's line on the invasion. In Bratislava, according to a former Czechoslovak propaganda official, Ladislav Bittman, they even put out a fabricated appeal from President Svoboda, urging people to co-operate with the invasion authorities[12].

Much effort went into neutralising about a dozen clandestine radio stations which Czechoslovak journalists and sympathisers in the Army signals corps managed to put on the air soon after the invasion. Tass accused the West of helping these transmitters and of

---

11. Jiri Valenta, interviewed by Don Larrimore, March 2, 1983.
12. Ladislav Bittman, *The Deception Game*, pp. 205–6.

jamming pro-Soviet stations. The KGB produced and distributed *Zpravy*, a special newspaper giving the occupation authorities' line. Many leading proponents of liberalisation fled to the West, but others were arrested by the security police, working closely with the KGB and anti-Dubcek hardliners. It was a far cry from the post-invasion terror in Hungary in 1956. This time the invasion had been much less bloody. This was in no way thanks to Andropov, but rather to the different circumstances of the reform movement. Whatever doubts he may have had about the invasion, Andropov loyally did his bit.

The next major crisis involving the KGB came in Afghanistan, a country which was not officially part of the Soviet sphere of influence. In April 1978 a group of Afghan Communist leaders engineered an armed coup against the non-Communist government of President Daoud. Although they had close links with Moscow, there is no evidence that the coup was planned or provoked by the Kremlin. Daoud had come to power with Communist support but in 1978 he turned against them, arrested their leaders, and planned to execute them.

Vladimir Kuzichkin, a former KGB major, who defected to Britain in 1982, takes up the story: "The Afghan Communists were in a desperate position. They consulted the Soviet embassy in Kabul. Moscow quickly confirmed that we would support their proposed coup against Daoud. Just before it was too late, the Communist leaders ordered the coup – in fact from their prison cells"[13]. The coup succeeded, but then, according to Kuzichkin, Brezhnev ignored warnings from Andropov's KGB that they should advise the coup leaders to proceed cautiously. The Politburo saw a chance to turn Afghanistan into a new member of the Communist family by pouring in money and advisers and severing its links with the West. "The KGB tried to explain tactfully that a Communist takeover in Afghanistan presented hair-raising problems. We pointed out that despite all his slaughter the tribes had accepted Daoud as a legitimate ruler. An openly Communist regime would arouse hostility that would then be directed against the Soviet Union", Kuzichkin says. The KGB also differed with the

---

13. *Time*, November 22, 1982.

majority in the Politburo over the choice of a new leader. It backed Babrak Karmal, a long-time KGB agent while Brezhnev preferred Nur Muhammad Taraki. Later as Taraki was coming under pressure from his ambitious deputy Hafizullah Amin, the KGB again gave a warning that was ignored. Amin, they said, was secretly pro-Western.

By December 1979 as armed resistance mounted against the regime, now headed by Amin, the Soviet Politburo finally accepted that the KGB had been right. Now the problem was to get rid of Amin. The KGB was ordered to poison him, but the cook they were dealing with lost his nerve. A less quiet method was then devised. Amin had already made several pleas to the Soviet Union for military assistance in dealing with the resistance. Now under cover of answering his request the KGB prepared to despatch him. Kuzichkin again:

> This time special Soviet troops were to storm the presidential palace. On December 26, 1979 Soviet paratroopers began arriving at Kabul airport. They strengthened the substantial garrison we had quietly been building there. The next day an armoured column moved out of the airport toward the palace. It consisted of a few hundred Soviet commandos, plus a specially trained assault group of KGB officers – rather like the United States' Green Berets.[14]

Kuzichkin says Andropov wanted no prisoners taken. Anybody leaving the building was to be shot on sight. Under the command of Colonel Bayeranov, the head of the KGB's commando training school, the troops stormed the palace. Amin was found with his girlfriend drinking in a bar on the top floor and promptly shot. Babrak Karmal was installed in his place.

Then the KGB made, according to Kuzichkin, its first serious mistake. It underestimated the strength of the armed resistance and overestimated the willingness of the Afghan army to fight. As a result, Moscow sent in too few troops. Once the Kremlin realised that its army was bogged down, the generals asked for re-

---

14. Ibid.

inforcements. The Politburo, stung by the international reaction to the invasion, turned them down. The failure to win a quick military victory at the start of the invasion would come to haunt Andropov later when he became Party leader.

After a decade of comparative calm, Poland returned to the forefront of Kremlin anxieties in 1980 with the birth of an independent trade union movement, Solidarity. By now, unlike at the time of the Czechoslovak crisis, Andropov was not only a voting member of the Politburo but one of its most important figures. Thirteen years of experience at the head of the KGB, and the fact of being proved right in his initial political assessment of the problems in Afghanistan gave his advice considerable weight. It can safely be assumed that he was as worried as any other member of the Politburo over the implications of the Solidarity movement and the virtual collapse of Communist Party authority in Poland in the winter of 1980. But it is unlikely that Andropov would have panicked and immediately thought of resorting to a Soviet invasion.

Instead, the KGB followed the well-tried path of co-ordinating hardline articles in the Soviet and Eastern European press, warning Poles not to go too far for fear of unspecified dire consequences. It strengthened its contacts with the more conservative members of the Polish Party leadership to try to encourage them not to give way totally in the face of the pressures for reform. As before, Andropov's message seemed to be: reform when necessary but never give up Party control. This was the line presumably laid down when Andropov joined Brezhnev and other key Soviet leaders for talks with the Polish Party and Government leaders, Stanislaw Kania and General Wojciech Jaruzelski, during the Twenty-Sixth Congress of the Soviet Communist Party in February 1981. Tass quoted Brezhnev as urging the Polish leadership to "turn the course of events".

Throughout the summer the Kremlin watched anxiously as the Polish leaders conspicuously failed to do so. At what point the decision to impose martial law was taken is not known for sure (October was almost certainly the latest date), but many experts believe that the idea was Andropov's. Its subtlety and efficiency, at least compared to outright Soviet invasion, have the hallmarks of intelligent political thinking. Of all the Soviet operations of the previous two and half decades, from Hungary and Czechoslovakia to Afghanistan, it was certainly the most successful. Working closely with the KGB, the Polish authorities arrested their opponents quickly and without any bloodshed. There was no need to change the Party leadership. The international outcry was relatively subdued. Above all, Soviet tanks had not been required to cross the Soviet frontier on to the territory of a so-called ally.

NATO AND THE THIRD WORLD

Beyond the borders of the Socialist world the KGB's success is hard to gauge. Its operations are murkier and less clear-cut, and the results are not easy to pin down. What is clear is that the NATO countries provide an important and growing focus for KGB activities. "NATO has been an open book for Moscow since the late 1950's", wrote former CIA official Harry Rositzke in 1981. "Low-level penetration of NATO and American field installations has been a routine exercise by the KGB for over twenty years"[15]. Estimates vary of the number of Soviet diplomats who are in reality spies, but Western counter-intelligence analysts claim it is at least a third of the staff of Soviet embassies and consulates[16]. (Their statements cannot be confirmed independently.) These 'legals' who operate under diplomatic cover receive support from other agents scattered through Soviet institutions, such as the Soviet press corps or Aeroflot offices. Every so often, and usually depending on the current state of political relations with Moscow, Western governments conduct a purge of these spies.

The largest of these purges was the expulsion of 105 Soviet diplomats from London in September 1971. For some months the Foreign Office had been preparing a list of undesirable diplomats, who were believed to be engaged in industrial and political espionage. Others were exposed by Oleg Lyalin, a KGB officer working in an export-import business in London, who was arrested

---

15. Harry Rositzke, *The KGB: The Eyes of Russia*, London, Sidgwick and Jackson, 1982, pp. 155–6.
16. *Time*, February 14, 1982.

by chance one night on a drunken driving charge. Fearing that he might be recalled to Moscow with his career possibly in ruins, Lyalin decided to defect along with his mistress, a married secretary at the Soviet trade mission. He co-operated eagerly with British counter-intelligence. The expulsions caused a major flurry of propaganda. The British Attorney-General Sir Peter Rawlinson told Parliament that Lyalin's tasks included the "organisation of sabotage within the United Kingdom" such as the destruction of British strategic nuclear bombers in advance of a surprise Soviet attack[17]. Tipped off by the Soviet authorities that the initially unidentified defector was Lyalin, the British press described him in less dramatic terms than Sir Peter as "a rather rootless young man who was too much beguiled by the glamour of the West" and began to turn to drink[18]. Nevertheless, Lyalin's exposures were highly damaging to the KGB, and after an emergency meeting of the Politburo, Andropov was ordered to recall many of his agents from the non-Communist world for fear that their cover was about to be blown.

The first year of Andropov's time at the KGB saw one of the more outrageous Soviet espionage coups against NATO. Two spies stole a 9-foot-long, 160-pound Sidewinder missile from a base in Bavaria. They drove hundreds of miles through West Germany with the rocket's nose wrapped in a carpet protruding through a car window. Then they dismantled the missile, and air-freighted the parts to Moscow[19]. An even more ambitious scheme the following year was a flop. Soviet military intelligence (the GRU) thought it had convinced a Lebanese fighter-pilot to fly his advanced Mirage interceptor to the Soviet Union for two million dollars. When a cheque for $200,000 was being handed over in Beirut in down-payment, Lebanese oficers burst in and wounded two Soviet agents in a shoot-out.

While this operation was an affair organised by the GRU, which works closely with the KGB, it is the KGB which is responsible for trying to limit the damage and retrieve spies, if things go wrong. The KGB quickly spread the word in the Lebanese case that the

17. *The Guardian*, October 2, 1971.
18. *The Sunday Times*, October 3, 1971.
19. *The Daily Telegraph*, October 30, 1968.

incident was nothing but an American provocation. The KGB makes a standard practice of urging defectors to return to the Soviet Union, usually by putting pressure on them through their wives and families. In 1971, for example, Anatoly Chebotarev, a GRU officer working as a trade delegate in Brussels, told Belgian police the names of more than thirty KGB and GRU agents operating against NATO. After Chebotarev was given asylum in the United States, Soviet officials asked for permission to see him. They handed him letters from his family which convinced him to change his mind and return to the Soviet Union. His wife and two children had been taken from their Brussels flat by the KGB and flown to Moscow shortly after Chebotarev walked into the US embassy[20].

In 1978 Andropov showed particular keenness to retrieve two Soviet employees of the United Nations, Valdik Enger and Rudolf Chernyayev, who had been arrested by the FBI in New Jersey in the act of collecting United States' submarine warfare secrets. They were tried and sentenced to fifty years in prison. The Soviet Ambassador in Washington, Anatoly Dobrynin, was instructed to press hard for their release. He persistently raised the subject at meetings with President Carter's National Security Adviser, Zbigniew Brzezinski. In April an astonishing deal was arranged in which the Russians exchanged five leading dissidents for the two Soviet spies, the first time that political prisoners had been released for spies and a clear sign of how urgently Andropov wanted his men back[21].

Many of the KGB's best results have come from so-called walkins, people who approach the Russians to offer secrets. In 1975 a 22-year-old American, Andrew Lee, contacted the Soviet embassy in Mexico, offering to sell information that a friend of his, Christopher Bryce, could pick up as a communications clerk with an electronics firm in California. The firm was working on spy and communications satellites for the CIA. Boyce was a college drop-out who became disillusioned with the American system over Vietnam and Watergate. Over a two-year period the two men supplied the Russians with highly sensitive information before carelessness by

20. Ibid., December 29, 1971.
21. Zbigniew Brzezinski, *Power and Principle*, London, Weidenfeld and Nicolson, 1983, pp. 338–9.

Lee attracted the attention of a Mexican policeman when he tried to contact his Soviet case office by throwing a briefcase through the gate of the Soviet embassy in Mexico City[22].

Geoffrey Prime offered his services to the KGB when serving with the Royal Air Force in West Berlin in 1968. For more than ten years he subsequently worked as a translator at the top-secret British electronic intelligence centre at Cheltenham. His spying was only discovered after he was arrested for a sex offence involving a 14-year-old girl. William Kampiles left his job at the CIA after less than year as a junior officer in the round-the-clock Watch Centre at CIA headquarters in Langley, Virginia. Disillusioned because he was not chosen for 'real' spy work, he walked out with one of the Watch Centre's secret manuals. He later sold it to a somewhat uncomprehending KGB station in Athens for a paltry $3,000[23].

Under Andropov the KGB made increasing efforts to modernise its techniques for spying on foreign embassies and governments. A report by an official commission appointed by the US Government and headed by Vice-President Nelson Rockefeller disclosed that the Russians were able to monitor official telephone calls in Washington, including the White House and Congress, thanks to a network of aerials erected on top of the Soviet embassy. Soviet buildings in New York, Maryland, and California were also picking up phone calls. KGB eavesdroppers benefited from the telecommunications revolution in the West and the increasing use of satellites and microwaves to transmit phone conversations. The Rockefeller Commission warned that in addition to the possible loss of sensitive information through the KGB's new expertise, private American telephone users "are potentially subject to blackmail that can seriously affect their actions, or even lead in some cases to recruitment as espionage agents"[24].

The KGB's use of microwaves against the United States embassy in Moscow caused a major row in 1976. The waves jammed American monitoring devices, similar to those deployed by the Russians in the United States, and may have activated hidden

---

22. Harry Rositzke, *The KGB*, pp. 202–4.
23. John Barron, *KGB Today*, New York, Reader's Digest Press, 1983, pp. 229–32.
24. *The Los Angeles Times*, June 27, 1975; *The Daily Telegraph*, June 24, 1975 and July 11, 1977.

microphones. Members of the US embassy staff complained to the State Department over the health risk posed by the electronic battlefield in which they worked. Washington and Moscow began negotiations and later reached an agreement for the KGB to reduce its radiation bombardment in return for the removal of some US listening devices, which were said to have picked up conversations by Brezhnev and other members of the Politburo on their car radios[25].

If bugging was a pastime in which both sides were engaged, at a continuously more advanced level of technology, the KGB had a monopoly of activity, for obvious reasons, at the newest frontier of espionage – the theft of industrial and computer information. Many of the Soviet diplomats expelled from Western countries in the last few years were accused of engaging in this kind of espionage. A particularly dramatic expulsion was President Mitterrand's clampdown on 47 Russians in April 1983. They were charged with forming a disciplined, professional network aimed at procuring information from the high-technology sectors of French industry and the armed forces[26]. The Soviet consulate in San Francisco, not far from Silicon Valley, is thought to be a centre of KGB efforts to obtain computer technology. The US Commerce Department estimated in 1983 that 70 per cent of computer microchips made in the Soviet Union are turned out on Western equipment, most of it shipped there illegally[27].

KGB specialists became adept at using the competitive instincts of Western middlemen who could see the financial possibilities of beating the embargoes imposed by NATO governments on technology sales to the Soviet Union. Many companies, of course, are not aware of the final destination of the goods they supply. Andropov's KGB scored a spectacular victory in 1982 with the disappearance of two machines, the size of cars, called projection mask aligners. They are used in the manufacture of microcircuitry for everything from digital watches to missile guidance systems. In March 1982 a Connecticut firm, Perkin-Elmer, received a routine purchase order from Favag, a Swiss company in the watch-making

25. *The Daily Telegraph*, February 28 and March 9, 1976.
26. *International Herald Tribune*, April 6, 1983.
27. *Time*, February 14, 1983.

town of Neuchatel. Perkin-Elmer reported the order to the US Commerce Department which investigated the deal for months before approving it in August. On delivery, Favag promptly sold the machines with a commission to a Paris-based export-import firm. They were shipped to Paris, and then vanished. They are assumed to have made their way to the Russians[28].

Like other intelligence agencies, the KGB attempts to recruit foreign decision-makers or those close to them, not only for the purpose of obtaining information, but also in the hope of exerting influence. A spectacular penetration of this kind, though it almost backfired, was the career of Günter Guillaume who left East Germany ostensibly as a refugee in 1956. He joined the Social Democratic Party (SPD) and eventually became an adviser in Chancellor Willy Brandt's office. For more than a year he was Brandt's personal assistant with access to West German and NATO defence secrets as well as political intelligence about the Bonn government's Ostpolitik. When he was arrested, along with his wife and several others in April 1974, Brandt found the scandal too intense and resigned. Brandt's departure had serious implications for the future of Soviet-West German relations, but the fact that Andropov had kept Guillaume on in Brandt's office in spite of the inevitable political explosion which his exposure would cause seemed to be a classic case of Moscow's trying to have its cake and eat it. The Kremlin put great store by its relations with Bonn, but it also could not resist the temptation of having a contact in so high a position. It simply hoped to escape the inherent contradiction.

Guillaume was the highest-placed political spy to emerge in the West throughout Andropov's KGB period. Whether there are others of comparable importance still in place is of course impossible to say. The law of probabilities, however, would suggest that over fifteen years others would by now have been unmasked, if they existed. The world has changed since the 1930's when many of the most notorious Soviet spies were recruited, particularly in Britain. At that time idealism about the Soviet Union was strong and there was concern on the Left about the trend in part of the Establishment to appease fascism. In the early post-war years there

---

28. *Time*, February 14, 1983.

was another potential group of ideologically motivated recruits, angry at the onset of the Cold War and the collapse of the war-time alliance with Moscow. By the late 1960's when Andropov took over the KGB these factors no longer applied. The Soviet model commanded no significant following in the West. Potential agents for the KGB would act for money or out of fear of blackmail rather than loyalty to Moscow's view of the world.

Andropov had little personal contact with his foreign agents, just as he largely avoided any direct involvement in particular KGB operations inside the Soviet Union (with the exception of a few cases, discussed in Chapter 5). The only reported case – and it rests entirely on the possibly exaggerated testimony of one demonstrably vain man – was that of a Canadian professor, Hugh Hambleton, who was recruited in the mid-1950's from a family of Soviet sympathisers and received a ten-year prison sentence in Britain in 1982. On a secret trip to Moscow in July 1975, Hambleton says he was told by his KGB contacts to expect an important guest to dinner that evening. The guest was a tall, grey man who arrived with two bodyguards. He asked Hambleton whether the United States could increase its military spending beyond present levels, whether Jews were badly persecuted in the United States, and whether young American radicals looked to the Soviet Union for inspiration. When the conversation turned to China, the visitor called Sino-Soviet relations a tragedy. He urged Hambleton to seek a job in an influential American research institute, such as the Hudson Institute. After an hour he left, and Hambleton says he was told by his contacts that the dinner guest had been Andropov[29].

Although Andropov tried to use the KGB to influence Western public opinion, there was little evidence that he succeeded. Western political movements are too varied, and on the whole sophisticated, while suspicions of the Kremlin are too deep-seated for the KGB to have much chance of making headway. Individuals acting for Moscow may be operating in Western political parties or protest movements, but they cannot set the agenda or control their direction.

Recent cases where Soviet agents of influence have been

---

29. John Barron, *KGB Today*, p. 14.

discovered in the West confirm the impression that such KGB activity is small-scale. In 1980 the French authorities imprisoned Pierre-Charles Pathé, of the aristocratic cinema family, for publishing KGB articles on international affairs over a twenty-year period. The following year Danish police uncovered a clandestine relationship between the KGB and Arne Herløv Petersen, an author and journalist. The KGB had paid him to place a series of advertisements in local papers in which Danish artists expressed support for a nuclear-free zone. Petersen also published a pamphlet attacking Mrs Thatcher without mentioning in the pamphlet that it came from the Soviet embassy.

More impressive was the operation conducted by Stanislav Levchenko in Tokyo from 1975 to 1979. Posing as a correspondent for the Soviet magazine *New Times* he was in charge of ten Japanese agents, four of whom he recruited himself. After he defected, he told Western officials that the agents whom he and his colleagues controlled included journalists, a former Cabinet minister, senior officials of the Japanese Socialist Party, and members of Parliament. Although he gathered information from them, more that half his time was spent in pushing Soviet propaganda, in some cases on the basis of forged documents. The KGB paid the salary of staff at a parliamentary association for Soviet-Japanese co-operation. It arranged the publication of a forged 'Will of Zhou Enlai'. It passed on a rumour that Italy was planning the secret sale of a nuclear reactor to China, a calculated effort at raising Japanese suspicions of China.

The combined effect of these so-called active measures in Western countries is hard to assess, though it is unlikely that it was great. Western intelligence sources believe such measures increased under Andropov, when the department which co-ordinated them was promoted in 1970 and re-named Service A, within the KGB's First (foreign intelligence) Chief Directorate. Service A works closely with the information departments of the Central Committee, so that the dividing line between what counts as KGB propaganda and what is Party propaganda is obscure. In general KGB propaganda is information which is either false, distorted, or forged (disinformation) or whose source is disguised, so that people do not realise that it originates in the Soviet Union. The expansion of the KGB's activities in this field in the 1960's and 1970's went hand in hand with the Soviet Union's increasingly active foreign policy then. As the global competition with the United States and the West developed, particularly in Africa, Asia and the Middle East, it was natural that the Kremlin would expand the general infrastructure of that policy in an effort to match the West. Active measures were part of the competiton.

In Western countries they were probably least successful. In an article in the *Nato Review* in 1983 Lawrence Eagleburger, the US Under-Secretary of State for Political Affairs, concluded that while they had to be opposed, "Active measures are not magic, nor does the West dance to a covert Soviet tune. Moscow does not dominate the political processes of Western democracies". The most that he was able to say of their value to the Soviet Union was that "the persistent Soviet attempts to influence our political agenda are not always without effect"[30].

In the Third World, where competition between East and West became intense from the 1960's onwards, Soviet efforts at disinformation and destabilisation were more effective than in the Western democracies with their more stable societies. But the KGB had a smaller impact in the Third World than its main rival, the CIA, which had a long record of toppling governments and attempting to assassinate foreign leaders[31]. Apart from Afghanistan, there is no known case outside the Soviet Union's post-war sphere of influence where the KGB has removed a foreign government. In Sudan in 1971 it seems to have tried to overthrow Numeiry, but the attempt was foiled and scores of Soviet diplomats including the Ambassador were told to leave the country. In Mexico in the same year five diplomats were declared *personae non gratae* after being found in contact with a local guerrilla movement. In 1979 Liberia charged three Soviet diplomats with inciting riots over food prices and

---

30. Lawrence Eagleburger, 'Unacceptable Intervention: Soviet Active Measures', *Nato Review*, Brussels, April 1983.
31. The CIA organised the overthrow of the Governments of Iran in 1953 and of Guatemala in 1954. It was involved in plots against President Ngo Dinh Diem of South Vietnam, Patrice Lumumba in the Congo, Rafael Trujillo in the Dominican Republic, and Sukarno in Indonesia. It organised the Bay of Pigs invasion of Cuba and made numerous efforts to kill Fidel Castro. It helped in the destabilisation efforts which led to the overthrow of Chile's President, Salvador Allende.

expelled them. Another trio was thrown out of Costa Rica that year for allegedly inciting a general strike. In 1980 Pakistan expelled more than one hundred Russians for subversive activities.

The Kremlin's main effort against established governments in the Third World is its support for national liberation movements. As well as supplying them with arms the KGB, along with the Soviet armed forces, runs training camps in the Soviet Union for their members. Among the clientele of these camps are believed to be groups which engage in terrorism, although the KGB is careful to ensure that it cannot be accused of inciting them to acts of terror, which it publicly denounces. John McMahon, Deputy Director of the CIA, told a United States Congressional committee in 1982 that after an extensive study of the Soviet Union's role in relation to terrorism "we concluded that the Soviets do not engage directly in terrorist activities"[32]. "We see evidence of Soviet complicity and indirect support to organisations which engage in terrorism...but we don't see the Soviet hand directly on the smoking gun". His statement does not answer the point whether the Kremlin privately supports terrorism but preserves a public position whereby it can deny it (so-called plausible denial), or whether it wishes to maintain links with groups which may one day be victorious and therefore turns a blind eye to methods which it considers risky or counter-productive.

One strong piece of evidence suggesting that the latter is the case came from the testimony of a Palestinian guerrilla captured by the Israelis in 1980. Adnan Jaber was offered for interview to a *New York Times* reporter, a rare chance to question a prisoner whom the Israelis presumably considered could strengthen their position. He commanded a guerrilla squad which killed six Jewish worshippers in a sabbath ambush in Hebron. He joined the PLO in 1969 and after training in Syria was sent to the Soviet Union in 1974. He told his interviewer that although most guerrillas were sent to the Soviet Union, Soviet training was not considered the best. "The training of the Vietnamese is better from the point of view of military experience. The experience of Vietnam is considered contemporary,

---

32. John McMahon, in *Soviet Active Measures: Hearings Before the Permanent Select Committee on Intelligence*, House of Representatives, 97th Congress, Second Session, Washington DC, July 13, 1982, p. 23.

and it resembles approximately the situation in which the Palestine Liberation Organisation finds itself, whereas the experience of the Soviet Union and China resembles more the experience of World War Two", he said[33]. The guerrillas attended political lectures in which they were encouraged to agree to a Palestinian state on the West Bank, the standard Soviet point of view. The Soviet instructors did not try to inspire them to emotional hatred. The target was the 'enemy'. Israel was never mentioned. The military part of the course emphasised conventional military techniques and not individual guerrilla acts or attacks on civilians. None of the exercises simulated an urban situation, except one in which they were taught how to take control of a building.

THE SHOOTING OF THE POPE

If the KGB's links to terrorism are at most indirect, what is one to make of its possible connection with the event which stunned the world on the afternoon of May 13, 1981? As the Pope was riding in his white jeep through a crowded St Peter's Square, a man fired a volley of bullets from close range. The Pope slumped, hit in the abdomen. The gunman was quickly caught. He turned out to be a 23-year-old Turk, Mehmet Ali Agca, a professional killer, wanted for murder in Turkey. Agca's motive for the attempted killing was not immediately obvious. "I am an international terrorist, ready to help other terrorists everywhere", he said in a signed statement. "I make no distinction between fascists or communists. The international terrorist, as I see it, is not bothered by ideological labels"[34]. Italian magistrates called the shooting "the tip of a conspiracy" and "the result of a complex plot orchestrated by hidden minds interested in destabilisation". In court the prosecution said "Agca was manipulated, trained, directed, helped and subsidised to kill the Pope".

As evidence for the conspiracy theory there was the fact that Agca

---

33. *International Herald Tribune*, November 1, 1980.
34. *The Man Who Shot the Pope: a Study in Terrorism*, transcript of a National Broadcasting Company documentary in the United States, broadcast on January 25, 1983.

had spent months before the shooting wandering around Europe spending money freely. Where had an unemployed Turk got all this money? Chance photographs taken by a tourist just seconds before Agca fired showed at least one, perhaps two, other men who appeared to be linked to him. Who were they? Were they meant to help him, or to kill him so that his secret could never emerge? Unfortunately the other man or men were not detained, and Agca at his trial refused to disclose any conspiracy.

But about a year after he started to serve a life sentence in an Italian prison, Agca began to talk. Now he said he was offered about $1.5 million to kill the Pope by Bekir Celenk, a Turkish businessman whom he had met at the expensive Hotel Vitosha-New Otani in the Bulgarian capital of Sofia in 1980. He also claimed that he later met Sergei Antonov, a Bulgarian Airlines official, in Rome and they discussed a plot to kill the Polish Solidarity trade union leader, Lech Walesa, and the Pope. Both Celenk and Antonov have denied the meetings took place.

Although Italian police arrested Antonov, he has not been brought to trial and the evidence in the case remains circumstantial. All that is known independently about Agca, apart from his own alleged confession, is this. In Istanbul in 1979 he had murdered a prominent liberal editor, Abdi Ipekci. Police found that about $10,000 had been deposited for him in an Istanbul bank shortly before the killing. A few days later he managed to escape from the high-security prison of Kartel-Maltepe. (The suggestion is that Agca was already a 'hired hand' or 'contract killer'.) In hiding, Agca immediately sent a letter to the dead Ipekci's newspaper threatening to kill the Pope, whom he sneeringly called the "Commander of the Crusades", and who was shortly due to visit Turkey. As a result of the threat, security on the Pope was tightened, and the visit passed off without incident.

Police later reconstructed some of Agca's movements. In February 1980 he crossed the Turkish border into Iran. In July he surfaced in Sofia for a prolonged stay at the Hotel Vitosha-New Otani, widely known as a meeting-place for arms and narcotic merchants and a regular stopping-place for Turks travelling up to Western Europe. Later Agca moved to Italy where he spent several months before the attempted papal assassination.

It is this period in Sofia which has provided the foundation on which a "Bulgarian connection" in the attempted killing of the Pope has been built. Is it possible, people ask, that the Bulgarian state security police would not have known that Agca, a killer who had threatened to murder the Pope, was living in Sofia? And if it knew, then surely the KGB must have known too? There is certainly no doubt that the two security services work very closely together. For almost forty years Bulgaria has been one of the Soviet Union's closest allies. The Soviet Ambassador to Bulgaria, appointed in 1979, was Nikita Tolubeyev, a friend of Andropov's deputy KGB chairman, and his eventual successor, Viktor Chebrikov. The two men had advanced together in the Ukrainian Party apparatus. But even without this personal connection close links between the two services were long-standing.

Agca developed his story a further stage in July 1983 when he claimed to reporters that both the Bulgarians and the KGB were involved in his attempt to kill the Pope. Tass quickly dismissed this claim as a "thread-bare propaganda canard" and said that alleged links between Agca and Communist countries were "nothing more than absurd insinuations"[35].

Certainly, the KGB had a motive for wanting to be rid of Pope John-Paul II. The first Pole to become Pope, he made a triumphant visit to his homeland in the summer of 1979, an emotional pilgrimage which brought millions of Poles into the streets for the most dignified and inspiring celebration of Polish nationalism that most Poles have ever experienced. The upsurge of pride and determination which greeted the birth of the Solidarity trade union movement the following year and turned it, almost overnight, from a strike movement in the Gdansk shipyard to a nation-wide organisation was widely considered to have been a consequence of the Pope's visit. Once in existence, the Solidarity movement gained immediate Vatican support. The Pope received Lech Walesa on January 15, 1981 with an emotional embrace televised around the world. Vatican money was channeled to Solidarity.

To a suspicious mind the Pope's activity may well have looked like a deliberate attempt to de-stabilise Poland. If two columnists in

---

35. Associated Press from Moscow, July 9, 1983.

the *Washington Post* are to be believed, the KGB had prepared a document for Andropov and the Politburo after the Pope's election, maintaining that Zbigniew Brzezinski, Carter's National Security Adviser, and Cardinal John Krol, both Polish-Americans, had engineered his election by lining up the West German and American cardinals behind him. The aim was said to be the fomenting of an anti-Soviet rebellion in Poland and the promotion of Polish-West German reconciliation[36]. Everything the Pope had done since 1979 would seem to fit into this gloomy analysis.

Establishing a motive, of course, is not enough to prove that Andropov would have ordered his men to arrange to have the Pope killed. Is the notion of a KGB plot any less wild than some of the speculation which the KGB's own disinformation people put out? *Pravda*, for example, linked Agca to unidentifed Italian neo-fascists; *Komsomolskaya Pravda* said Americans were training hit-men in Turkey; a Soviet monthly said Italian church conservatives would have wanted to kill the Pope; a Novosti Press Agency article suggested that the Reagan Administration had tried to kill him because he disagreed with US foreign policy[37].

In favour of the theory that the KGB was behind Agca there is, first, the trouble the Pope was causing. Secondly, there are historical precedents, admittedly scanty. The Bulgarian secret police was widely thought (though never proved) to have arranged the murder with a poison-tipped umbrella of a prominent exile broadcaster, Georgi Markov, in London in September 1978. Further back in time, the KGB's predecessors had been ruthless in tracking down and killing irritating exiles, the most famous, of course, being Leon Trotsky who was murdered in Mexico.

Against the notion of KGB guilt is the fact that Soviet murders have concentrated on those whom Moscow considers traitors – political dissidents, defectors, and exiles engaged in anti-Soviet or anti-Communist activity. The KGB does not have a history of assassinating foreign heads of government or state. (But then the Pope is in a unique position. As a Pole in the Vatican, he fits somewhere between the anti-Communist exile, and the head of government. The KGB could safely have calculated that his

36. *Washington Post*, March 30, 1983.
37. Cited by Paul B. Henze, *Christian Science Monitor*, March 21, 1983.

successor would not be another Pole, and therefore his charisma and political symbolism for Poland would have died with him.)

More important is the fact that the Kremlin risked enormous damage from public exposure if it took part in any assassination attempts, whether or not it succeeded. The CIA is inclined to doubt the KGB link. According to the *Los Angeles Times*, CIA professionals concluded that the Bulgarians must have known that Agca wanted to kill the Pope. (He was on the public record as saying so.) They chose not to stop him, because they regarded him as an unstable person who would probably be captured[38]. Unless new evidence emerges, the verdict on the KGB's alleged role in the papal shooting has to be 'Not Proven'.

---

38. *International Herald Tribune*, May 28-9, 1983.

7
The Rise to Supreme Power

Konstantin Chernenko, the man whom Brezhnev had hoped to have as his successor, addressed a special meeting of the Central Committee two days after Brezhnev's death. It was one of those rare times when Politburo members allow themselves a display of public emotion and Chernenko rose to the occasion. "Words fail to express the bitterness of our loss"[1], he said as he launched into extravagant praise of his dead friend. Brezhnev had been a man of courage and principle. The keenness of his mind, his quick wit and love of life had taught much to those who had worked hand in hand with him. The Politburo owed it to Brezhnev's memory to treasure and develop his style of guidance and everything bequeathed by him.

Well might Chernenko have felt emotional, for the most important part of his speech was about to come. The Politburo, he went on, "has entrusted me to propose to the meeting to elect Comrade Yuri Vladimirovich Andropov General Secretary of the Central Committee."[2]. It was a hard moment, since Chernenko knew at that point that Andropov's election was a formality. The Kremlin gives little instruction in how to be a good loser and Chernenko showed his disappointment clearly when he grudgingly went on to remind his victorious rival of the "modesty required of a Party member" and the need to "respect the opinion of other comrades"[3].

If November 12, 1982 was a black day for Chernenko, it was one of triumph for Andropov, the culmination of a long rise to power

1. *Pravda*, November 13, 1982.
2. Ibid.
3. Ibid.

which had moved into top gear only ten months earlier with the death of Mikhail Suslov. Suslov's departure left a gap which Chernenko and Andropov had each tried to fill at the other's expense, in what proved to be a trial run for the contest for the more important prize, the job held by Brezhnev.

It can hardly be doubted, of course, that Andropov had long had ambitions to occupy Brezhnev's position. At least since his elevation to full membership in the Politburo in 1973, if not earlier, Andropov must have realised that he was one of the younger, more intelligent, and experienced top decision-makers in the Soviet Union. As head of the KGB he had a seat on the Defence Council and in 1976 he became an army general. But Andropov also knew that he was not Brezhnev's most likely successor. In the early 1970's Brezhnev's closest ally was Andrei Kirilenko. An associate of Brezhnev's since the 1930's when they worked together in the Ukraine, Kirilenko had been a Secretary of the Central Committee and a member of the Politburo since 1966. Brezhnev told a group of American reporters at an impromptu press conference shortly before his June 1973 visit to the United States that Kirilenko or Suslov chaired the Politburo if he was absent himself[4].

Later, Brezhnev's favour switched to Chernenko, whose promotion was signalled when he became a Central Committee Secretary in 1976. At the end of 1978 Chernenko was made a full member of the Politburo and was frequently seen in public at Brezhnev's side. Like Kirilenko, Chernenko was a friend from Brezhnev's pre-Moscow days. He had worked with Brezhnev in Moldavia in the 1950's and then followed him to the capital where he was appointed head of the general department of the Central Committee in 1965, in effect Brezhnev's chief of staff.

By the end of the 1970's most observers assumed that Chernenko was the most probable heir to Brezhnev's job. Brezhnev had had a stroke in 1975 and began to cut down his work load. From 1978 he seemed to suffer a further decline and during his meeting with President Carter at Vienna in June 1979, his last summit encounter with an American president, he was no longer in full command of

---

4. *New York Times*, June 15, 1973.

his brief and relied heavily on advisers. The main difficulty for Chernenko was that he needed Brezhnev to retire and hand over power. If Brezhnev died in office, much of Chernenko's political influence would fade with his patron's. Chernenko's strategy therefore was to persuade Brezhnev to retire. Andropov's was to try to discredit Brezhnev and if possible, by extension, all those, Chernenko included, who were close to him.

Chernenko's problem was that Brezhnev showed no interest in retiring. None of the Soviet Union's previous leaders had retired. They had either died in harness or been removed by their colleagues. Indeed it is one of the many faults of the Soviet system that it has developed no tradition of honourable retirement. Even members of the Politburo who have given up their jobs because they became ill and not because of disagreements with their colleagues have found that they became to all intents and purposes 'unpeople'. Their names drop out of public life and they only rarely, if ever, receive invitations for important receptions. They lose access to the special bulletins of home and foreign news which are circulated to a restricted group of senior officials. Instead, they are reduced to reading *Pravda* and the rest of the Soviet press. They may retain some of their material privileges, including pensions and dachas, but public recognition is removed from one day to the next. The most they can look forward to is an obituary in the newspapers and burial in the Kremlin wall or one of the other graveyards of distinction.

As long as Brezhnev was determined to stay on, Chernenko's strategy had its risks. If he tried to persuade the old man to retire, he courted the danger of falling out of favour either as a result of direct confrontation with Brezhnev or if Brezhnev's other colleagues passed the word to him that Chernenko was plotting. Andropov's strategy also involved risks. He too could face the charge of plotting if his efforts to discredit Brezhnev and Chernenko became too obvious.

Andropov's credentials were more impressive than Chernenko's, although both shared limitations in their colleagues' eyes. Neither had combat experience in the Second World War. Neither had run a factory or a collective farm. A ruddy-faced peasant's son with a broad Slavic face and strong white hair brushed back from his forehead, Chernenko was the more personable of the two. Although he was almost three years younger than Chernenko, Andropov looked older and less healthy.

But whereas Chernenko was a classic apparatchik who had spent his entire career in the Party bureaucracy, Andropov had served as a diplomat and adviser on foreign affairs, and as head of the KGB. He had considerable experience of foreign policy and in the KGB job had forged important links with the armed forces. It is the KGB which guards the Soviet Union's missile sites and every significant military installation. KGB officers form part of the missile launching teams. The KGB also has its own troops in the shape of fifteen specially trained divisions of border guards.

Andropov's background gave him the advantage of being able to project himself as independent of Brezhnev. He had held important offices of Party and State in his own right, and could distance himself from Brezhnev. Chernenko, by contrast, was nothing but a Brezhnev associate, tainted by the increasing sense of failure that characterised the last years of the Brezhnev era. The crisis in Afghanistan and Poland, agricultural stagnation and economic inefficiency – these all seemed to redound to Brezhnev's discredit, and it was natural that other members of the Politburo would like to suggest that they were less responsible for allowing them to happen than Brezhnev and his immediate friends, such as Chernenko.

The first small hint that Chernenko had begun to see Andropov as a direct rival for power emerged in 1981. At the Twenty-Sixth Party Congress in February, which Chernenko was responsible for organising, Andropov was the only Politburo member who did not get to chair a session[5]. During the summer rumours were rife that Brezhnev's health was poor but he was resisting retirement. In December the rumours appeared to receive official sanction. A literary magazine in Leningrad called *Aurora* dedicated its monthly issue to Brezhnev's seventy-fifth birthday. Amused readers discovered that on page 75 the magazine printed a satirical story about a very old writer who "does not plan to die"[6]. The story-teller made it clear that he hoped the writer would hurry up and die. He had

---

5. Boris Meissner, 'Transition in the Kremlin', *Problems of Communism*, January–February 1983, p. 8.
6. Viktor Golyavkin, 'Jubilee Speech', *Aurora*, Leningrad, December 1981.

heard the writer was dead, but found the report was false: "My delight was premature. But I don't think we have long to wait. He will not disappoint us. We all believe in him. We wish he would finish off his unfinished business, and be as quick as possible in providing us with the happy event". The magazine immediately became a collector's item and was passed eagerly from hand to hand among Moscow's intelligentsia. Was the story about the elderly writer mere coincidence? Or a witty jab at the aging Brezhnev and, if so, by whom?

In January 1982 more startling rumours began to circulate in Moscow. Brezhnev's daughter, Galina, was said to be involved in a spectacular corruption scandal. Stories about corruption among the élite are, of course, common currency in the Soviet Union. In a society which draws so tight a veil over the private lives and personalities of its leaders and where economic scarcities are well known, it is hardly surprising that many citizens suspect that members of the *nachalstvo* – the authorities – are going beyond their normal Party privileges and becoming rich on the side. At every level of officialdom bribes and favours are regularly accepted as routine. Why should people believe it to be any different at the very top? Nevertheless scandals involving senior figures in or near the Kremlin are usually hushed up. The last time a scandal emerged was a decade earlier when it was revealed by Soviet sources that Ekaterina Furtseva, Khrushchev's Minister of Culture and the only woman ever to join the Politburo, had built herself a luxurious dacha at the state's expense.

The rumour that the General Secretary's daughter was involved in corruption was a sensation. Whether true or false, Muscovites found it significant that the rumour was going round. Who had started it? The scandal was said to have been discovered shortly after the funeral of Nikolai Asanov, a former director of the Soviet national circus, on December 27. One of the mourners, Irina Bugrimova, a lion tamer with an unusual collection of diamonds, returned home to find some missing. She told the police who found them in the flat of a playboy friend of Galina's named Boris Buryatia, or Boris the Gypsy. He had started out as a minor actor in Moscow's gypsy theatre (hence the nickname) but thanks to Galina's influence had obtained a minor position at the Bolshoi.

Galina had always been something of an *enfant terrible*. In addition to rumours of several affairs she had been married three times, her most recent husband being General Yuri Churbanov, a Deputy Minister of Internal Affairs, in effect the second in command of the MVD, the uniformed police. For a time she worked in the Ministry of Foreign Affairs section which arranges trips and receptions for diplomats and foreigners. This provided the opportunity for unofficial deals and her friends, like Boris the Gypsy, used her to obtain luxury goods.

As head of the KGB Andropov must have been aware of the scandal. But officially any action by his agency had to be taken by the First Deputy Chairman of the KGB responsible for internal security, General Semyon Tsvigun. Tsvigun was in an extremely awkward position as he was Brezhnev's brother-in-law. At this point the story becomes more obscure. What is known for certain is that on January 19 Tsvigun died, and when his official obituary was published it was seen that neither Brezhnev nor Suslov had signed it, although four other Politburo members did. Something was clearly wrong since, as General Secretary of the Central Committee, Brezhnev was expected to sign the obituary of every Central Committee member. A second clue was that Tsvigun was not buried in the cemetery at Novodevichi where all senior officials of similar rank are interred.

Western reporters in Moscow were told by Soviet sources that Tsvigun had killed himself but there were conflicting reports of the reason. Some said that Tsvigun had been involved in a cover-up of Galina's misdemeanours for some time but realised he was now too vulnerable himself. Others brought Suslov into the picture. It was said that Andropov put the file on the whole case in front of Suslov who confronted Tsvigun with it and told him he faced prosecution. The encounter not only led to Tsvigun's suicide but may also have brought on Suslov's death. On January 25 it was announced that Suslov had died of a stroke. It had always been Suslov who had protected the good names of the élite and made sure that no scandals involving them became publicly known. Andropov's decision to make an issue of the Galina case put Suslov in a position where he had to break with his normal practice. The shock to him, and to Tsvigun, was apparently severe.

Ten days after Tsvigun's death Boris the Gypsy was arrested and on February 17 the police also detained Anatoly Kolevatov, the director of the circus. Kolevatov was said to have been found in possession of an astonishing $1.4 million worth of illicitly obtained diamonds and foreign currency. He had apparently used his position to extort bribes from performers who wanted to join foreign tours by the circus. Meanwhile Galina denied any complicity in the various scandals. She was spared arrest.

Many details of this murky sequence of events remain obscure, as do the exact political consequences of the scandal. The Brezhnev family clearly did not come well out of it. As a crony of Brezhnev Chernenko was also indirectly tainted. Andropov appeared to gain most. He had a personal reputation as one of the least corruptible and most honest members of the Politburo, and was able to stand aloof from the scandal as someone who had tried, in as much as it was in his power to do so, to punish the guilty. It was probably his KGB which had kept the rumours of the scandal going, providing an indirect warning that Andropov was beginning to flex his muscles in the succession struggle.

The death of Suslov, the number two man in the Kremlin hierarchy, opened the way for the next round of manoeuvring. As Secretary of the Central Committee responsible for enforcing ideological rectitude in every sphere, from the conduct of the armed forces, economic management, education, culture, to the administration of Eastern Europe, Suslov left an enormous and crucial gap. Brezhnev's own health was deteriorating fast and this could no longer be concealed from the public. At Suslov's funeral he was shown on television looking weak and depressed. Three weeks later he was seen publicly in tears again, this time at the funeral of an old war-time comrade, General Konstantin Grushevoi.

Three months older than Brezhnev, Kirilenko was also weakening physically as a result of progressive arteriosclerosis. He failed to appear with the rest of the Politburo on March 3 at a performance of an unusual anti-Stalinist play by Mikhail Shatrov at the Moscow Arts Theatre, called *This Is How We Shall Win*. Ironically the play showed a sick Lenin worrying over the undesirable qualities of Stalin, whose succession he was too weak to prevent. Andropov and Chernenko watched the play with Brezhnev. At the beginning of

March the ailing Brezhnev flew to Uzbekistan to award that Central Asian republic the Order of Lenin. In Tashkent he delivered an important speech offering reconciliation with China. But the flight to Tashkent, the round of public appearances, and the change of climate affected his health. When he flew back to Moscow the usual live television pictures of his arrival in Moscow were unavailable. Soviet sources told Western reporters that the Party leader had suffered a mild stroke on the plane and been carried from it on a stretcher. He was rushed to a special section of the Kremlin hospital in a coma. For several days he lost the power of speech.

Brezhnev's incapacity forced a postponement of the normal spring meeting of the Central Committee until May. The meeting was due to resolve the crucial issue of who would take over Suslov's position in the Secretariat. In January Chernenko had already tried to move into the gap left by Suslov's death. At Suslov's lying-in-state he put himself in the place of most importance next to Brezhnev. In March he engineered the removal of Alexei Shibayev, the head of the Soviet trade union organisation, and a Kirilenko appointee. In April he published an important ideological article on the question of pluralism under socialism in *Kommunist*. In early May, in Brezhnev's absence, he read the Party leader's message of greetings to a conference of Secretaries of primary Party organisations in the armed services.

But Andropov was also moving forward. The Politburo chose him to give the speech on the anniversary of Lenin's death in April at the prestigious annual ceremony attended by the Party leadership and all senior officials. Chernenko had made the speech the previous year. Comparison of Andropov's speech and Chernenko's *Kommunist* article reveals a subtle difference of approach between them, almost as though they were campaigning to inherit Suslov's mantle[7]. Both denied the need for political pluralism under 'real' socialism and repeated Suslov's favourite line that the Leninist model of socialist construction is universally applicable. But Andropov went on to say that the development of democracy depended on "the successes of socialist construction", suggesting that economic performance was more important at the current stage

---

7. For more detail, see Elizabeth Teague, *Signs of Rivalry between Andropov and Chernenko*, Radio Liberty Research, RL 214/82, May 25, 1982.

than more democracy[8]. Chernenko by contrast pointed out that "it is sometimes possible to hear people asking whether we do not already have too much democracy in our society, and whether it is not leading to a weakening of discipline"[9]. He rejected these ideas (which are presumably found at all levels of the KGB and the Party's ideological departments) as a "witting or unwitting confusion of democracy with petty-bourgeois notions".

While coming over as somewhat more disciplinarian than Chernenko, Andropov was careful to stress that he was not an old-fashioned Stalinist police chief. With an eye to reformers within the Party who might be concerned at his KGB image, he said that the mistakes of the Stalinist past were over. "As is well known, at one time there were problems, not simple ones, associated with a departure from Leninist norms. Our Party under the guidance of the Central Committee has overcome the negative consequences of that. We have done this work and learned the necessary lessons from the difficult record of historical experience"[10], he said. His only direct mention of crime was a reference to corruption – a not too subtle reminder of the scandals which had just rocked the Brezhnev entourage. Projecting himself as Mr Clean, he declared that "Soviet citizens are justly indignant at instances of embezzlement, bribery, red tape, a disrespectful attitude to people and other antisocial acts....The Soviet people fully support measures taken by the Party to uproot these phenomena"[11].

If it did nothing else, Andropov's speech put his hat in the ring as a candidate for Suslov's job. If he was to succeed the ailing Brezhnev, Andropov had to return to the Central Committee Secretariat. It would have been unprecedented to move straight from the KGB to the Party's highest post. A spell back in the Secretariat was essential.

The key moment for decision came at a session of the Politburo shortly before the Central Committee met on May 25. By one account there was a heated debate[12]. Brezhnev suggested Cher-

8. *Pravda*, April 23, 1982.
9. *Kommunist*, No. 6, 1982, pp. 25, 43.
10. *Pravda*, April 23, 1982.
11. Ibid.
12. Zhores Medvedev, 'Yuri Andropov and His Ways', *Labour Focus on Eastern Europe*, London, Vol. 5, Nos. 5–6, Winter 1982–3.

nenko for the job but was overruled. Ustinov, Gorbachev, and Gromyko were against Chernenko, as were even two of Brezhnev's closest friends, Dinmukhamed Kunaev and Vladimir Shcherbitsky, who objected to working under someone they regarded as their junior[13]. Other accounts put Kirilenko in the anti-Chernenko faction also[14]. Kirilenko was still smarting under Brezhnev's promotion of Chernenko as his favoured successor. Kirilenko had the best contacts within the Party apparatus and could act as a bridge to Andropov.

While there is general agreement among observers that Ustinov supported Andropov, the degree of his enthusiasm is disputed. Some argue that Ustinov was strongly against Chernenko on the grounds that he had no authority among military leaders, having spent the war thousands of miles from the front as Party Secretary in the Krasnoyarsk region of Siberia[15]. Andropov had at least been nearer the front line during the war, although he had no direct combat experience. Ustinov was also said to be upset at the way Brezhnev exaggerated his own war record, particularly in his later years, and continually awarded himself new medals.

On the other hand, it is argued that the history of rivalry between the KGB and the armed forces must have tempered Ustinov's enthusiasm[16]. A clue to this may be found in the way the job of KGB chief was handled after Andropov's transfer back to the Secretariat. Two days after Andropov's move, Vitaly Fedorchuk, the head of the KGB in the Ukraine, was appointed to succeed him. This appointment, it is said, cannot have reassured the military since Fedorchuk had spent a quarter of a century until 1970 specialising in counter-intelligence in the armed forces and supervising the officer corps. Fedorchuk's shift six months later from the KGB job to head the Ministry of Internal Affairs may have been caused by senior military criticism of the first appointment.

In spite of these possible reservations Ustinov probably supported Andropov because he was abler than Chernenko and seemed more likely to be a strong promoter of efficiency. Like the rest of

13. Zhores Medvedev, *Andropov*, Oxford, Basil Blackwell, 1983, p. 11.
14. Myron Rush, 'Succeeding Brezhnev', *Problems of Communism*, January–February 1983, p. 4.
15. Zhores Medvedev, *Andropov*, pp. 103–5.
16. Myron Rush, *Problems of Communism*, p. 4.

the Politburo Ustinov must have realised that in bringing Andropov back into the Secretariat they were in a sense already selecting him as Brezhnev's successor. Andropov had done well as head of the KGB by keeping the security services firmly under Party control. He was a disciplinarian in contrast to Brezhnev's easy-going manner and, of course, he had had considerable experience of foreign policy and international military issues through his membership of the Politburo and the Defence Council.

Ustinov may also have approved of Andropov's sophisticated line on detente. It is sometimes assumed in the West that the Soviet military is automatically suspicious of detente and prefers the maximum possible spending on arms. This is an over-simplification. The perceived need to maintain military parity with the United States imposes severe strains on the Soviet economy and keeps the military establishment at full stretch in trying to test and develop new weaponry. Andropov himself had long been a firm champion of detente. In 1975 he argued that "detente is a continuous process which demands constant movement forward"[17]. A year later, in his Lenin Anniversary speech he stated that "the policy of peaceful co-existence implies negotiating agreements, a quest for mutually acceptable, at times compromise solutions" and, in a clear reference to the disadvantages of unlimited arms spending, he went on "It is easier to build a new society with a relaxation of tensions and a reduction in the arms burden"[18]. In 1980 he was the only Politburo member to warn that detente was in serious danger[19].

It was noticeable, too, that in his first speeches on becoming General Secretary Andropov took a balanced position on defence spending. While arguing that "it was indispensable to give the armed services everything they need" he put this after his mention of improving people's living conditions as the Party's number one priority[20]. Ustinov's closeness to Andropov was signalled by the fact that the Defence Minister was the first speaker to follow Andropov in addressing the nation at Brezhnev's funeral. Chernenko was not chosen to give a speech at all. If there were any doubt that Ustinov

17. *Pravda*, June 10, 1975.
18. *Ibid.*, April 23, 1976.
19. Ibid., February 18, 1980.
20. Ibid., November 23, 1982.

and Andropov had become allies, the funeral arrangements surely dispelled it.

In May 1982, six months before Brezhnev's death, things were not yet quite so clear cut. Although Andropov had inherited the vacancy left by Suslov, he did not take over all Suslov's functions in charge of culture, ideology, and foreign affairs. Some were still held by Chernenko. In foreign affairs the division was that Andropov supervised Soviet relations with non-ruling Communist Parties while Chernenko looked after the more important aspect – relations with Parties in power. In June and July Andropov met with visiting delegations from the Communist Parties of India, Syria, and West Germany. In August he met a delegation from the Greek Communist Party. This was especially revealing since the Greek delegation had been received by Chernenko on its previous visit a few days after Suslov's death. But Chernenko attended Brezhnev's meeting with the Czechoslovak Party leader, Gustav Husak, in June. Andropov was not present. Chernenko also accompanied Brezhnev to the Crimea in the summer and took part in the Soviet leader's meetings with Erich Honecker of East Germany and General Wojciech Jaruzelski of Poland.

In the ideological field Chernenko had to give up some of his power to Andropov. In April and mid-May Chernenko signed the obituaries of two prominent actors and an actress but at the end of May, after Andropov's return to the Central Committee, when another leading actor died, Kremlin-watchers observed that Andropov and Chernenko both signed the death notice printed in *Pravda*[21]. Soviet sources told Western correspondents that the longer-term allotment of Suslov's responsibilities was still being worked out[22]. Interest focused on one particular occasion when Andropov spoke in Brezhnev's absence in front of the rest of the Politburo at a ceremony celebrating the 1,500th anniversary of the city of Kiev on June 24. Andropov was deputising for the General Secretary in front of Chernenko. But the ceremony was given scant coverage on Soviet television, perhaps a sign that Chernenko still controlled the media.

21. Ibid., June 1, 1982.
22. *Christian Science Monitor*, June 30, 1982.

Little is known for sure about the jockeying which went on throughout the summer. Chernenko still seemed prominent right up to the moment of Brezhnev's death. In July an expanded and revised version of Chernenko's book, *Questions to do with the Work of the Party and Government Apparatus*, was given longer and more lavish reviews in the press than the first edition had received two years earlier. In October Chernenko was ranked ahead of Andropov in the presidium of a special meeting of the Politburo, Defence Council, and the military leadership. In November Viktor Grishin, the Moscow city Party leader, who was thought to be closer to Chernenko than Andropov, gave the speech in celebration of the anniversary of the Revolution. Andropov, meanwhile, was relatively inconspicuous. Between August 31, when he greeted Brezhnev on the Soviet leader's return from spending the summer at his dacha in the Crimea and October 26, he was not seen on Soviet television or mentioned as attending any public gathering.

The most significant indicator of Andropov's power was the removal from office of Sergei Medunov, the Party First Secretary in Krasnodar. This apparently minor shift was, in fact, a powerful blow at Brezhnev and his entourage. The Krasnodar region covers much of the Black Sea coast, including the resort of Sochi, and takes in the area where many Party officials have their summer villas. Medunov was said to have taken money in return for giving building permission. He was also implicated in what was labelled the Great Caviare Scandal, which had allegedly lasted for several years and put millions of roubles and hard currency into the pockets of hundreds of officials[23]. The essence of this huge operation, which was uncovered in 1979, was that caviare was packed in tins marked herring, which were distributed to special restaurants and shops and recorded as such in the books. The contents were sold abroad for hard currency and the price difference between the herring and caviare was divided up among the syndicate, which was headed by the Deputy Minister of Fisheries. When the illegal operation was discovered, he was sentenced to death, several of his deputies received prison sentences, and the Minister of Fisheries, Aleksander Ishkov, was obliged to retire. Sergei Medunov, as Krasnodar First

---

23. This episode is recounted in detail in Medvedev, *Andropov*, pp. 139–41.

Secretary, was also involved but the local KGB office was prevented from investigating his role by Brezhnev, who was an old friend of his. At some point in August Medunov's official protection slipped, and he was removed from his job in Krasnodar. It seems likely that Andropov had forced the move, just as he had done with the Galina case earlier in the year, as part of his general effort to press the issue of cleaning up corruption into a campaign to undermine Brezhnev.

During this time Chernenko was still plotting against Kirilenko to remove his already dwindling chances of succeeding Brezhnev. Kirilenko's picture disappeared from the usual display of Politburo portraits put up on the eve of the anniversary of the Revolution, a clear hint that his membership of the Politburo had been suspended. Soviet sources told Western reporters that Kirilenko's son, a foreign trade official, had defected to the West. Although the rumour proved wrong, it was seen as a way of undermining Kirilenko's standing among his colleagues. Who was behind this move against Kirilenko? The evidence suggests that it was Chernenko, rather than Andropov. Firstly, there had been a long-standing rivalry between Chernenko and Kirilenko. Secondly, it was seen that Kirilenko was allowed to attend Brezhnev's funeral. Although he stood apart from the leadership at Brezhnev's lying-in-state and walked with the Brezhnev family in the funeral procession, it was remarkable for a politician who had fallen from grace to be given any public position at all. Andropov, as the new General Secretary, must have approved it. When Kirilenko's retirement from the Politburo was announced on November 22 "because of the state of his health and at his own request", Andropov paid tribute to his "services to the Party and the country"[24]. This expression of gratitude was in marked contrast to the silent send-off usually given to retiring Politburo members. It seemed to show both that Andropov had not been Kirilenko's main opponent and that he intended to allow him an honourable departure.

When Brezhnev died of a heart attack in the morning of November 10, 1982, Andropov and Chernenko were the only two serious candidates to succeed him. Mikhail Gorbachev, the

---

24. *Pravda*, November 23, 1982.

Secretary in charge of agriculture, was the only other Politburo member who also headed a section of the Central Committee. But at the age of 51 he was by far the youngest man in the Politburo. His relative youth and his limited experience of issues outside agriculture made him an improbable successor. Ustinov, the Defence Minister, was a man of experience who was in charge of a vital element of the Soviet state, but he was probably disqualified by the fact that no previous Defence Minister had become General Secretary. The Party had always feared the distortion of the Revolution, known as Bonapartism, and this made it unlikely that a military man could jump in one move into the top civilian job. Although Ustinov was not a professional soldier and had spent most of his career in defence procurement, he had always appeared in public in uniform since becoming Defence Minister in 1976 and was clearly identified as a military figure. Gromyko, the Foreign Minister, was also a man with vast knowledge and considerable prestige, but his long service in diplomacy and foreign affairs had left him short of experience in other fields and without any powerful internal constituency.

Brezhnev's death was not made public until twenty-six hours later, when a weeping Igor Kirillov, the main television news announcer, appeared on the screen at 11 a.m. Moscow time, with a black-bordered portrait of the dead leader. He read out the brief formal statement: "The Central Committee of the Communist Party of the Soviet Union, the Presidium of the USSR Supreme Soviet and the Council of Ministers of the USSR inform with deep sorrow the Party and the entire Soviet people that Leonid Ilyich Brezhnev, General Secretary of the Soviet Communist Party Central Committee and President of the Presidium of the USSR Supreme Soviet, died a sudden death at 8.30 a.m. on November 10, 1982". The first hint had come at 7.15 p.m. the night before when television viewers waiting for a live pop concert found the programme had been replaced without explanation by a film about Lenin. At 9 p.m. the announcers for the usual evening news programme, *Vremya (Time)*, wore dark jackets. After the news, the first channel showed an unscheduled film of war reminiscences. On the second channel an ice hockey game gave way to Tchaikovsky's mournful *Pathetique* symphony.

Rumours buzzed round the Soviet capital that a senior Politburo figure had died, yet no-one was sure if it was Kirilenko, the 83-year-old Arvid Pelshe, or Brezhnev himself. By that time, in fact, in typical Kremlin secrecy, Andropov had already been chosen to take over. The decision was taken at an emergency Politburo meeting on the evening of the day Brezhnev died. Under Party rules the 300-member Central Committee is supposed to have the decisive voice but when it convened the day after the official announcement of Brezhnev's death it was simply to ratify a choice that was already made. The Central Committee rarely over-rules anything decided by the Politburo. On this occasion the fact that Andropov's election as General Secretary was proposed by Chernenko, the only serious rival, eliminated any discussion. While the Central Committee met, the centre of Moscow was sealed off by police and troops, a signal that all was under control.

Little is known of the Politburo session which picked Andropov. Ustinov, it is assumed, supported him for the General Secretaryship. Gromyko was also an ally, at least to judge from the fact that Andropov promoted him to become First Deputy Prime Minister a few months later. They chose him over Chernenko on the basis of his superior experience and intellect. With these two men in Andropov's camp Chernenko had little chance. In the interest of preserving a facade of unity and achieving as smooth and dignified a transition as possible at a time of considerable tension with the United States, they no doubt argued that a quick and unchallenged succession was important. Chernenko was asked to nominate Andropov at the Central Committee meeting which they would schedule for the day after next.

No word of the Politburo decision was published, but sharp-eyed observers guessed its outcome when the official news agency Tass reported shortly after the announcement of Brezhnev's death that a committee to organise his funeral had been formed. Those who remembered the precedent set when Stalin died twenty-nine years earlier recalled that the chairman of the funeral committee had been Nikita Khrushchev. Soon afterwards he was confirmed as Party leader. When Tass announced that the chairman of the Brezhnev funeral committee would be Andropov, it was clear who had won. After months of jockeying, Brezhnev's successor was in place.

8
Taking Charge at Home

It was an ordinary Friday afternoon at the Ordzhonikidze machine-tool plant in Moscow. Workers were standing at their lathes – in all probability casting their minds forward to the coming weekend. Suddenly down the line came a small group of managers and trade union officials, accompanied by a tall, grey-haired man in glasses. Without security guards and the large retinue of officials who usually walk beside Soviet leaders, Yuri Andropov was on an impromptu, unannounced tour of inspection.

He stopped here and there to chat to workers and ask questions. "How much do machine operators earn?" "Do lathe-workers get more?" "What technical help does your factory give to enterprises in the other socialist countries?" "Have you worked here long?" He asked one man about his family, another about his education, and joked with a woman worker about the low representation of men in the factory paint shop[1]. Later, during a work break, he gave a short speech, drawing a laugh at one point when he said it was standard procedure to "adjust the plan" which set production targets: "I must admit that I never heard of an upward adjustment of the established plan". Targets were always lowered. Becoming serious, he warned that the results this led to were obvious. Output went down while wages stayed the same. The consequence nationally – though he did not put it in quite those words – was excess demand, leading in the Soviet context not to inflation but to shortages and queues: "This results in a gap between the volume of

---

1. Reuters from Moscow, February 1, 1983.

goods in the shops and the amount of money held by the population"[2].

Productivity in the Soviet Union was not high enough:

> Everything we do and produce must be done and produced, as far as possible, at minimum cost and high quality, quickly and durably. We must produce more goods to fill the shelves.... Miracles, as they say, don't happen. You understand that the government can only provide as many goods as are produced. A wage increase cannot provide a real improvement in the standard of living, unless it goes together with a better supply of good-quality products which people want and unless services improve.[3]

Andropov ended his pep-talk with the comment: "Comrades, I'd like you to understand me correctly. Strengthening discipline is not just an issue for workers or engineers and technicians. It applies to everyone, starting with Ministers".

By Western standards Andropov's visit to the Ordzhonikidze plant was hardly remarkable. With his simplistic explanation of inflation, and his appeals for hard work and higher productivity, he could have been any Western politician or manager on a factory tour. But in the Soviet context the tour was unusual, reminiscent only of the occasional sallies Khrushchev had made to talk to workers and peasants on the job. When Brezhnev visited factories, the occasion was prepared in advance and usually included a political rally, at which he announced policy decisions. Television coverage was heavy.

Andropov's tour, by contrast, was unrehearsed. The Soviet press and censorship organs were caught so much off-guard that they let one worker's answer through, embarrassingly unchecked. When Andropov asked an elderly fitter how much he earned per month, the man replied – according to the verbatim transcript put out by the official news agency, Tass: "Enough – 380 Roubles, including my pension". In fact, the man's earnings were way beyond the legal

---

2. *Washington Post*, February 2, 1983.
3. *New York Times*, February 2, 1983.

maximum of 300 Roubles for people who stay at work beyond retirement age but also draw their pension. By the time the next morning's Soviet newspapers appeared, the fitter was reported as having described his wages only as "Enough". Evidently the full answer was deleted to avoid embarrassment for Andropov and to prevent complaints from other working pensioners whose income had been restricted to the legal maximum[4].

No photographers went with Andropov on his tour, perhaps because he was afraid of appearing awkward on camera or because he assumed the cameras might inhibit the workers he talked to. Perhaps he just wanted people to read the content of his remarks, and not be distracted by pictures. In its own way, of course, the factory visit was a publicity stunt. The message was probably intended to be a double one: firstly, to present the impression of Andropov as a down-to-earth, 'working' leader, genuinely interested in day-to-day issues; secondly, to stress that his main concern as General Secretary was with improving the economy.

His factory outing took place at the end of January 1983. But, as early as his first speech after succeeding Brezhnev in November 1982, Andropov had signalled that his priority was to raise the Soviet Union's economic performance. Indeed, no assessment of Andropov's first year in office can come close to being accurate unless it focuses on his approach to the economy. Although the West naturally watched his first moves in the foreign policy and arms control field with special attention, the heart of Andropov's programme lay in the domestic arena – in his effort to make some repairs to the ailing Soviet economy.

In that November speech Andropov specifically argued that everything, including the Soviet Union's ability to help Third World nations and cut a powerful international figure, depended on an improvement of the economy. It was not primarily through having a huge military arsenal or an ocean-going Navy that the Soviet Union exercised influence in the world. "A steady growth of the economy and improvement of the welfare of the people are both our duty to the Soviet people and our internationalist duty....The Party is guided by Lenin's far-sighted injunction that we exercise

---

4. Reuters from Moscow, February 1, 1983. 380 Roubles = 527 Dollars = 351 Pounds.

our main influence on the world revolutionary process through our economic policy"[5].

Many Western commentators commonly make two mistakes in analysing Soviet politics. One is to over-emphasise foreign policy, with the result that they overlook the more important, domestic impact that any Soviet leadership has on Soviet society. In the West Khrushchev is remembered largely for his foreign policy fireworks, such as the Cuban missile crisis, the military intervention in Hungary, his ebullient tour of the United States, and his cocky, anti-Western comment "We will bury you". But his ending of Stalin's terror and the release of millions of political prisoners were a far more lasting and profound achievement in the Soviet Union. Similarly, Brezhnev may be remembered abroad for the invasions of Czechoslovakia and Afghanistan, and the brief era of detente with the United States, symbolised by his summit meetings with Presidents Nixon, Ford, and Carter. But the economic stability he provided at home, the provision of pensions and other social benefits to peasants, and the massive injection of funds into Soviet agriculture under his leadership meant a great deal more for the Soviet population, even though by the end of his period in power stability had become stagnation, and agriculture, in spite of huge investment, was still not producing enough.

The other common Western mistake is to consider Kremlin politics almost exclusively in terms of a hidden power struggle. While the official Soviet line, which claims that discussions in the Politburo are a model of unity and comradely consensus, is obviously absurd, it is also wrong to assume that any Soviet General Secretary spends most of his time trying to remove rivals and defuse opponents' plots. The end of the Brezhnev era when the General Secretary's health was visibly failing and no successor had been chosen was certainly a time of leadership instability, as Chapter 7 has described. But this was an exceptional phase. For most of the Brezhnev era there was no challenge to his rule. The view that there is permanent instability in the Kremlin is wide of the mark. This is not to deny that Andropov has had problems with his colleagues since he took office. He has. But they have not been his

5. *Pravda*, November 23, 1983.

overwhelming concern, nor have they created a serious obstacle to his plans for domestic change, in particular in the economy which he inherited from his predecessor.

In his November 1982 speech Andropov gave an honest but gloomy account of the problem:

> The chief indicator of the economy's efficiency – labour productivity – is growing at an unsatisfactory rate. Co-ordination between the branches which extract raw materials and those which process them is still a problem....Plan targets continue to be met only through massive investment and high production costs....Inertia and conservatism are still dominant....Some people just do not know how to set about doing the job properly.[6]

Andropov gave no figures, but the picture would have been bleaker if he had. There has been a gradual decline in Soviet economic growth since the mid-1970's, even judging by the Soviet Union's own calculations. This applies to both industry and agriculture. Between 1950 and 1973 the gross national product per employed civilian grew annually by 4 per cent. Between 1973 and 1978 it grew at only 1.6 per cent per year[7]. Manufacturing output per person-hour rose between 1950 and 1973 by 5.2 per cent, contrasted with 3.2 per cent between 1973 and 1978. As for farm production, meat and milk output rose at only 1.4 per cent per year in the 1970's, while the Soviet Union's urban population went up by 2.1 per cent per year. Worse was to come. Since 1978 there have been four bad harvests in a row. The reasons for shortages of meat and dairy products in Soviet cities are therefore clear.

Faced with this legacy, any Soviet leader who wished to get results would be expected to take firm action. Andropov argued in his November speech that changes should be made to encourage initiative, enterprise, and better quality work. Shoddy work and

---

6. *Pravda*, November 23, 1982.
7. We are indebted to Philip Hanson, 'Economic Constraints on Soviet Policies', *International Affairs*, London, Vol. 57, No. 1, Winter 1980-1, for these statistics. He cites the annual publication, *Narodnoe Khoziaistvo SSSR*, Moscow, for the various years.

irresponsibility should be penalised in terms of "the earnings, official status, and moral prestige of workers" – in other words, by loss of a worker's bonus and promotion prospects[8]. He called for a general tightening of labour discipline. On the energy and raw materials front, he proposed the introduction of energy-saving technology, and tighter controls on firms which wasted energy. He made a strong attack on the inefficient performance of the Ministry of Railways, which obviously plays a major role in transporting the Soviet Union's raw materials.

As for economic reform in general, Andropov's remarks were circumspect and cautious. The word 'reform' was not mentioned as such. He touched only briefly on the question of freeing factories and farms from the dictates of the central planners. "A lot has been said of late about the necessity of broadening the independence of associations and enterprises, of collective farms and state farms"[9], Andropov declared. "It is thought that the time has come to take practical steps to resolve this problem. The Politburo has instructed the Council of Ministers and Gosplan (the State Planning Commission) to do this. In this matter it is necessary to act with circumspection; carry out, if necessary, experiments; weigh and take into account the experience of fraternal countries".

At the time many Western commentators gave Andropov high marks for his honest appraisal of the Soviet economy's problems, but low ones for his programme of action, or rather lack of a programme. It was said that similar exhortations to better performance had been heard all too often before. Andropov seemed to have no new ideas. With hindsight, that judgement appears to have been too hasty. In particular, Andropov's comments about the need for careful experiments and close study of other Socialist countries were revealing. Beneath a general framework of caution and without using the politically loaded word 'reform', Andropov was arguing for openness to new ideas and a willingness to take controlled risks.

We have argued earlier that the picture of Andropov which emerges from close study of his career is that of a cautious moderniser, a man who has the intellectual ability to recognise

8. *Pravda*, November 23, 1982.
9. Ibid.

problems, the common sense and realism to admit them (at least some of them) publicly, the imagination to look for, or to ask his aides to look for, workable solutions, and the political will to try to implement them. When it comes to managing the Soviet economy, Andropov appears to be acting true to the form displayed earlier in his career.

Of course one should not exaggerate Andropov's dynamism. He believes in slow and steady progress, not in impetuous bursts of (often misplaced) energy like Khrushchev. In terms of the Soviet economy, this may well be enough. Philip Hanson, one of its leading Western analysts, has pointed out that

> it is quite widely held – both in the West and in the Soviet Union – that the Soviet economic slowdown is a phenomenon whose origins are 'systemic'; specifically, it is argued that the root of the problem is an increasing lack of 'fit' between a highly centralised system of planning and management, devised in an earlier era of rapid, forced industrialisation, and the demands of a complex, modern economy.[10]

Hanson argues that this is not the whole story, and that two important reasons for the Soviet slowdown can be identified which are not systemic. One is the decline in the growth of the labour force. With most working-age women and a fair proportion of pensioners (like Andropov's contented fitter at the Ordzhonikidze plant) already employed, there are no reserves left. Moreover, the population of industrial Russia is hardly growing. The only areas with a high birth-rate are the Central Asian republics which have a low industrial base and few natural resources to exploit. Put crudely, Central Asia's people are in the wrong place, though for cultural reasons they are not prone to migration, nor is the non-Asian remainder of the Soviet population very anxious that they should move.

The second 'non-systemic' factor is geography. The Soviet Union's future energy and raw material sources will cost more to produce because they are mainly in inaccessible terrain in Siberia.

10. Philip Hanson, *International Affairs*, p. 26.

The cheaper, longer-established reserves of oil, natural gas, coal, and iron-ore are running out. Although other resources exist in plenty, they are hard to extract and transport. The result is that the Soviet Union is developing an energy problem. As Hanson puts it, "What the Arabs have done to the West, Mother Nature has done to the Soviet Union"[11]. The conclusions to be drawn from this analysis and the statistics that lie behind it are these. Firstly, a major reform of the Soviet economy towards greater de-centralisation would not deal with some of its most important problems and, secondly, the Soviet economy is not deteriorating catastrophically. Soviet growth rates, though declining, are still positive.

At the end of Andropov's first nine months in power he had taken a number of small but significant steps in the economic field which largely reflected the above analysis of an economy which is not 'in crisis' but does require some change. He announced a discipline campaign and a drive against slackness and corruption. He formed a new team of Party economic policy-makers. He produced a new law on labour collectives, which appeared to be designed to forestall any possible tendency towards 'Solidarity-style' trade unionism in the Soviet Union. In March 1983 the Politburo gave its support for the nation-wide introduction of the 'collective contract' system in agriculture, under which small teams of peasants are given more freedom to decide what crops to produce, and are paid by results. In July the Central Committee and the Council of Ministers announced a limited experiment in industrial planning and management, which was also based on the principles of giving greater autonomy to smaller units and offering the incentive of payment by results.

Andropov's discipline campaign excited great interest in the West, partly because it was his first measure but also because it fitted most obviously with his image as a KGB man. Here was the old police chief, now in supreme control in the Kremlin, and what does he do about the Soviet economy? He cracks the whip and orders the police to round up shirkers and malingerers. The campaign began in mid-December when the Politburo announced that at its regular weekly meeting it had discussed "workers'

11. Ibid.

letters" which urged the leadership to organise "a strengthening of state, labour, and production discipline"[12]. Suddenly, the press printed scores of such letters while the main evening news programme on television, *Vremya*, showed workers at a Moscow factory complaining about the lateness and drunkenness of fellow employees. In January, the first corrective action was taken. Local Party vigilantes, who are often used to help the police with crowd control at sports events, were drafted in to hairdressing salons, cinemas, and even public bath-houses to search for people who had improperly taken time off from work. Wearing their official red armbands and often joined by uniformed police, they checked the identity papers of people who were queuing for food in shops. Suspected offenders had their names taken. The police then phoned their employers, and in some cases people were dismissed as a result.

The sudden searches angered many people, particularly shoppers, who complained that shopping during work-time was the only way to avoid the worst of the queues. After a few weeks the searches tailed off, and the authorities took a few longer-term measures to try to alleviate daytime queuing. Some shops were ordered to extend their opening hours into the evening to make it easier for customers. Some larger factories were told to set up outlets for repairing shoes and clothes on the premises to save people time.

But the discipline campaign remained in force. Employers were ordered to keep closer controls on absenteeism, and to insist on workers clocking-in and clocking-out. Professionals and research assistants working at institutes who often used to write at home had to spend more time at their offices. In August the Central Committee and the Council of Ministers announced tough new penalties for slackers. Workers absent without good cause would lose a day of holiday for every day missed at work. People absent for more than three hours a day would be treated as having missed the whole day. They could also face demotion, loss of their share in bonuses, and the threat of having to pay "compensation for loss of production" of as much as a third of their monthly pay.

The discipline campaign was also used as a warning to inefficient or corrupt officials. Six days after the November 1982 Central

---

12. *The Observer*, January 15, 1983.

Taking Charge at Home   161

Committee meeting, Ivan Pavlovsky, the Minister of Railways, was sacked. Two weeks later Nikolai Shchelokov, Minister of Internal Affairs and one of Brezhnev's political allies, was also sacked. The move came as Soviet newspapers published expressions of Politburo concern that the streets of some Soviet cities were not safe and part of the reason was due to poor performance by the police and prosecutors. More ministers were dismissed in the first few months of 1983. Out went Valentin Makeyev, a Deputy Prime Minister in charge of light industry and the production of consumer goods, food, and clothing. Out went Alexander Struyev, the Minister of Trade, who was responsible for the internal distribution of food and other merchandise to the shops – clearly another area of consumer dissatisfaction. Out went Mikhail Mikhailov, the Deputy Minister of the Aviation Industry, who was said to have allowed his subordinates to get away with bribery and corruption[13]. Out went Anatoly Yershov, the Deputy Minister of Light Industry, for incompetence and corruption. In July 1983 it was the turn of Ignaty Novikov, the Chairman of the State Committee for Construction Affairs, who played a prominent role in 1980 as head of the organising committee for the Moscow Olympics and was one of the group of officials who came from Brezhnev's home town in the Ukraine[14]. Several of these men were over seventy. Andropov wanted to show that the comfortable Brezhnev days, when inefficiency and corruption could hide behind the general air of stagnation at the top, and when friendship with the boss was sure protection, were over.

Andropov set about creating a younger team to oversee the economy. The November Central Committee meeting appointed Nikolai Ryzhkov, 53, the former Director of Uralmash, one of the largest industrial complexes in the Soviet Union, and a senior official of the State Planning Commission since 1979, as a Secretary of the Central Committee. He was to work with Vladimir Dolgikh, 58, who had been a Secretary since 1972, and took charge of heavy industry in 1976. Dolgikh had earlier made an outstanding reputation as the leading economic administrator in the Krasnoyarsk region of Siberia, one of the Soviet Union's richest regions of

13. *Baltimore Sun*, March 24, 1983.
14. *New York Times*, August 1, 1983.

raw materials. He now took on the supervision of all industrial performance, the job previously held by the 76-year-old Kirilenko. In overall charge of the economy was Mikhail Gorbachev, aged 51, who was previously Secretary in charge of agriculture but who received general responsibility for economic policy under Andropov. While only one of these three men was new to the Secretariat, Andropov re-organised their duties. Another key appointment was the transfer in June 1983 of the First Party Secretary of Leningrad, Grigori Romanov, aged 60, to Moscow to become a Secretary. Although his responsibilities were not revealed officially, they are thought to be in the area of defence procurement[15]. Important, too, was the transfer to Moscow of Geidar Aliyev, 59, who spent two years as head of the KGB in the Republic of Azerbaijan in Andropov's early phase at the KGB. Later he was Party leader in Azerbaijan. At the November Central Committee meeting he was promoted from candidate to full member of the Politburo and made a Deputy Prime Minister, apparently in charge of re-organising the railway system[16]. This new team has considerable experience and is not conspicuously old.

On the labour relations front Andropov's first moves reflected all the contradictions of life in Soviet factories. A new law on 'work collectives' was published in draft form in April 1983 and passed by the Supreme Soviet in July. Taken together with the tough new regulations on absenteeism and indiscipline, the law produced – in the words of one Western observer – "a schizophrenic picture of the Soviet worker: on the one hand alleged master of his socialist fate; on the other a chronic slacker who has to be watched every minute"[17]. The law on work collectives was described by the new Deputy Prime Minister, Geidar Aliyev, as widening the circle of questions which organised groups of workers could discuss and promoting the concept of "self-management", though he was careful to deny it had any similarity to the Yugoslav system of the same name[18].

---

15. Peter Taylor, *Central Committee Plenum: More Influence for the Military-Industrial Sector?* Radio Liberty Research, RL 236/83, June 15, 1983.
16. *New York Times*, March 25, 1983.
17. Mark Frankland, 'The Workers' Paradise is Running Out of Workers', *The Observer*, August 14, 1983.
18. *Pravda*, June 18, 1983.

As with so many of the other changes introduced by Andropov, the purpose of the new law appeared to be to modernise an existing Soviet practice without offering major concessions or watering down Party control[19]. It fleshed out in legal form the broad principles of industrial democracy already contained in the new Soviet Constitution of 1977. The law was partly a reaction to the fact that the Soviet work-force is better educated than it used to be, and that some workers have been asking for a greater say in decision-making. Under the law work collectives are permitted to "propose, advise, and suggest" changes which managers must "consider" and "respond to". Meetings of the collectives can be held whenever necessary, and not less than twice a year. However, managers still retain the final say, and the subjects which the collectives may discuss do not include the appointment of managers, wage levels, or the setting of production norms. What then is left? Mainly problems of industrial safety, the choice of which workers should receive bonuses, and the ubiquitous question of 'discipline'. Workers are encouraged to discuss the state of work discipline, and propose ways of punishing slackers.

They are also urged to form work brigades. These are one of the most important developments in the Soviet economy, and have been growing up piecemeal for a number of years. A brigade is a group of workers in the same part of the production process who are allowed to decide for themselves how to organise the work and distribute the pay. Their earnings depend on results. The building industry, where each project is different and work-arrangements are less structured, is a good area for this kind of informal, *ad hoc* organisation, and much of it is already run on the brigade system. The Andropov plan was to extend the brigade system throughout Soviet industry, wherever possible, in the hope of giving workers a greater sense of responsibility and identification with their work, and some chance for the hardest-working to earn most pay. (Under the new law, however, brigades cannot appoint their own leaders. That remains a prerogative of the management, which in effect means the Party.)

19. For a useful discussion on the new law, see Elizabeth Teague, *Draft Law on Workers' Collectives*, Radio Liberty Research, RL 160/83, April 20, 1983.

Andropov also showed interest in extending the brigade system in agriculture. Its possibilities here are considerable, and before Andropov came to power the system was already being tried in several regions of the country. Known as the 'collective contract' system, the basic idea is that a group of peasants, ranging in size from fifty to a hundred, is offered a piece of land, given seed and fertiliser, and lent some equipment. They are assigned some output targets. After that, they are free to decide how to organise the work, what hours to work, and whether to grow other crops besides those specified in their contract. They earn a profit on any crops produced above the contract. Clearly the aim is to harness the energy which millions of Soviet peasants already devote to their private plots and vegetable gardens into something wider, while maintaining the ideologically respectable facade that it is 'collective'.

The system has aroused considerable controversy in the Soviet Union, and articles have appeared in the Soviet press over the last few years attacking and defending it. Its critics claim it is politically dangerous since it creates resentment among farm-workers who are not part of it and therefore have less chance to earn so much. If it develops, the critics say, the system will give rise to a new class of 'kulaks' or rich peasants and provoke dissension in the countryside. Some local Party officials and farm managers are suspicious of it, because they see their power over peasants reduced.

Nevertheless, Mikhail Gorbachev, the Central Committee Secretary in charge of agriculture, has been a consistent supporter of the collective contract system as a way of boosting the Soviet Union's flagging farm production. He has tended to favour it over the more grandiose 'Food Programme' launched by Brezhnev at a Central Committee meeting in May 1982, and strongly supported by Brezhnev's friend, Chernenko. Under Brezhnev the Soviet Union devoted a greater share of resources to agriculture than ever before in history. The policy began in 1965 almost immediately after Brezhnev came to power, and in the last full Five-Year Plan of his time in office (1976-80) the share of total investment represented by agriculture rose to 27 per cent. A large part of the money went on expensive irrigation and land-reclamation projects, but the bulk was designed to achieve a kind of industrialisation of agriculture by creating vast mechanised livestock farms, and developing agricultural machine-building and huge vegetable plantations and processing plants. Under the Food Programme announced in 1982 almost a third of the investment sums allocated for agriculture were to go to rural road-building, and the building of better houses, schools, and communal facilities for people in the countryside. Part of the aim was to try to reduce the emigration of young people from the countryside, a trend which had been encouraged ironically by one of Brezhnev's important social advances, the relaxation of the rules tying peasants to the collective farms.

When Andropov took over supreme power, there were thus two alternative approaches to agriculture. One was the policy favoured by Brezhnev and Chernenko of throwing money at the problem and going for large-scale units. The other, favoured by Gorbachev, was to encourage decentralisation and local initiative. He had promoted the collective contract system widely between 1970 and 1978 when he served as First Party Secretary in his home region of Stavropol.

Andropov had taken no public position on the issue before he became Party leader. In his first speech in his new capacity, he endorsed the Brezhnev Food Programme, though without much sign of enthusiasm. But by March 1983 it became clear that he also favoured extending the Gorbachev approach. It may not be entirely coincidence that Gorbachev's region, Stavropol, was also Andropov's home base, the place where he was born and spent the first sixteen years of his life. Knowing the area, Andropov may well have kept a close interest in it, and concluded that if the collective contract system could work well there, it was worth promoting it elsewhere. In March the Politburo backed the system and called for its nation-wide extension.

Andropov also endorsed the idea of giving encouragement to peasants' private plots. This had already begun in the last years of Brezhnev. Collective farms were permitted to 'lease' a cow or pigs to peasants who fattened them on their private land, and could keep part of the profit. More land had also been made available for the plots.

At the same time Andropov continued to give public support to the Food Programme, making it clear that his increased support for local initiative was not intended to replace the Brezhnev approach but to supplement it. In this he was being typically cautious, willing to endorse and develop a new experimental idea, if it seemed to be promising, but not throwing out an old system altogether.

His plans for industrial reform, which were the last to be announced, reflected a similar attitude. Contained in a decree of the Central Committee and the Council of Ministers published on July 26, 1983, they authorised a limited and controlled experiment, to be adopted in five ministries[20]. The stated aims were to reduce the number of centrally imposed indicators which a factory had to fulfil, and to give managers more say in the planning process. A greater share of the factory's profits would be left to the plant, and managers would have more freedom to decide whether to spend these funds on investment, social benefits, or bonuses for workers. The experiments were also meant to encourage managers to introduce new technology and compensate them more generously for losses incurred while new processes were installed and started up. On the wages front, there was to be an increase in differentials to reward higher qualifications. Perhaps most controversial, the experiment was intended to encourage factories to reduce their work-force and pay the remaining workers more for greater productivity. The five ministries were the USSR Ministry of Heavy and Transport Machine-Building; the USSR Ministry of the Electrical Equipment Industry; the Ukrainian Ministry of the Food Industry; the Belorussian Ministry of Light Industry, and the Lithuanian Ministry of Local Industry. In charge of the USSR Ministry of Heavy and Transport Machine-Building, Andropov appointed Sergei Afanasyev, the man who master-minded Soviet missile development for nearly twenty years and was in charge of some of the country's best designers and engineers.

The experiment revived some of the provisions of an earlier economic reform introduced in September 1965 which was never fully implemented, as well as a so-called reform of the reform launched in July 1979[21]. But it fell a long way short of the Hungarian economic reform, and showed little evidence that Andropov's expressed openness to lessons from the other Socialist countries had yet yielded concrete results. Unlike the Hungarian

---

20. *Pravda*, July 26, 1983.
21. Keith Bush, *Andropov's Industrial Reform*, Radio Liberty Research, RL 290/83, August 1, 1983.

reform, the new Soviet experiment made no move away from the system of centrally administered prices, nor did it give enterprises direct access to foreign suppliers. Foreign trade remained with the ministries and organisations in Moscow.

A broad judgement on Andropov's first moves in the economic field would have to be that he was willing to tolerate some experimentation, and that he favoured a limited decentralisation and greater encouragement of lower-level initiative, whether among private peasants, workers' brigades, or factory managers. At the same time he was insisting on greater social and industrial discipline – more rewards, in other words, for those who try, and more penalties for those who do not. At a meeting of the Central Committee in June, only the second one held since he came to power, he spelt it out in appropriately stern language: "Every citizen of our country has a right only to those material benefits as correspond to the quantity and quality of his socially useful work. Strict accounting and strict observance of this principle are important"[22]. Dealing with the issue of corruption, he said "the law must be implacable and its application inevitable". Yet he also showed that he was well aware that in order to deal with corruption one had to provide people with a higher standard of living and a better choice of consumer goods. It was not enough to pay people more, he said, if they could not buy the high quality goods they wanted except by going to the black market. "It is vexing to see that although the initial inputs are good the quality of the products is often such that people prefer to overpay a profiteer for decent, tastefully made things. This situation must be corrected".

Shortly after the new industrial experiments were announced, Western reporters in Moscow were given a leaked study of the Soviet economy which had been presented in April to a closed-door seminar organised by the Academy of Sciences, the economic departments of the Central Committee, and the State Planning Commission[23]. The report was one of a number of papers discussed at the seminar. It called for sweeping reforms, including the abolition of administrative management methods which failed to take local conditions and the requirements of individual enterprises

22. *Pravda,* June 16, 1983.
23. *International Herald Tribune,* August 4, 1983; *The Times,* August 6, 1983.

into account. It warned that economic changes could not be carried out without social conflict. "A fundamental restructuring of the system of economic management touches significantly on the interests of many social groups, some of which see in it hopes for an improvement in their positions while others see a worsening", it said. The timing of the leak suggested that it resulted from disappointment among some economists at the limited scope of the announced reforms.

Some Western commentators have argued that the modest nature of Andropov's changes are the result of the opposition which he has faced from colleagues in the Politburo, the State Planning Commission, and the Party bureaucracy. (One analysis even claimed that Andropov was an ally of those who leaked the reform paper[24].) The assumption is that Andropov is a dynamic and impatient man who would like to move faster and cannot. Our argument is that Andropov is more cautious than the 'impatience' model claims. As a former head of the KGB, he must know the political limitations of the Soviet system better than anyone else. This is not to say that in an ideal world he would not wish to make reforms. But he is a realist. Rather than constantly suggesting changes and being blocked, he tends to anticipate problems and therefore draws back from confronting them all at once.

In dealing with his colleagues, Andropov deliberately decided to act gingerly. Kirilenko was dropped from the Politburo in November 1982, a move that had already been agreed before Brezhnev's death. But he was the only casualty, and Andropov let him fall with some dignity. Arvid Pelshe, whose health was extremely poor at the age of 84, was allowed to remain in the Politburo until he died in May 1983. Andropov was also cautious about assuming all Brezhnev's functions immediately. When the Supreme Soviet met two weeks after Brezhnev's death, it did not fill the post of Chairman (the Chairman or President of the Presidium of the Supreme Soviet is the Head of State). Some Western observers speculated that the Politburo could not agree on a replacement[25]. Others said that Chernenko had originally been

---

24. *The Times*, August 6, 1983.
25. Mark Frankland, *The Observer*, November 28, 1983.

promised it, but Andropov felt strong enough to renege on this[26]. A more likely explanation is that Andropov wanted to preserve a decent interval before taking on the job. The November meeting merely nominated him to be a member of the 39-member Presidium, but not its Chairman. In 1977 Brezhnev had created the precedent of combining the top Party and State functions, a move which made sense given the increasingly public role which the Party leader has to play in meeting foreign leaders. It seems logical that Andropov would want to follow this precedent, but for tactical reasons he decided to wait a few months. When he was chosen to become President in June 1983, Chernenko nominated him, as he had done for the post of General Secretary seven months earlier. Chernenko said the Central Committee had unanimously decided that Andropov should be chosen as Head of State in addition to being Party leader "as evidence of the indivisibility of the prestige of the Party and the state, as an expression of the unity of the reason and will of the Party and the people"[27]. In May Ustinov, the Defence Minister, had revealed that Andropov held Brezhnev's third job, the Chairmanship of the Defence Council. This body, which is hardly ever mentioned in the Soviet press, includes the Defence Minister, the Foreign Minister, the Prime Minister, the head of the KGB, and some other full members of the Politburo. Its membership suggests that it considers all major security and foreign policy issues and makes recommendations to the Politburo, acting in effect as the supreme authority on international and defence issues.

Chernenko's position was the subject of considerable Western speculation in the early months of 1983. Politically, he suffered a partial eclipse after Andropov won the top Party job. He gave up the powerful post of head of the Central Committee's general department, which he had held throughout the Brezhnev years. While remaining in charge of ideology, he did not have control of all aspects of culture. His physical health was also under stress. In April he missed a conference in East Berlin on the centenary of Karl Marx's death as well as the Lenin Anniversary in Moscow. He also failed to appear for the May Day parade. But Andropov gave him

26. Zhores Medvedev, *Andropov*, Oxford, Basil Blackwell, 1983, p. 117.
27. *Pravda*, June 17, 1983.

the important and prestigious task of making the opening speech at the Central Committee meeting in June. This was an unusual concession. Under Brezhnev it had almost invariably been the General Secretary who read the main report. Was this a forced concession, a recognition of Chernenko's considerable power to obstruct and block, if necessary?

In one sense, perhaps it was. For the surprising thing about Andropov's tenure of power is not how few people he has dropped from the Politburo but how few he has appointed. Apart from the promotion from candidate to full member of the Politburo of Aliyev in November, no-one else was chosen for full voting membership in the Politburo at that Central Committee meeting or the one in June. By then, as a result of deaths over the previous eighteen months, membership in the Politburo had dropped to eleven. In June Vitaly Vorotnikov, a former Deputy Chairman of the Council of Ministers in the Russian Federation, became a candidate member of the Politburo. Western observers also noted how few Party Secretaries in the republics and the regions had been replaced since Andropov took over. This also may be a sign of Chernenko's continuing power, since as a former head of the general department of the Central Committee, he had better links with these officials than Andropov had.

Did Andropov want to replace more of these people, and was he being prevented, or had he not bothered to try? At this stage the answer is not clear. What is clear is that in his first few months he saw the economy as his main priority. He set about appointing new people in the economic field and creating new policy guidelines for them to work to. While it is true that a determined Party opponent of Andropov's new policies has the power at almost any level of the bureaucracy to obstruct and undermine economic changes, this was not a problem which Andropov seemed to want to confront so early in his time at the top, especially when his own health was not good. His initial preference seemed to be to bypass the Party, and concentrate on improving the Government instead.

One other important area of domestic policy must be mentioned – Andropov's tightening-up on the ideological front. Surprisingly, just as there were some Soviet intellectuals who welcomed Andropov's appointment to the KGB in 1967 on the grounds that

Taking Charge at Home

he might be more tolerant than his predecessors, some looked to his promotion into the General Secretaryship in 1982 as a possible occasion for hope. This time the argument was different. It was said that precisely because of his long period as head of the KGB Andropov would want to adjust his image in the West. The best way would be to make some liberal moves towards dissidents, such as allowing Academician Andrei Sakharov to return to Moscow from exile in the closed city of Gorky, or releasing some political prisoners.

In the event, none of these hopes bore fruit. An amnesty proclaimed by the Presidium of the Supreme Soviet on December 27, 1982 to mark the sixtieth anniversary of the formation of the USSR did not apply to any prisoners convicted of "especially dangerous crimes against the state" or of "crimes against the administration", the two categories which cover political prisoners. In May 1983 Tass put out a tough statement denying Western speculation that Sakharov might be allowed to emigrate from the Soviet Union. It reaffirmed the standard Soviet line that Sakharov was a security risk because of his past association with the hydrogen-bomb programme, and could never leave the country[28].

While these moves merely confirmed the hard-line status quo, there were others which marked a more determined attempt to eliminate the last vestiges of the dissident groups and movements. Georgy Vladimov, one of the few dissident writers remaining in the Soviet Union, was told in January that he had been implicated in a case involving the anti-Soviet emigre organisation, NTS, and that he would be put on trial unless he emigrated. In 1977 Vladimov had become head of the Soviet section of Amnesty International. Vladimov took the warning seriously, and left in May. Also in January Roy Medvedev, who had been untouched by the authorities for several years, was summoned by the Deputy Procurator-General of the USSR and warned that he must cease his "anti-Soviet activities". In February the USSR resigned from the World Psychiatric Association in a clear attempt to avoid further pressure from foreign psychiatrists for an end to its incarceration of dissidents in mental hospitals. In March and April there were

---

28. *The Daily Telegraph*, May 12, 1983.

reports of house searches, arrests, and trials in the Baltic states. In May the authorities in Leningrad put Valery Repin on trial for treason. Repin had managed the so-called Solzhenitsyn Fund, set up by the exiled writer to help the families of detained dissidents. In May Alexei Smirnov was tried in Moscow for helping to compile a new edition of the *Chronicle of Current Events* and a new publication of dissident information called *Express-Information*. In spite of his numerous arms control proposals Andropov disappointed Western peace activists by the tough line taken against the small, unofficial peace group in the Soviet Union known as 'The Group to Establish Trust between the USSR and the USA'.

There were few signs of softness in the first months of Andropov's rule. One was the release after almost a year's detention of a small group of so-called 'Euro-Communists', young academics who had advocated a liberalisation of the Soviet system and who were related to prominent figures in the Establishment. Another was the permission to emigrate given to the group of Siberian Pentecostalists who had lived for some years in the basement of the American Embassy in Moscow after running in past the Soviet police guards. In general, though, the emigration picture started off by being even bleaker than it had been in the last years of Andropov's time at the KGB. In January and February 1983 only 204 Jews were permitted to leave, an annual rate of half the already low 1982 figure. In April the authorities announced the creation of a "Soviet Public Anti-Zionist Committee"[29]. Although the official Soviet media often say that there is a difference between anti-semitism and anti-Zionism, the tone of much Soviet media comment blurs the distinction. It was not clear whether the new committee which was intended to arouse public indignation against Israel would be scrupulous in preserving the difference. Its founding declaration said that "Jewish citizens of the USSR are an inseparable part of the Soviet people". On its face a legitimate statement, it was interpreted in some Western quarters as a warning that Jewish emigration might come to a complete halt. This view appeared to be given credence by a report of a press conference held by the new committee and published by the Soviet press agency,

---

29. Tass, April 21, 1983.

Taking Charge at Home 173

Novosti, which stated "Some Western correspondents insistently tried to find out why emigration of persons of Jewish nationality from the USSR has now fallen off so sharply. They were told that the people who left were mainly those whose families had been split up during World War Two. This process of re-uniting families is, for the most part, now complete"[30].

A stiffening was also seen in the Party's approach to theatre and the arts. The fact that Andropov's son-in-law was an actor, and that through him he must have had an entrée into the thinking of the drama world, did not prevent a tightening of censorship in the theatre at the beginning of 1983. Several plays were scrapped. In February the Minister of Culture, Pyotr Demichev, told a meeting of leading cultural figures that there was an ideological crisis in the Soviet theatre[31]. Party organisations would exercise closer oversight in future to ensure that there were more plays on industrial production themes. Andropov was also reported to have talked to Georgy Markov, the Chairman of the Soviet Writers' Union, in January. During the conversation he criticised a popular writer, the late Yuri Trifonov, and said that writers must help the Party in struggling for more order and discipline[32].

Order and discipline – those were two of the most important themes of Andropov's opening phase in office. Whether it was the economy, the arts, or public life as a whole, Andropov showed himself determined to draw a contrast with the looseness of his predecessor's rule. In the economy the demand for order could be seen as a prerequisite for efficiency. If it was to deliver the goods which the Soviet public wanted, 'order' was an ingredient which no-one could seriously complain of. In the rest of Soviet life, however, 'order' was a value which was bound to be interpreted as a sign of repression.

---

30. Novosti Press Agency, June 7, 1983.
31. *Sovetskaya Kultura*, March 5, 1983. For more details, see Nataliya Gross, *The New Soviet Leadership and the Theatre*, Radio Liberty Research, RL 155/83, April 15, 1983.
32. Zhores Medvedev, *Andropov*, p. 154.

9
First Steps in Foreign Policy

It is hard to describe as anything but gloomy the foreign policy legacy which Andropov took over from Brezhnev. On the central issue, Soviet relations with the West, Andropov faced a daunting prospect. Detente, which had seemed to promise so much in the early 1970's, had collapsed. The United States and the Soviet Union had embarked on a new cold war, marked by a ferocity of hostile rhetoric on both sides which was reminiscent of the worst excesses of the late 1940's and early 1950's. The three most important states in Western Europe, though more willing than Washington to maintain normal political and economic ties with Moscow, were led by strongly anti-Soviet governments. Prime Minister Margaret Thatcher, Chancellor Helmut Kohl and President François Mitterrand were all less committed to dialogue with Moscow than their counterparts had been five years earlier.

In the early 1970's relations with the West had been Brezhnev's most successful area. As a result of a massive build-up in Soviet nuclear strength in the preceding years – a trend started by Khrushchev after the Cuban missile crisis – the Soviet Union had achieved strategic parity with the United States. This laid the basis for a series of arms control negotiations which created the agenda for regular and almost routine US-Soviet summit meetings and consultations between 1972 and 1975. In Western Europe Brezhnev succeeded in negotiating a settlement of most of the political issues left unresolved since the Second World War. With the peace treaty with West Germany in 1970, the Berlin Agreement in 1971, and the Helsinki Accords in 1975 Moscow obtained Western recognition of the territorial status quo and a more stable *modus vivendi* with Western Europe.

But detente did not last. Andropov had to adjust to the central paradox of the Brezhnev era. While the Soviet Union's military power increased during the 1960's and 1970's, its political influence declined. In Eastern Europe Moscow intervened by force in Czechoslovakia in 1968 to restore Party control, and in Poland in 1981 it prevailed on a weak and uncertain ally to impose martial law for the same purpose. In both countries it was clear that the Soviet Union could not rely on a majority consensus for its form of socialism. The recurring danger of national rebellion and consumer unrest seemed set to sharpen because of growing economic problems. Higher prices for imported energy, declining growth rates, and the rigidity of a centrally planned economy limited the chance of trying to win popular loyalty through a steady increase in living standards. In Western Europe Soviet influence on the hearts and minds of the Left continued to slip. Communist Parties found they could only prosper if they loosened their ties to Moscow. The peace movements were critical of the Soviet position on arms control and began to forge links with fledgling peace groups within the Warsaw Pact.

In the Third World the Soviet invasion of Afghanistan had been condemned by the vast majority of Islamic nations and most members of the non-aligned movement. It spoiled Moscow's relations with one of the Soviet Union's most important neighbours, Iran. Elsewhere in the Middle East Soviet political influence was small. Moscow had been powerless to prevent the Israeli encirclement of Beirut in 1982, and was offered no serious role in the diplomatic search for peace. In Africa the Soviet Union had not capitalised on its backing for the MPLA in the Angolan civil war and for the Ethiopian Government in its resistance to Somali invasion. Apart from Madagascar and Mozambique no other countries in sub-Saharan Africa developed significant links with Moscow in the years which followed. In Latin America Cuba was still largely isolated more than twenty years after Castro's revolution and was costing Moscow millions in annual subsidies. The revolutions in Grenada and Nicaragua were encouraging, but because of the hostility they had aroused in Washington they presented Moscow with an awkward issue of how far to go in their support. In Asia the Soviet Union had begun a process of normalising relations with China but the prospects were unclear. In Indochina Moscow's ally, Vietnam, had failed to establish international legitimacy for its military presence in Kampuchea.

No wonder that in his speech at Brezhnev's funeral Andropov described the international situation as "complicated"[1]. Andropov, of course, could hardly pretend that he did not share responsibility for the foreign policy position which he inherited. As a full member of the Politburo since 1973 he must have had to endorse Kremlin policy, even though on a few particular issues he may have disagreed with it.

In the case of Afghanistan, for example – as was discussed in Chapter 6 – there is evidence that Andropov was unhappy about Brezhnev's policy before the invasion. But once the mistakes had been made, Andropov went along with the collective Politburo decision. On other issues Andropov took a leading role. The notion that the crisis in Poland in 1981 could best be handled by the Polish army through the imposition of martial law rather than by outright Soviet intervention is said to have been Andropov's. The device, which was unprecedented in Eastern Europe, achieved its goal of suppressing the independent trade union, Solidarity, and can be counted a qualified success.

Whether he was a quiet supporter, an initiator, or, in a few cases, an opponent of the choices Brezhnev's Politburo made, Andropov seemed anxious to make his own mark on foreign policy as soon as he took power. On Afghanistan he showed more urgency than Brezhnev had done in seeking an arrangement with Pakistan that might lead to a Soviet troop withdrawal. With China there were signs that the Kremlin was willing to be more flexible about offering concessions to end the long rift between the two major Communist powers. In the Middle East Andropov took a more vigorous role, sending SAM-5 ground-to-air missiles to Syria (the first time these advanced weapons had been allowed out of the Warsaw Pact) and receiving several Arab leaders in the Kremlin within weeks of assuming office. In the East-West arms control field

---

1. *Pravda*, November 16, 1982.

he surprised NATO governments with a battery of new and newly packaged proposals that were designed to appeal to large sections of the Western public and put pressure on the West for matching moves. General Edward Rowny, Reagan's negotiator in the Strategic Arms Reduction Talks (START) piquantly called it "Trial by Yuri"[2]. Overall, Andropov appeared more flexible, energetic, and imaginative than his predecessor.

EAST-WEST RELATIONS AND THE NUCLEAR ISSUE

No issue was more urgent than arms control and relations with the West when Andropov succeeded Brezhnev. Little more than a year was left before NATO was due to deploy a new generation of land-based medium-range nuclear missiles in West Germany and other countries of Western Europe. In Moscow's view the 108 Pershing-II and 464 ground-launched cruise missiles raised the prospect that NATO might be able to launch a successful pre-emptive strike against the Soviet Union. According to Moscow's calculations of the existing balance of nuclear weapons in Europe, they also threatened to give NATO a numerical superiority of nuclear delivery systems. In the three years since NATO's decision to deploy the weapons, Moscow had repeatedly tried to persuade the West to cancel it, in particular by offering a moratorium on the deployment of more of its new weapons, the SS-20's.

By November 1982 these efforts had still not changed NATO's mind, even though public protests in most of the countries which were due to receive the new American weapons were strong. In Britain the opposition Labour Party was committed to rejecting the weapons. In Holland and Denmark there was considerable disquiet in Parliament. In West Germany, which faced a general election in March 1983, the Social Democratic Party was under strong pressure from its own left wing as well as from supporters of the environmentalists, the Greens, to refuse to take the new missiles. But NATO was only willing to give up its deployment plans on

---

2. *The Guardian*, January 7, 1983.

condition that the Soviet Union also dismantled its SS-20's. This was Reagan's so-called zero option.

Andropov had three choices at the negotiations. He could accept the zero option, look for a compromise, or do nothing. But he was well aware that the negotiations were being closely followed by public opinion in Western Europe. Soviet proposals, if properly crafted, and launched with enough publicity, could influence the debate in the West and put pressure on NATO to change its plans. Thus Andropov's fourth option was to tailor his proposals with public opinion more than the negotiators in mind. Andropov chose a combination of the second and fourth options.

Within five weeks of taking office he used the occasion of a speech celebrating the sixtieth anniversary of the founding of the Soviet Union to announce that Moscow was ready to cut its SS-20's in Europe down to the number of missiles held by Britain and France; that is, 162. He did not make clear what would happen to the surplus missiles. Would they be scrapped, or moved to Asia? According to Western officials, the offer of a substantial reduction in its SS-20's was not a completely new Soviet move. Even before Brezhnev's death the Soviet negotiators at Geneva had hinted at it. But no-one had expected that Moscow would link its proposal directly to the British and French arsenals. Andropov's offer was shrewd. It drew attention to the non-American nuclear systems in Europe, reminding people that they too were pointed at the Soviet Union. It also served to start a new debate within NATO, creating extra problems for the alliance. While being ostensibly a Soviet compromise, it required NATO to abandon the 1979 decision.

Two weeks later Andropov made another departure. A long editorial in *Pravda* for the first time disclosed details of the Soviet position at the Geneva strategic arms reduction talks. Moscow was offering a stage-by-stage reduction that would cut heavy bombers as well as land- and submarine-based intercontinental missiles to 1,800 units on each side, a 25 per cent drop from the level agreed in the 1979 Salt II treaty. The Soviet proposal would also cut the number of warheads to an equal level. The position of course was known to the American negotiators, but the Soviet decision to go public forced Washington on to the defensive, making it try to refute the Soviet charge that its proposals were one-sided. Later in January

First Steps in Foreign Policy

Andropov called his Warsaw Pact allies together for a summit meeting in Prague. The meeting ended with a battery of proposals, the most radical of which was the suggestion that NATO and the Warsaw Pact should sign a non-aggression pact pledging not to be the first to use any kind of force, whether nuclear or conventional.

Taken together these three initiatives, made in rapid succession, gave the Western public an impression that the new Soviet leader was being flexible, reasonable, and ready for compromise. By contrast, the Reagan Administration appeared to be stuck fast on a series of take-it-or-leave-it propositions which made people question Washington's good faith. In order to dispel this impression Reagan found himself obliged to send Vice-President Bush on a mission to Europe to spread the word that the Americans were indeed negotiating genuinely and seriously.

Andropov did not stop at public declarations. He also tried his hand at diplomacy – with the target as West Germany. When Hans-Jochen Vogel, the newly selected candidate of the opposition Social Democrats (SPD) indicated a wish to travel to Moscow and Washington to boost his credibility as a statesman, he was promptly promised that he would be received in Moscow by the new Soviet leader. As a result he became the first Western politician since Brezhnev's funeral to hold full-scale talks with Andropov. During the talks Andropov gave a number of vague but subtle hints of flexibility on some of the key issues then vexing the West. He hinted that Moscow would dismantle the SS-20's that might be negotiated away rather than merely re-deploy them in Siberia, from where they could be brought back at a time of crisis.

In addition, Andropov asked the West German Government if he might send his Foreign Minister, Andrei Gromyko, to Bonn. A few days after Vogel returned home, the Soviet position was thus once again in the news in the Federal Republic with less than two months to go before the election. Gromyko's message to the conservative government, spelt out at a rare press conference in Bonn in a further headline-making move, was tougher than Andropov's had been to Vogel. Gromyko talked darkly of some form of retaliation if West Germany went ahead with the NATO plans to deploy the new missiles. This was not so much the language of compromise, but that of threat. Its aim was the same – to try to influence the election debate.

On March 6 West Germany went to the polls. The outcome was an increased majority for the governing Christian Democrats. Although the main issue in the election was the economy rather than the missile question, the SPD defeat was clearly a blow for Moscow. Andropov's tactics of directly appealing to the West German electorate had not worked, and there was some evidence that it may have backfired by upsetting some West German voters who thought Moscow was interfering in the election. When the next important election campaign took place two months later in Britain Moscow stayed aloof. A letter written by the British Labour Party asking the Kremlin to clarify what reciprocal steps it would take if Britain unilaterally gave up its nuclear weapons was left unanswered.

But Andropov had not given up his efforts to influence the Western debate. At a less direct level than he had done during the West German election he still hoped that Western public opinion could put pressure on the governments concerned. In early May he made a major shift in the Soviet position by offering to count warheads rather than missiles as the basic unit in assessing the relative arsenals – the Soviet Union would be willing to cut its warhead total down to the level of the British and French. Although the new position was a modification of Andropov's December offer which had already been rejected by NATO, it was an intelligent adjustment. It met head-on one of the West's major objections to earlier Soviet proposals, which was precisely that they did not count warheads. Since each SS-20 has three warheads, any ceiling on warheads rather than missiles would clearly require a larger Soviet reduction. The new Soviet proposal was also a reminder that the British and French arsenals were in the process of being modernised, and that their combined warhead totals would soon dramatically increase. By focusing on warheads the Kremlin was drawing attention to the growing number involved in British and French plans.

The new offer turned out to be as ineffective as the others, and by the middle of June after Mrs Thatcher had won the British election it was clear that NATO was not going to forgo its plans to deploy the cruise and Pershing-II. All NATO had done was to come up with an offer to cut back on its plans for full implementation of the 1979 decision if the Russians cut back on their SS-20's. For their part the Russians showed no sign of wishing to find a compromise on the basis of an equal match of SS-20's for the cruise and Pershing-II. To do so would require them to reverse all their previous arguments and accept the equation of SS-20's with the new NATO weapons. Andropov appeared to calculate that it would be better to let NATO deploy its weapons and take whatever countermeasures might seem appropriate rather than 'legitimise' them by reaching a formal agreement at Geneva. As the summer continued, the Kremlin stepped up its warnings that it would also deploy new missiles, possibly in Eastern Europe, if NATO went ahead with its deployments. On the eve of the opening of the autumn session of the Geneva talks, which were expected to be the last before NATO's deployments began, Andropov made a substantial new offer. In an interview with *Pravda* on August 27, he promised that the Soviet Union would liquidate all the surplus missiles above the number retained by Britain and France if NATO cancelled its plans. What previously had only been Soviet hints of possible dismantling were now explicit. The offer, which also involved the dismantling of the older SS-4 and SS-5 missiles, meant that Moscow would have fewer warheads targeted on Western Europe than in 1976.

Another sign of Andropov's adaptability to sensitive issues in the West's public debate came on the question of nuclear-free zones. The idea of creating such a zone in Central Europe had been current in the mid-1960's but then dropped out of sight. The peace movement revived it in 1981 and it was later endorsed by a commission of politicians headed by the Swedish Prime Minister, Olof Palme. In January 1983 Andropov proposed a 300-mile-wide zone free of nuclear weapons in Central Europe, roughly double the area suggested by Palme. Later in the spring he told the President of Finland, Mauno Koivisto, that the Soviet Union was prepared to discuss the question of making the Baltic a nuclear-free zone. His offer was vague but it seemed designed to assuage some of the concerns aroused by the activities of Soviet nuclear submarines near the Swedish coast.

On the general issue of relations with the United States, Andropov showed similar skill at achieving headline-catching publicity, although here too results were meagre. The battle-ground was not the question of medium-range missiles as it was in Europe, but the movement for a nuclear freeze. Andropov's tactics were to appeal to Americans over the heads of the White House and to suggest that the Reagan Administration was being impossibly intransigent. He answered a series of written questions submitted by an American journalist at the end of 1982 with a message "congratulating every American family on the onset of the new year of 1983 and sincerely wishing them well-being and happiness. Today the Soviet people and the Americans have one common enemy – the threat of war and everything that enhances it"[3]. He briefly outlined the Soviet position on arms control and exressed the hope that the "United States will reciprocate this fair and constructive position with a manifestation of goodwill on its part"[4].

In April when an American schoolgirl from Maine wrote to him about the danger of nuclear war, Andropov replied in person and had his reply published.

> Yes, Samantha, we in the Soviet Union are endeavouring and doing everything so that there will be no war between our two countries, so that there will be no war at all on earth....We want peace. We have a lot to do: grow grain, build, invent, write books and make space flights. We want peace for ourselves, and for all people of the planet, for our own kids and for you.[5]

He concluded by inviting the girl and her parents to visit the Soviet Union. The visit took place in the summer but Andropov himself did not receive them.

A month later Andropov pitched an invitation at a higher level, but the purpose was still to send the same message to the American public that it was their President who was responsible for all the

---

3. *International Herald Tribune*, December 31, 1982.
4. Ibid.
5. *Summary of World Broadcasts*, BBC, Caversham Park, SU 7318/A1/1, April 1983.

trouble between Moscow and Washington. Averell Harriman, the 91-year-old doyen of United States diplomacy and a former US Ambassador in Moscow, was invited to the Kremlin for a chat with Andropov. He told Harriman that the United States must stop trying "to gain military superiority over the Soviet Union and dictating to it"[6]. Soviet policy aimed at good-neighbourly relations with Washington. "Unfortunately we do not see the present American administration displaying such a responsible approach"[7], he added. Harriman's visit was given extensive coverage in the American media, as Andropov had hoped.

While this soft-sell was underway, Andropov's direct communications with the Reagan administration were contrastingly blunt. He reacted quickly to White House statements with unusual promptness. The day after Vice-President Bush released an "Open Letter to the People of Europe" from President Reagan in January offering to meet Andropov to sign an accord banning all Soviet and American land-based medium-range missiles, the Soviet leader gave an interview to *Pravda* saying the Reagan offer was unrealistic and a "propaganda game"[8]. When Reagan made a speech two months later which raised the possibility of building an anti-ballistic missile defence system using laser beams in space (quickly dubbed Reagan's 'Star Wars' speech by the Western press), Andropov rounded on him in another *Pravda* interview. This time he described American policy as "not just irresponsible but insane"[9]. He also called the President's charge that the Soviet Union was continuing to deploy SS-20's in Europe in spite of a declared moratorium "a deliberate lie"[10]. It was the first time for more than a decade that a Soviet leader had made such a personal attack on his American counterpart.

Andropov's tough language, fiercer than anything used by Brezhnev in his last years, suggested that the Kremlin was writing off any chance of reaching a political accommodation with the Reagan administration. Many Western commentators agreed with Soviet ones in describing it as the most anti-Soviet administration in

6. *International Herald Tribune*, June 3, 1983.
7. Tass in English, June 2, 1983.
8. *Pravda*, February, 2, 1983.
9. Ibid., March 27, 1983.
10. Ibid.

Washington for at least twenty years. While going through the motions of maintaining arms control negotiations, the Soviet side doubted whether there was any genuine willingness for compromise on the American side. Moscow was afraid that if it made sufficient concessions to reach an agreement it might only end up by helping Reagan's re-election. For the same reason it was suspicious of any talk about a US-Soviet summit meeting unless it was well prepared and seemed to indicate a lasting switch by the United States administration back towards detente. The Politburo felt badly burned by the Carter Administration which had come to a summit meeting in Vienna in June 1979 to sign the Salt II treaty and then, after a row developed in Washington over the presence of a Soviet combat brigade in Cuba, failed to press for its ratification in the US Senate. Once bitten, twice shy, the Kremlin would need strong evidence that Reagan was radically shifting United States policy before they would agree to meet him.

Andropov confirmed this line at two separate meetings in August, first with an American trade union leader, William Winpisinger, and then with a group of nine Democratic Senators. He also took the opportunity to make another headline-catching proposal. This time it was an offer for a joint US-Soviet ban on the testing and deployment of any weapons in space. The Soviet Union also promised not to be the first country to put any anti-satellite weapons into space. Andropov's willingness to see these Americans contrasted sharply with the low-level reception given to the US Secretary for Agriculture, John Block, who was in Moscow during the same period to sign a new long-term US-Soviet grain agreement. Although the agreement was the first significant commercial pact between the two countries since Reagan took over, it was barely mentioned in the Soviet media. Part of the reason was the Soviet Union's general embarrassment over the issue of grain imports from the West, on which it has always been coy. But the cold-shouldering of Block was also meant as a signal to Washington, designed to express the Kremlin's continuing suspicions of the Reagan Administration's political intentions. A commercial agreement was not enough to convince Moscow that the political climate was improving.

Soviet suspicions were given a boost at the beginning of September when the United States led the international outcry over the shooting down of a South Korean Boeing 747 airliner, with the loss of 269 lives, near the Soviet island of Sakhalin. The plane had strayed for more than two hours into Soviet air-space. The Russians initially refused to admit they had shot it down, although they said their fighters had fired tracer bullets in front of it to warn it to land. Indeed, their reaction was almost identical to the way they had acted in April 1978 when another South Korean airliner penetrated Soviet air-space over the Kola Peninsula near the Arctic circle. Then too they fired, although the plane was able to make an emergency landing. Their diplomatic reaction both then and in September 1983 was marked by delay in acknowledging the incident, evasiveness in explaining it, and no admission of error. The difference in the Sakhalin disaster was that their statements, first put out by Tass, and later expanded in an unprecedented news conference by Marshal Ogarkov, the Chief of the General Staff, contained an ambiguous expression of regret for the loss of life, and a strong attack on the United States for conducting espionage operations in the Sakhalin area.

According to Leonid Zamyatin, the head of the International Information Department of the Central Committee, who attended the press conference with Ogartzov, Andropov had not been consulted before the shooting (which occurred shortly before midnight in Central Russia). The Soviet ground control command, which told the fighter pilot to shoot, was acting according to local rules of engagement after referring to regional air defence command[11]. Officers higher up the chain were informed afterwards. The Soviet reaction to the international outcry was tough and aggressive. As the Kremlin saw it, the incident was being blown up out of all proportion by the White House as a way of fanning anti-Soviet sentiments in the rest of the world. The fact that this happened on the eve of a meeting in Madrid between Gromyko and the US Secretary of State, George Shultz – the first for almost a year – tended only to convince the Russians that Washington was not serious about improving relations.

At Madrid Shultz gave Gromyko a stern lecture about the airliner incident and then told the press that the Soviet Foreign

11. *Summary of World Broadcasts*, BBC, Caversham Park, SU 7436/C/15, September 12, 1983.

Ministers' explanations were "totally unacceptable"[12]. After Gromyko's planned Aeroflot flight to New York to attend the annual session of the United Nations General Assembly was blocked from landing at a civilian airfield in the United States as part of a widespread international boycott, Soviet anger mounted. The Foreign Minister cancelled his trip to the United Nations, an unprecedented move in his 26-year period in office. At the end of September Andropov revealed his own position for the first time. Throughout the crisis he had kept silent, leaving most public comment to senior military spokesmen and press commentators.

Some Western observers saw this as a sign that Andropov was embarrassed or was out of step with the Soviet military, which wanted to take a hard line in trying to pin the blame for the incident on the United States. But it is more likely to have been caused by Andropov's hope that the crisis would blow over more quickly if he stayed aloof and above the fray. After Reagan addressed the United Nations on September 26, delivering another fierce attack on the Soviet system, Andropov held back no longer. Denied a comparable platform for an authoritative Kremlin reply at the United Nations by the restrictions on Gromyko's flight, the Soviet leader used the unusual device of authorising a statement to be read out in his name on Moscow's television news two days after Reagan's speech. It was the toughest rebuke to the United States he had yet delivered. While condemning the latest American arms control proposals as "a deception", and accusing the United States of having blood on its hands as a result of its interventions in Lebanon and El Salvador, Andropov pronounced the key sentence: "Even if someone had any illusions as to the possible evolution for the better in the policy of the present American administration, the latest developments have finally dispelled them"[13].

Andropov's statement left little doubt that the Politburo had ended its long debate on whether it could do business with the Reagan Administration with a decisive 'No'. Andropov seemed particularly stung by Reagan's references to the Soviet Union as an "evil empire", which the Soviet leader denounced as a new

---

12. *The Guardian*, September 9, 1983.
13. *Pravda*, September 29, 1983.

American "crusade against socialism as a social system"[14]. His statement was meant to stress that the Soviet Union had its own pride too and had lost patience with being endlessly vilified. Although he maintained that the Soviet Union still had "good will and a desire to come to agreement", it was clear he had little hope left[15].

Already in Lenin's day Soviet analysts had treated Western policy towards the Soviet Union as a struggle between two trends – the realists who were prepared to accept the Soviet Union as a fact and deal with it as any other state, and the reactionaries who hoped to isolate the Soviet Union and somehow provoke or encourage counter-revolution. Nixon's election in 1968 and his Republican Administration's support for detente led the Kremlin to believe that the realists had won a permanent victory. If even American conservatives were willing to deal with the Soviet Union on a routine basis, then a major change had occurred in US policy-making and attitudes towards relations with the Soviet Union.

The collapse of detente less than a decade later was a bitter disappointment. The Russians felt the blame lay with the Americans. Even before his tough statement on September 28, Andropov had suggested, in a speech to the Central Committee in June 1983, that he saw the Reagan Administration as incurably reactionary. Describing the world as divided by "a social barricade" between socialism and imperialism, he said "the aggressiveness of ultra-reactionary forces led by US imperialism has sharply increased. Attempts are being made to reverse the course of history at all costs. Of course this policy will not bring the imperialists success, but because it is adventurist it is extremely dangerous to mankind"[16]. Somewhat more optimistically he added that "other politicians" in the capitalist world took a more realistic line and accepted the "necessity and mutual benefit of long-term peaceful co-existence between states with different social systems".

The trouble for Andropov was that he was hard pressed to name them. The governments of all the major capitalist states were in the hands of conservatives, suspicious of detente. Two of them had

14. Ibid.
15. Ibid.
16. *Pravda*, June 16, 1983.

been confirmed in office by their electorates during his first seven months in power. Even Japan was under a more right-wing government. Yasuhiro Nakasone, who took over as head of the Liberal Democratic Party two weeks after Andropov's own accession, was a more enthusiastic proponent of a strong national defence than his predecessors. It was not a healthy balance sheet for Andropov's first year at the helm.

CHINA

If Soviet relations with the West were bleak when Andropov took over, China seemed to offer a somewhat more hopeful prospect. Already in the last few months of Brezhnev's rule the Kremlin had offered a number of olive-branches to Peking. There were signs that a major debate over foreign policy was underway in Peking, as disillusionment set in with the country's one-sided reliance on the West over the previous decade. The excessive optimism of the mid-1970's when Chinese leaders thought that imported Western technology could solve many of their problems had given way to a more sober feeling that development would take time. There might be some benefit in reviving contacts with the Soviet Union which had supplied the first generation of China's post-war industrial infrastructure. At the same time some leaders argued that the cost of endless military confrontation with the Soviet Union was too high. A new *modus vivendi* was needed. On top of it all came Reagan's insistence on preserving close American links with Taiwan.

Andropov had been closely involved with the issue of China in the 1960's. He had been on delegations to China, had helped to draft the Soviet Communist Party's letters to the Chinese, and had attended many of the unsuccessful negotiations which finally led to the break in relations. As an intelligent man, he must have realised that a reconciliation with China could be of almost as much significance to the Soviet Union as detente with the West had been a decade earlier. It made no sense to have a major confrontation on both the Soviet Union's flanks. Just as China had moved to open relations with Nixon in the early 1970's at the height of its confrontation with the Soviet Union, Moscow now felt a similar

First Steps in Foreign Policy

compulsion as tension with the Reagan Administration increased. "Triangular diplomacy" was still in force. This time it was Moscow rather than Washington which was playing the China card.

For the first time for several years China and the Soviet Union both perceived an interest in improving their relations. When Brezhnev died, Peking made the gesture of sending its Foreign Minister Huang Hua to the funeral. Andropov reciprocated by greeting Huang warmly at the reception in St George's Hall which followed the funeral. Other diplomats watched curiously as Andropov deliberately engaged Huang in conversation and held up the line of waiting Heads of Government. He asked Gromyko to see Huang for a full meeting the next day. Another symbol, small though it was, was the handling of a collection of Andropov's speeches prepared soon afterwards for foreign readers. Selected in Moscow, the anthology carefully doctored the speech made by Andropov on the anniversary of Lenin's birth in April 1964. As recently as 1979 a collection of Andropov's speeches in Russian had included his 1964 references to the way "the Chinese leaders in their struggle for hegemony are more and more openly replacing Leninism with Maoism" and publishing "slanderous calumnies" about the Soviet Union[17]. In the 1982 English version these passages were excised. All that is left in the anthology are the measured tones of the statesman-like and far-sighted Andropov, speaking in 1964 almost the same words as he could use in 1982 – "The party is willing, as before, to search for ways of normalising relations with the Communist party of China....We will continue to work for strengthening Sino-Soviet friendship on the Leninist principles of proletarian internationalism"[18].

Of course Andropov is no Khrushchev. In 1955 seven years after the break between the Soviet Union and Yugoslavia – a break which had led to Soviet economic and diplomatic sanctions against Tito and a massive rounding up of alleged Titoist agents throughout Eastern Europe – Khrushchev had flown to Belgrade and publicly apologised. It was a typically dramatic, personal gesture, made easier perhaps by the fact that Khrushchev could legitimately

---

17. *Pravda*, April 23, 1964.
18. Yuri Andropov, *Andropov, Selected Speeches and Writings*, Oxford, Pergamon, 1983, p. 51.

distance himself from Stalin's action in condemning Yugoslavia originally. Stalin's rule was a one-man dictatorship. Andropov was a different man, not given to such flamboyant actions. He was closely involved in the past hostility to China. Nevertheless he too, in a smaller way, made his apology for Moscow's arrogance in the past. He told the Soviet Central Committee in June that the past twenty years had shown how diverse and complex the world of socialism was: "Between individual socialist countries there are big distinctions as regards their economies, culture, ways and methods of solving the tasks of socialist development. This is only natural, even if it seemed to us at one time that it would be more uniform"[19].

Andropov's muted apology came shortly after hints from the Chinese side that Peking was willing to consider a restoration of Party-to-Party and not just Government-to-Government links. In May the Chinese had also demonstrated a clear interest in improving their relations, not only with Moscow, but also with Moscow's allies in Eastern Europe. Qian Qichen, the Deputy Foreign Minister who headed the Chinese delegation to the Sino-Soviet talks, visited East Germany, Hungary, and Poland, the first such move for more than twenty years.

Qian's talks in Moscow in March, the second round in the consultations which had begun before Brezhnev's death, were shrouded in secrecy but apparently produced further progress. Qian met with Gromyko before leaving Moscow and a brief Tass statement afterwards said that both sides saw "positive significance" in the dialogue. A separate set of talks between trade delegations from both countries was opened while Qian was in Moscow. It ended with agreement for a big increase in trade, a rise of more than 150 per cent in 1983 compared to the previous year. Other signs of progress appeared. China invited a Soviet chess team for the first time for eighteen years. It showed interest in taking part in the Moscow book fair. Alexander Bovin, a senior Soviet journalist and a former colleague of Andropov's from his days as head of the Central Committee's Liaison Department with the Communist and Workers' Parties of Socialist Countries became the first high-level Soviet commentator to travel to China since the break in relations. The

---

19. *Pravda*, June 16, 1983.

two countries agreed to re-open two border crossing-points in Central Asia. In September, in advance of the third round of consultations, a Soviet Deputy Foreign Minister, Mikhail Kapitsa, arrived in Peking. He was the highest-ranking Soviet official invited to China since the 1960's.

In many ways China had made the greater concessions in developing the new dialogue. China had broken off a dialogue three years earlier after the invasion of Afghanistan and its resumption now, while Soviet troops were still in the country, was a change of line. China was still demanding a Soviet withdrawal from Afghanistan. It also insisted on a Vietnamese withdrawal from Kampuchea, and a major scaling-down of Soviet troop deployments on the Sino-Soviet border. But the Russians were told that these were no longer pre-conditions for the talks. They were negotiable. Andropov's line in reply was to say that the issues of Afghanistan and Vietnam were separate problems that should not affect the main question – bilateral problems between China and the Soviet Union.

Here the substance of the matter was the border issue and the presence of more than half a million Soviet troops. China was only asking for the return of some river islands and about 25,000 square kilometres of mountainous land in the Pamirs, but it wanted Moscow to admit that the original nineteenth-century Tsarist treaties under which Moscow obtained other vast tracts of land had been negotiated under duress, and were "unequal". It also called for a significant cut in the Soviet troops. Andropov remained undecided on the point, although there were hints that the subject was under debate in Moscow. Lev Delyusin, the head of the China department of the Institute of Oriental Studies in Moscow and another close associate of Andropov's from the 1960's, told a reporter from *The Guardian* that his personal view was that a unilateral troop reduction by the Soviet Union could help[20]. The Defence Minister, Ustinov, conferred with his Mongolian counterpart and shortly thereafter the Mongolians expelled roughly a third of the six thousand Chinese nationals living in Mongolia for more than twenty-five years. The Mongolian move was puzzling, but

20. *The Guardian*, March 22, 1983.

observers speculated that the authorities were concerned at Moscow's growing reconciliation with Peking, and were trying to provoke tension. Four divisions of Soviet troops are based in Mongolia, whose government has always been closer to Moscow and fears Peking.

Andropov's failure to announce any cut in Soviet troops on the border during his first ten months in power may have been due to opposition within the Politburo, or from the Mongolians. Or it may have been that he was not yet convinced of the wisdom of a one-sided Soviet concession. Certainly it gave the lie to speculation that the new Soviet leader was in a hurry to improve relations with Peking. A troop cut could have been the single most obvious way of signalling that his approach was different from Brezhnev's. After a year in office, an assessment of Andropov's policy on China would have to be modest. A new flexibility, yes. A strategy of small steps, yes. But nothing radical or dramatic.

AFGHANISTAN

Essential continuity, marked by a touch of flexibility, was also the hallmark of Andropov's policy on the damaging issue of Afghanistan. When Andropov took over, Soviet troops had been in Afghanistan for almost three years. Although the Kremlin had resisted the temptation to send in more and more troops, as the Americans had done in Vietnam (by November 1982 the original Soviet contingent of 85,000 men had inched up to 105,000), it was having little success in pacifying the country. Soviet forces controlled the capital, Kabul, and a few other provincial centres. Thanks to total air superiority they could set helicopter-borne troops down wherever they liked, but the key task of winning and maintaining control of the countryside eluded them. Faced with a military stalemate in the struggle against the Moslem resistance, the Kremlin was working on a long-term political strategy of Soviet-financed economic and social modernisation, of necessity mainly in the cities. Some 9,000 Afghans were on training courses in the Soviet Union as well as an unknown number at Soviet military institutes. The aim was to build up sufficient pro-Soviet cadres to run the country, in the hope that time would eventually leave the rebels isolated.

Simultaneously, the Kremlin was trying to promote a regional solution by persuading Pakistan to do a deal with the Afghan regime of Babrak Karmal, under which the three million refugees in Pakistan could return home and arms supplies to the Pakistan-based resistance would cease in return for a phased Soviet withdrawal. A major difficulty was that President Zia refused to recognise the Karmal regime. Another was the rebels' apparent determination not to give up the fight. A special United Nations mediator, Diego Cordovez, had held one round of indirect talks with the Afghan and Pakistani Foreign Ministers in Geneva in June 1982 by shuttling between the respective delegations. No progress had been reported.

This was the situation which Andropov inherited. He signalled an immediate interest in the issue when he met with Zia and Karmal after the funeral of Brezhnev. In January he encouraged the UN mediator to start a new round of consultations by travelling to Islamabad, Kabul, and Tehran. (Iran refused to take part in the indirect shuttle diplomacy, although it asked to be kept informed.) In March he invited the UN Secretary General Perez de Cuellar to visit Moscow and in April a new round of shuttling opened in Geneva. According to Cordovez, this produced provisional agreement on 95 per cent of a settlement package in line with the four principles laid down by the United Nations – a withdrawal of foreign troops, the voluntary return of the refugees, re-affirmation of Afghanistan's non-aligned status, and a representative government. In June the Pakistani Foreign Minister visited Moscow and the capitals of the other four permanent members of the Security Council, and later that month the Geneva consultations resumed.

This stepped-up pace of discussions clearly indicated that chances of a breakthrough had risen, although Western diplomats not directly involved in the talks remained sceptical. The impression of movement helped Moscow in two directions. At the summit conference of the Non-Aligned movement in New Delhi in March, the Afghan issue was low on the agenda, while member governments focused most of their attention on crises where the United

States was playing a negative role. Soviet overtures to Pakistan also served to unsettle the Reagan Administration, which was more willing than the Carter Administration to support the Afghan resistance with the apparent aim of tying the Russians down in Afghanistan. This was part of the Reagan Administration's more assertive policy of confronting Moscow wherever it could. During the spring US officials told reporters that CIA arms supplies to the resistance had increased at the end of 1982[21].

Details of the secret discussions in Geneva remained obscure. It was not clear what concessions, if any, were being made, and which side was giving up the most. Press reports which appeared on the eve of the talks in June implied that Zia had moved a considerable way, mainly because of the internal economic and social problems created by the refugees in Pakistan and under the prompting of the Chinese. The Pakistani President had gone on record as saying that the Russians were entitled to a "friendly Afghanistan"[22]. The draft agreement was reported to provide for the resignation of Karmal as a sop to Pakistani and international opinion, but the retention of a Communist-led regime, broadened to include some tribal and religious figures. Soviet troops would withdraw over a six- to eighteen-month period but the Russians would be entitled to retain some military advisers and facilities in Afghanistan. Such an arrangement would continue to give Moscow the dominant role in the country's affairs, and could be described as a victory for the Russians. In addition, they would be promised that arms supplies for the resistance would cease. The main Soviet concessions would be the removal of Karmal, and the phased withdrawal of Soviet troops. The second one could of course be reversed. After the June talks there was a lull. The UN mediator prepared to visit the various capitals again in the autumn.

The Soviet media's approach to the war also changed under Andropov. Previously, reporting of the war had been vague and indirect. The Soviet press did not even confirm that Soviet troops were engaged in combat. The impression was left that they acted entirely in an advisory or logistical role, giving help to the Afghan

---

21. *International Herald Tribune*, May 5, 1983.
22. *Far Eastern Economic Review*, June 9, 1983.

army. In February and March 1983 the army newspaper *Krasnaya Zvezda* as well as *Komsomolskaya Pravda*, the paper mainly read by Soviet young people, that is, the group most threatened by concern over the prospect of serving in Afghanistan, carried a number of articles praising the bravery of Russians in the field. The articles mentioned ambushes in which Russians were caught, the problems facing helicopter pilots, and the ordeal of Soviet nurses in remote parts of Afghanistan while carrying out their "international mission". A letter from seven guards officers published in *Krasnaya Zvezda* complained of the long delays that held up correspondence between soldiers and their families.

The new frankness about the war fitted in with Andropov's general campaign to use the columns of the press for a more open and honest discussion of the problems facing ordinary Soviet citizens. At the same time it was reported that Soviet war casualties were being treated in Moscow hospitals, another sign that the war was no longer being deliberately hidden[23]. Neither of these trends meant that Andropov was planning to withdraw Soviet troops. The opposite policy was equally possible. He might have been planning to accustom the Soviet public to the reality of the war and the prospect that it would be a long and difficult struggle in order to prepare them for a deeper Soviet commitment. The same interpretation could be made of his accelerated efforts to find a settlement with Pakistan. No intelligent leader would want to leave untested the chances of a negotiated solution, especially if it required the other side to make the larger concessions.

THE MIDDLE EAST

There were signs of renewed Soviet interest in the Middle East after Andropov came to power. Under Brezhnev it had been the region of greatest failure. As a result largely of Henry Kissinger's efforts, Egypt had been persuaded to shut the Soviet Union out of the negotiations for peace. The Americans had also encouraged Israel's

---

23. *The Guardian*, March 28, 1983.

preference for a series of bilateral deals with each of its Arab neighbours rather than the comprehensive peace settlement which Moscow wanted. In Lebanon, while the Israelis drove the PLO out of Beirut, the Kremlin confined itself to vague warnings but took no action. Its failure to influence the crisis annoyed the Kremlin, especially as it coincided with private criticism it was receiving from many Arabs. Gromyko told the Supreme Soviet in June that "the role of the Soviet Union in that region, adjacent to our borders, is not merely that of a passive spectator. Our country has formulated just principles for a political settlement, including the proposal for an international conference on the Middle East. They are known to the whole world"[24].

Gromyko's brief and touchy reference to Soviet policy in the Middle East did not spell out the various steps Andropov took to regain a Soviet foothold in the region. One was to project himself into the front-line of Soviet diplomacy. In December he received a seven-member delegation from the Arab League, which included the Foreign Minister of Saudi Arabia, Saud al-Faisal. It was the first such meeting between Soviet and Saudi officials for fifty years, a signal that Andropov hoped to gain some influence in one of the most conservative Arab states. That month he also played host in Moscow to King Hussein of Jordan. In January he held talks with the PLO Chairman, Yasser Arafat.

In spite of his obvious interest in the Middle East, Andropov made no public statements on the subject – a sign that on this issue at least he was not interested so much in public relations as in concrete diplomacy. Indeed, there were persistent rumours that the Syrian President, Hafez Assad, paid secret visits to Moscow during the winter. Andropov was also anxious to restore relations with Egypt since the expulsion of the Soviet Ambassador in September 1981. A visit by Anatoly Gromyko, the Director of Moscow's Africa Institute, and the Foreign Minister's son, to Cairo in January marked an improvement in the atmosphere between the two countries. When the Libyan Prime Minister Major Abdel Jalloud visited Moscow in March to discuss a possible Soviet-Libyan friendship treaty, his talks were held with the Soviet Prime Minister

24. *Pravda*, June 17, 1983.

Nikolai Tikhonov rather than Andropov. The Soviet Union did not support Libya's hardline attitude against Egypt.

The main aim of Andropov's new diplomacy was to oppose the Reagan plan under which the process of bilateral Arab-Israeli negotiations would switch to Jordan, with King Hussein cast in the role of representing the Palestinians. The Kremlin also hoped to capitalise on Egyptian concern over the Israeli occupation of southern Lebanon and persuade President Mubarak to repudiate the Camp David process. Finally, Andropov wanted to buttress Syria against any possible temptation to go along with the Americans. It was not that Andropov was against a peaceful settlement. Moscow had repeatedly urged its Arab friends to recognise the existence of Israel. What it wanted was to be included in a peace settlement as a co-guarantor with the United States on the lines of the short-lived Geneva conference of 1973. Moscow was not prepared to tolerate a Pax Americana in the Middle East, a region, as Gromyko had said, which was close to the Soviet Union.

"I shall oppose the Reagan plan, and we will use all our resources to oppose it", Hussein quoted Andropov as having told him in December. "With due respect, all the weight will be on your shoulders, and they aren't broad enough to bear it"[25]. "We will not allow Lebanon to be an American monopoly", he told Assad[26]. Syria was the Soviet Union's main ally among the front-line states in the Middle East. During the winter Andropov acceded to Assad's request for restoration of the aircraft, tanks, anti-aircraft missiles, and other weaponry lost by the Syrians during the Israeli invasion of the Lebanon. Moscow also delivered the powerful Sam-5 missile for installation on Syria's borders against a possible Israeli attack. The missiles remained in the control of Soviet military advisers. Earlier Soviet supplies of weaponry to Arab states over the past twenty years did not guarantee the Kremlin control over Arab military tactics, and there was no evidence that Andropov's decision to give Syria some of its most advanced defensive weaponry would allow him a veto over Syrian policy. Andropov was taking a gamble, as Brezhnev had done before him, that he could at least exercise

25. *Jerusalem Post*, April 17, 1983.
26. *Le Monde*, April 22, 1983.

some influence on Syrian actions. He must have calculated that the arms supplies would discourage Assad from any temptation to go along with the agreement between Israel and Lebanon which Washington was trying to negotiate. The danger was that the new missile emplacements might provoke the Israeli government into a new military strike, facing the Russians once again with the choice of being involved in a wider war or appearing impotent.

The first success for Andropov's policy of blocking Reagan's diplomacy came in April when the PLO Chairman Yasser Arafat withdrew from his discussions with Hussein on a joint negotiating approach for the projected talks between Jordan and Israel. Success number two came in May when the US Secretary of State George Shultz completed an agreement between Israel and Lebanon. Syria promptly refused to go along with it. Andropov was faced with a serious difficulty when a revolt against Arafat's leadership broke out within the ranks of the PLO. In many ways Moscow sympathised with the PLO hardliners. On the other hand Arafat had always been the man with whom it had had dealings and it would have been reluctant to see him removed. Accordingly, Moscow sent him messages of support and made it publicly clear that it backed him still.

Compared with Brezhnev's Middle Eastern policy, Andropov's first year in office showed some important shifts. He was more involved in face-to-face discussions than the ailing Brezhnev had dared to be. It was remarkable how quickly Andropov trusted himself to enter the thicket of Middle Eastern politics, given that this was not an area in which he had specialised in the past. He took a high-risk decision to re-supply Syria and install new missiles in the face of an ultra hard-line Israeli Government. Finally, he had no compunction about deliberately challenging and obstructing American policy. Under Brezhnev the Kremlin had frequently shown restraint in the Middle East in the interests of trying to preserve detente. With detente virtually dead Andropov was not willing to be as accommodating to the United States as his predecessor had been.

AFRICA AND CENTRAL AMERICA

Developments in Africa and Central America in the first year of Andropov's rule were marked by a significant increase in pressure on two of the Soviet Union's friends. In Africa the South African Government stepped up its support for the Angolan rebel movement, UNITA, as well as continuing its occupation of large parts of southern Angola. In alleged pursuit of guerrillas from the African National Congress (ANC) the South Africans also mounted a commando raid on the capital of Lesotho and bombed targets close to the Mozambican capital, Maputo. There were unconfirmed reports that South Africa was involved in backing dissidents in Zimbabwe. In Central America the CIA helped to finance and arm a series of incursions into Nicaragua against the Sandinista Government by disaffected former members of the pre-revolutionary Somoza regime's National Guard.

In the face of these moves Andropov reacted with no less caution than Brezhnev had done. In contrast to the Middle East, which was close to the Soviet Union's borders, Southern Africa and Central America had little geopolitical interest for the Soviet Union. Andropov received the Angolan President, Jose Eduardo dos Santos, for talks in the Kremlin in May and promised that Moscow would continue to defend him. But there was no sign that the Kremlin was prepared to endorse or encourage a direct effort to drive the South Africans out of Angola with the aid of the roughly 20,000 Cuban troops stationed in Angola. Andropov made no public statement during the dos Santos visit, and left Tikhonov to host the Kremlin dinner. The Russians continued to approve the United Nations plan for Namibia, and criticised Washington for linking it to the issue of the Cuban troops in Angola. Here too there was no indication of any real Soviet interest in a breakthrough after years of stalemate both on the diplomatic front and in the guerrilla war waged by SWAPO, the Namibian liberation movement.

Andropov's position on Nicaragua was also a direct continuation of Brezhnev's. In March he met Daniel Ortega, one of the main Sandinista leaders, as he passed through Moscow on his way back from the summit conference of the Non-Aligned movement. The communique on their talks was markedly less warm than that on Angola, reflecting the fact that in the Soviet view Nicaragua was not yet a Socialist country. It also made no mention of any Soviet military help. On the contrary, it said that Ortega "emphasised that the revolutionary government of Nicaragua has all the necessary resources to defend the country and rout the invaders" while Andropov merely expressed his "solidarity"[27]. While these public statements clearly cannot be said to cover the whole story, they do reflect a difference in the Kremlin's perception of Angola and Nicaragua. Angola is an ally. Nicaragua is not. Moscow was willing to supply arms but was not prepared to commit itself publicly to Nicaragua's defence. Nicaragua's Interior Ministry, Tomas Borge, said in August that Andropov's advice was that the Sandinistas "should not artificially radicalise the process" of internal change in the country for fear of provoking the United States[28].

The Pentagon claimed in March 1983 that Nicaragua had received fifty Soviet tanks, a thousand East German trucks, one hundred anti-aircraft guns, and three brigades of Soviet artillery as well as Soviet-built assault helicopters and transport aircraft[29]. Whatever exaggeration there may have been in these figures, which were given in testimony to a sceptical Senate committee which was debating whether to approve a White House request for more military aid to El Salvador, none of the items mentioned were of the kind which could easily be passed on to El Salvador's guerrillas, given that there is no land frontier between the two countries. The Pentagon failed to provide convincing evidence that the Russians or the Cubans were aiding the El Salvador guerrillas rather than defending Nicaragua against pressures from outside. In July and August Castro and Andropov came out in support of the efforts led by Mexico, Colombia, Venezuela, and Panama to find a negotiated solution to the tension in Central America. Castro offered to withdraw his advisers from Nicaragua if Reagan pulled his out of El Salvador.

27. *Pravda*, March 26, 1983.
28. *The Guardian*, August 9, 1983.
29. *International Herald Tribune*, March 16, 1983.

Eastern Europe

Eastern Europe was the area of foreign affairs that Andropov knew best thanks to his experience in the 1960s. But there was no sign that he wished to change the Kremlin's prevailing line when he succeeded Brezhnev. He saw all his Eastern European allies three times within two months of taking power, first at Brezhnev's funeral, then at the sixtieth anniversary celebrations of the formation of the Soviet Union in December, and finally at the summit meeting of the Warsaw Pact in Prague at the end of January. In June he met them again at a summit meeting in Moscow, called to discuss the talks on controlling medium-range missiles in Europe. He also invited the East German leader, Erich Honecker, and the Hungarian leader, Janos Kadar, to Moscow. But he dropped Brezhnev's regular summer meetings in the Crimea with each Eastern European leader.

The only difficult country was Poland. Shortly before Andropov took over the Polish authorities had embarked on a policy of calculated risk in trying to regain public support. In mid-November Lech Walesa, the leader of the banned trade union organisation, Solidarity, was released from internment. A month later martial law was suspended. In January 1983 the authorities gave their provisional approval for a second visit by the Polish Pope. Andropov had helped to devise the concept of martial law in Poland in 1981 and presumably approved its suspension. But in May the Kremlin signalled a marginally tougher new policy after the May Day celebrations in Poland had shown that Solidarity was still active. An article in the periodical *New Times* criticised the Polish weekly *Polityka* for allegedly supporting "pluralism"[30]. This was followed by a piece in the Soviet Party's journal *Kommunist* which approvingly reprinted a Polish Party article that called for a firm line against "rightist forces"[31]. It seemed clear that the Kremlin thought the Polish gamble was not working and that the authorities were once again losing control. On the eve of the Pope's visit in June Gromyko made a stern speech in Moscow accusing the West

---

30. Cited in *The Observer*, May 29, 1983.
31. Ibid.

of practising ideological subversion against Poland. "Poland was and remains an inalienable part of the socialist community"[32], he declared. But after the Pope's visit, the Kremlin relaxed again. The Polish leader, General Jaruzelski, was awarded the Order of Lenin in July, a clear sign of approval.

A similar general toughening was visible in Hungary in April. Andropov and Kadar were of course old colleagues from the days of Andropov's ambassadorship in Budapest in 1956. It was noticeable that the communique on the meeting during the December celebrations in Moscow was warmer than that of any other encounter Andropov had. Andropov had backed Kadar's economic reform programme in the 1970's. When Kadar visited Moscow in July he was again warmly praised by Andropov.

In the spring Kadar had shown signs of irritation at the way the West was focusing on Hungary as a maverick in the Warsaw Pact, a country which was somehow re-introducing capitalism behind a socialist facade. Kadar told the Central Committee in April that there was to be no "reform of the reform", the Party would retain the decisive role in shaping economic policy, and the media should observe a one-year moratorium on discussion of Hungary's small handicraft, trade, and other enterprises where individual and co-operative owners are allowed to employ paid staff and retain their own profit. The Western press was paying too much attention to this small-scale private enterprise. Kadar also warned the burgeoning group of perhaps two-to-three hundred intellectuals, who openly circulated Western political literature and had formed an independent peace movement, not to go too far. Kadar was clearly acting in line with Andropov's wishes.

It was not that Andropov was against the Hungarian economic experiment. Indeed the Soviet Union was studying it closely with a view to possibly copying some of its features eventually. What was unacceptable was the way that Western commentators and some Hungarians themselves were beginning to invest it with excessive political content, as though it was a benign cancer eating away at the Socialist system.

In February a high-level meeting in Moscow of the Council for

---

32. *Pravda*, June 17, 1983.

Mutual Economic Assistance (Comecon) had given a new impetus to the snail-like progress towards economic integration and coordinated national plans which Eastern Europe had been trying to make for years. The message in all these changes was that reform was tolerable only if the Party authorities remained in control and gave no suggestion that the socialist economic system was in serious trouble.

Conclusion

To sum up, the foreign policy of Andropov's first year remained broadly on the same lines as Brezhnev's. In style there were clear differences, as Andropov quickly sought to exert his own authority on the decision-making process. He was visibly more vigorous and in better control of the detail of Soviet positions than Brezhnev had been in his later years. Politicians and diplomats who met him found Andropov confident, interested, and alert. On the European missile issue he showed greater flexibility and imagination, more willingness to adjust the Soviet position, and a more skilful use of public relations.

It was hard, however, to see significant changes in the substance of his foreign policy. In the Middle East he was more willing to obstruct the United States, perhaps partly in retaliation for continuing US efforts to exclude the Soviet Union from any influence in the region. On Afghanistan there were signs of a more energetic search for a political settlement with Pakistan, but no real evidence of willingness to make major concessions. The same contradictory mixture of dynamic persistence was true for Soviet relations with China. Andropov was not ready for a unilateral reduction in Soviet troops on the border – a gesture which would not have affected Soviet security but could have given a powerful push to the process of reconciliation. In Africa and Central America Andropov's policy showed no change. In Eastern Europe he advocated, and was beginning to enforce, a gradual closing of the ranks.

Towards countries and regions on or close to Soviet borders such as China and Western Europe Andropov looked for improvements in relations but not at the price of substantial concessions. Towards the United States the strategy was one of defensive confrontation. At the back of it all there were hints that Moscow would fall back on traditional Soviet isolationism if necessary – a Fortress Russia policy. In June he told the Central Committee that the Soviet Union must try to become self-sufficient in food production, a hint that he wanted to make the country immune from Western sanctions. He expressed disillusionment with Moscow's friends in the Third World, the countries of so-called "socialist orientation", when he said that the Soviet Union "sees the complexity of their position and the difficulties of their revolutionary development. It is one thing to proclaim socialism as one's goal and quite another thing to build it"[33]. The Soviet Union helped towards their economic development "to the extent of our possibilities" but their advance depended on hard work by their own people and the adoption of correct policies by their leaders.

As for defence and security issues, Andropov stressed that the Soviet Union would stick by the nuclear and strategic parity which was established between East and West a decade earlier. If an arms race was forced on it, then "we shall enhance the combat power of the Soviet armed forces"[34], he pledged. He held out little hope of seeing a revival of detente with the West. Behind a wall of self-sufficiency and massive military might, Fortress Russia would watch and wait.

---

33. Pravda, June 16, 1983.
34. Ibid.

Conclusion

When Andropov succeeded Brezhnev in November 1982, many observers wrote him off as a care-taker who would probably make little impact on the Soviet or world scene. There were doubts about the degree of his power, and whether he would ever be as strong as Brezhnev had been at his height. There were doubts about his health. There were doubts about the loyalty of his colleagues.

A year later, many of these doubts have been resolved. Andropov faces no serious challenge from any potential rival. While he is ten years older than Brezhnev had been when he took over in 1964, Andropov's colleagues are older too. Only two members of the Politburo are energetic enough to have the will to challenge him, and they are still too young to need to bother. While there are signs that not all his colleagues agree with Andropov's aims, he has ensured that they do not feel alienated or threatened enough to plot to remove him, in the pattern of Khrushchev's sudden replacement in 1964.

Physically, Andropov's condition was weak when he took over, and his health deteriorated further in the first few months of 1983. But the consensus of the medical experts in the Western community who have studied his behaviour closely is that he is likely to remain in charge for several years longer. No-one has questioned the quality of his mind.

Indeed, if and when President Reagan or his successor ever meets his Soviet counterpart, he will find a Soviet leader who is in many ways the most formidable Kremlin figure that the West has had to deal with for thirty years. Khrushchev's impetuosity, his earthy turn of phrase, his cockiness and bombast are as foreign to

Andropov as are Brezhnev's stolid sentimentality and inferiority complex. The man who now runs the Kremlin is reserved in manner but more intelligent and self-confident than either of his predecessors.

Where there are uncertainties, they centre on the problems facing the Soviet Union in general – problems which would confront any Kremlin leader. How far is the current downturn in relations with the West going to go? Can they worsen much beyond the present level, already the coolest period of East-West relations since the Cuban missile crisis of 1962? If the nuclear arms race continues, what effect will this have on the Soviet economy, as it enters a period of lower growth? Are the Soviet Union's internal problems likely to provoke domestic upheaval, focused on economic discontent or tension between the different nationalities? Is the leadership of the powerful Soviet military machine going to demand a greater say in political decisions?

It is premature to speculate how far these trends will go, and whether they will overwhelm Andropov. What is clear is that he has already begun to try to counteract at least some of them. Of course, by no stretch of the imagination is he a 'liberal', as some analysts dubbed him when he first took over. But, at least in Kremlin terms, he is no conservative either. Throughout his varied career and in his first year in power as General Secretary, he has acted as a cautious advocate of change. After the stagnation of the last years of Brezhnev, he has shown himself willing to move gradually to try to solve some of the country's economic problems. His actions in the economic field fit the pattern already visible in the days when he was operating in Hungary and later as the Central Committee Secretary in charge of relations with Eastern Europe and China. He is a man who looks for sophisticated advice and is prepared to identify problems and seek detailed analysis rather than accept the conventional wisdom without thought.

In choosing solutions, however, Andropov usually avoids risks. The economic changes which he has announced are limited in scope and ambition. By conducting a controlled experiment in only a few parts of the economy, he minimises the danger of failure but also hopes that by demonstrating undeniable results he can persuade the Party bureaucracy and the economic administrators to accept reform. A more imaginative man would have gone for bigger changes. A more impatient man would have acted faster. Andropov is neither.

As a team leader, he has acted in equally cautious style. He has been tolerant of his Politburo colleagues. None has been sacked so far during his period in power. Towards the Party apparatus he has also been soft. With the exception only of the most outstanding cases of corruption there have been no significant dismissals from the Central Committee. The government structure has been dealt with somewhat more vigorously, partly because its political resistance is smaller. His calls for a tightening of discipline throughout Soviet society, and the modest moves he has made to enforce them, betray the mentality of a puritan and a policeman, and may have some effect in the initial phase of a new leadership. There was a widespread feeling that the indecision of Brezhnev's last few years had produced a sense of drift. But Andropov will have to show that the reward for discipline is a higher standard of living if his campaign is to succeed. He will also have to recognise the inherent contradiction in his effort to enhance discipline while also encouraging incentives. Unless there is some loosening-up on the ideological front, so that the scientific and technical communities can dare to try out new methods, Andropov's cautious experiments will be still-born.

Towards the largely hostile world beyond the Soviet Union's heavily guarded borders, Andropov has acted no more rashly than his predecessor. He seems well aware of the limits of Soviet power. It can safely be assumed that he will continue to maintain Soviet defence spending at a level high enough to prevent the United States from regaining the nuclear superiority it enjoyed in the 1960's. The entire leadership is united in the view that the achievement of nuclear parity at the end of the 1960's laid the basis for detente and brought the Soviet Union the international status which it had long coveted. Andropov will insist that parity be maintained. In this he has the backing of Marshal Ustinov and the military leadership which has a vested interest in not permitting the Soviet Union to slip back. In the arms control field, Andropov has taken some initiatives and has shown more flexibility than Brezhnev in tailoring his offers to Western public opinion. But the gap between what he was prepared to give and what the United States has demanded has been too wide, and seems set to remain so.

Elsewhere, Soviet policy under Andropov has mainly been one of retrenchment. With the exception of its heightened involvement in Syria, an area of considerable volatility, the Kremlin has sought to minimise the risks of any serious clash with the United States. In general, Andropov's foreign record has been to maintain a posture, rather than a policy. Heavily armed, touchy about any conceivable threats to its security, and reluctant to make any concessions, the Soviet Union under his leadership seems to be hoping that the international situation will change, but is not prepared to do much to bring about change. There is an old Soviet joke about Stalin, Khrushchev, and Brezhnev sitting in a train that suddenly stopped. Nothing seemed able to make it move again. "Shoot the driver", shouted Stalin. Still the train did not move. "Tell the driver's mate that Communism is just round the next corner", shouted Khrushchev. Again the train failed to budge. "Let's pull down the blinds and pretend the train is moving", Brezhnev murmured.

Now it is the turn of a man born on a railway station himself. Can Andropov do any better? So far he has only changed a few signals. Time will tell if the train begins to move.

Select Bibliography

Andropov, Y. *Selected Speeches and Articles*, Moscow, Polizdat, 1979.
Andropov, Y. *Andropov, Selected Speeches and Writings*, Oxford, Pergamon, 1983.
Barron, J. *KGB Today*, New York, Reader's Digest Press, 1983.
Brzezinski, Z. *Power and Principle*, London, Weidenfeld and Nicolson, 1983.
Calvocoressi, P. *World Politics since 1945*, 3 edn, London, Longman, 1977.
Crankshaw, E. *The New Cold War: Moscow v. Peking*, Harmondsworth, Penguin, 1963.
Gittings, J. *Survey of the Sino-Soviet Dispute*, London, Oxford University Press, 1968.
Irving, D. *Uprising*, London, Hodder and Stoughton, 1981.
Jakobson, M. *The Diplomacy of the Winter War*, Cambridge. Mass., Harvard University Press, 1961.
Krasin, V. *Sud (Trial)*, New York, Chalidze Publications, 1983.
Kupriyanov, G.N. *Ot Barentsego Morya do Ladogi (From the Barent Sea to Ladoga)*, Leningrad, Lenizdat, 1972.
Lomax, B. *Hungary 1956*, London, Allison and Busby, 1976.
Medvedev, Z. *Andropov*, Oxford, Basil Blackwell, 1983.
Micunovic, V. *Moscow Diary*, tr. David Floyd, New York, Doubleday, 1980
Platonov, S.P. *Taistelut Suomen Rintamalla 1941-4 (The Battles on the Finnish Front 1941-4)*, Helsinki, Kirjayhtymä, 1972.
Rigby, T.H., Brown, A. and Reddaway, P. (eds) *Authority, Power and Policy in the USSR*, London, Macmillan, 1980.
Rositzke, H. *The KGB: The Eyes of Russia*, London, Sidgwick and Jackson, 1982.
Segal, G. *The China Factor: Peking and the Superpowers*, London, Croom Helm, 1982.
Shawcross, W. *Crime and Compromise: Janos Kadar and the Politics of Hungary Since the Revolution*, London, Weidenfeld and Nicolson, 1974.
Steele, J. *World Power: Soviet Foreign Policy under Brezhnev and Andropov*, London, Michael Joseph, 1983.
Windsor, P. and Roberts, A. *Czechoslovakia 1968*, London, Chatto and Windus, 1969.

Index

Aaltonen, Aimo 37
Afanasyev, Sergei 166
Afghanistan 111, 118, 121, 129:
  Andropov's policy 176, 192–5, 203;
  invasion of 2, 105, 107, 119–20, 139,
  155, 175–6, 191
Agca, Mehmet Ali 131–3, 134–5
agriculture 18, 80, 155–6: Andropov's
  interest in 16, 48, 139, 156–7, 164–6,
  204; collective contract system 159,
  164–6; collectivisation 20–2, 39, 45, 49;
  in Hungary 45, 48–9; in Karelia 39,
  42
Albania, Soviet relations with 74–5
Aliyev, Geidar 162, 170
Alliluyeva, Svetlana 87, 109
Amin, Hafizullah 119
Amnesty International 94, 105, 171
Andropov, Igor (Andropov's son) 9,
  10–11, 12, 82
Andropova, Irina (Andropov's daughter),
  see Filippova, Irina
Andropov, Konstantin (Andropov's
  grandson) 11
Andropov, Vladimir (Andropov's
  father) 19–20, 21
Andropov, Yuri Vladimirovich: appointed
  as General Secretary 1–3, 16, 105,
  136–7, 146, 149, 151, 152–4, 169, 171,
  206: assessments, Eastern 4–5, 7–9, 142;
  assessments, Western 3–5, 111, 157–9,
  168; breadth of experience 14–15,
  17–18, 88, 138–9; compared with
  Brezhnev 4–6, 13, 176, 192, 203–4,
  205–7; early life 19–22, 165;
  education 15, 22, 27–8, 81;
  flexibility 177, 179, 181, 192, 203;
  foreign policy 77, 88, 109, 139, 147,
  154–5, 174–204. 207–8; health 2, 3,
12–14, 18, 139, 170, 205; internal
  affairs 152–73, 206–7; knowledge of
  languages 8, 16, 30, 48–9;
  limitations 17–18, 138–9; as
  moderate 6, 66, 95, 102, 171, 206; as
  moderniser 18, 113, 124, 157–8, 163,
  206; private life 1–2, 6–7, 9–12, 30; as
  realist 5, 18, 115, 158, 168; see also
  agriculture; arms control; Brezhnev,
  succession to; Central Committee;
  Communist Party; detente; economy,
  Soviet; Hungary; Karelia; KGB;
  Komsomol; Politburo
Andropova, Tatyana (Andropov's
  wife) 11–12, 30
Andropova, Tanya (Andropov's daughter-
  in-law) 11
Andropova, Tanya (Andropov's
  granddaughter) 11
Angola, Soviet relations with 175, 199
Antonov, Sergei 132
Antonyuk, Lt.-General M.A. 28
Arafat, Yasser 195–8
Arbatov, Georgy 11, 82, 112
arms control: Andropov 154, 172, 176–88,
  201, 204, 207; Brezhnev 174–5, 178
Asanov, Nikolai 140
Assad, Hafez 196–8
Augstein, Rudolf 3

Bayeranov, Colonel 119
Begin, Menahim, see Israel
Beria, Lavrenti 88
Bittman, Vladislaw 117
Block, John 184
Bogomolov, Oleg 83
Borge, Tomas 200
Bovin, Alexander 82–3, 190
Boyce, Christopher 123–4

Index

Brandt, Willy 126
Brezhneva, Galina 140-2, 149
Brezhnev, Leonid 72, 86-8, 125, 146, 150-1, 153-4, 161, 164-5, 168, 170, 205-8: and Afghanistan 118-19, 155, 176, 192-3; assessments of 4-6, 13, 16, 18, 136, 155; and China 80-1, 143, 188-9, 192; contact with foreign leaders 3, 155; and Czechoslovakia 113, 115, 147, 155, 175; foreign policy 174-6, 183, 188, 195, 197-201, 203-4; funeral 1, 5, 109, 146-7, 149, 151, 179, 189; health 13, 137-9, 142-4, 155; and Poland 120, 175-6; private life 11-12, 140-2, 144; relations with Andropov 88, 95-6, 148; succession to 2, 15, 35, 108, 136-40, 142-51, 155, 168-9; and Yugoslavia 77
Brezhneva, Viktoria (Brezhnev's wife) 11-12
Britain 77-8, 124, 126-7, 174, 177-8, 180-1; *see also* NATO
Brzezinski, Zbigniew 123, 134
Bugrimova, Irina 140
Bukovsky, Vladimir 10, 66, 95, 103
Bulgaria: Soviet relations with 56; and attempted killing of Pope John Paul II 132-3, 134-5
Burlatsky, Fedor 82
Buryatia, Boris 140-2
Bush, George 1-2, 109, 179, 183

Carstens, Karl 1-2
Carter, Jimmy 105, 107, 112, 123, 134, 137-8, 155, 184, 194
Castro, Fidel 175, 200
Gelenk, Bekir 132
Central Committee 128, 137, 141-3, 151, 185, 204: Andropov on 4, 6, 15-16, 17, 43-4, 75, 88, 113, 147, 206; Department for Liaison with the Communist and Workers' Parties of the Socialist Countries 16-18, 47, 64-76, 80-5, 86, 190; Head of Fourth European Department 44; International Department 64-5, 69; Secretariat 64-5, 67, 77-8, 82, 86, 89, 143-7, 162
Chebotarev, Anatoly 123
Chebrikov, Viktor 133
Chernenko, Konstantin, as Andropov's main rival 2, 15, 136-9, 142-9, 151-2, 164-5, 168-70
Chernyayev, Rudolf 123
Chervonenko, Stepan 115

Cheysson, Claude 3-4
China: Soviet relations with 16, 18, 56, 64-5, 67-8, 127, 128, 143, 176: Andropov's attitudes towards 67-8, 72, 78-80, 82, 176, 188-92, 203-4, 206; border troops 191, 203; break with 65, 70-5, 76-8, 86
Chronicle of Current Events 105-6, 172
Churbanov, General Yuri 141
CIA (Central Intelligence Agency) 96, 109, 111-12, 123-4, 129-30, 135, 194: in Central America 199; lack of knowledge of Andropov 1, 13-14
Colby, William 17, 111-12
Comecon (Council for Mutual Economic Assistance) 76, 203
communism, transition to 52-3, 55, 70-2, 75, 188-9, 204
Communist Party 64, 112, 120, 150, 163-4, 168-9, 175, 202-3: Andropov's relationship with 17, 81, 95-6, 170, 206-7; Control of KGB 17, 88-9, 96, 146; membership, 1920's-1930's 21, 22-3
Cordovez, Diego 193-4
corruption: under Andropov 96, 144, 159-61, 167, 207; under Brezhnev 4, 105, 140-2, 148-9
Corvalan, Luis 95
Costa Rica, Soviet relations with 130
Crimean Tatars 92, 100-2, 103
Cuba, Soviet relations with 77, 80, 107, 155, 174-5, 184, 199-200, 206
Cuellar, Perez de 193
Czechoslovakia 49, 56, 147: Andropov's relations with 44, 113-16, 121; reforms in 80, 103, 113-15, 116-18; Soviet invasion 53, 103, 114-18, 120, 155, 175

Daniel, Yuli 84, 87, 92-3
Daoud, President Muhammad 118
defectors 13, 87, 109, 134, 149: from KGB 110-12, 118, 122-3, 128
defence expenditure 18, 146, 162, 204, 207; *see also* arms control; nuclear weapons
Defence Council 137, 146, 148: Andropov as Chairman 169
Delyusin, L.P. 83, 191
Demichev, Pyotr 173
demonstrations 46, 65, 103
Deng Xiaoping 74, 78
de-Stalinisation 50-1, 54, 67, 69, 75, 77, 81-2, 92, 113, 144, 155; *see also* liberalisation; re-Stalinisation

Index

detente, East-West 1-2, 146, 184, 186-8, 198, 201, 203, 205-6: 1950's 73, 82: 1960's 79, 92, 187; 1970's 79, 95-6, 104-5, 107-8, 155, 174-5
Dildenkin, N.A. 35
discipline, labour 18, 153, 156-7, 159-60, 162-3, 167, 173, 207
dissent 93-4, 123, 134: and Andropov 17, 84, 86, 88-92, 94-5, 97-108, 171-2; religious 92, 103, 106-8; Stalin's moves against 23; *see also* human rights; peace groups
Dobrynin, Anatoly 123
'dogmatism' and Sino-Soviet dispute 71-2, 73-6, 79
Dolgikh, Vladimir 161-2
Dolgoruki, Yuri (Andropov's nickname) 2
Dubcek, Alexander 80, 113, 115-18
Dzerzhinsky, Felix 89

Eagleburger, Lawrence 129
East Germany 49, 80, 147, 201-2
economic policy, Soviet 5, 76, 143-4, 146, 154-6, 175, 206-7: falling growth rate 18, 139, 156; New Economic Policy 19-20; reform in 18, 83, 157-9, 161-8, 170, 173, 202-3; *see also* Hungary: economy
economic policy, Chinese 72
Egypt, Soviet relations with 18, 195-6
Eisenhower, Dwight 72
El Salvador 199
emigration from USSR 93, 94, 172: Jews 95, 103-5, 172-3; Soviet Germans 3, 104-5
Enger, Valdik 123
Epatko, Vasily 110
Erishtein (Andropov's mother) 19
ethnic groups 205: in Karelia 26, 31-2, 36
European Security Conference, Madrid 11
exile: external 19, 92, 94, 171; internal 91, 98-9, 107, 171

al-Faisal, Saud 196
Fedorchuk, Vitaly 145
Filippov, Mikhail 10, 173
Filippova, Irina (Andropov's daughter) 10
Finland: post-war relations with 38; war with USSR 24-38
Ford, Gerald 155

France, nuclear weapons in 178, 180-1
Furtseva, Ekaterina 140

Galanskov, Yuri 103
Geneva intermediate-range nuclear force (INF) reduction talks 177-83
Geneva strategic arms reduction talks (START) 177, 178
Georgadze 100-1
Germany, war with 25-38
Gero, Erno 50, 51-2, 54-5
Ginzburg, Alexander 97, 100, 103, 107
Gomulka, Wladyslaw 53, 65
Gorbachev, Mikhail 145, 149-50, 162, 164-5
Grenada 175
Grishin, Viktor 148
Gromyko, Anatoly 195
Gromyko, Andrei 2-3, 11, 145, 150-1, 179, 185, 189, 196-7, 201
Grushevoi, Konstantin 142
Guillaume, Günter 126

Hambleton, Hugh 127
Hanson, Philip 158-9
Harriman, Averell 183
Hegedus, Andras 9, 48-51, 52, 53-5
Helsinki agreement 106-7, 174
Heltai, George 46-7, 58
Ho Chi Minh 77
Honecker, Erich 147, 201
Hoxha, Enver 75
Huang Hua 189
human rights 107: activists 98, 103; *see also* dissent
Hungary: Andropov as Ambassador 5, 7-9, 16, 46-50, 57, 64, 67, 76, 113-14, 201, 206; Andropov as counsellor 16, 46; Andropov's role during uprising 47-8, 50-63, 88, 101, 115, 121; economy 50, 80, 166-7, 202; relations with USSR 80, 155, 201-3; uprising 1956 7, 16, 56-63, 65, 69, 118
Husak, Gustav 53, 147
Hussein, King of Jordan 196-7

imprisonment, political 17, 91, 98-9, 105-6, 171
industrialisation 20-3, 80, 158: Hungary 45, 50
industry, Andropov's concern with 156-7, 159, 162-3, 166-7; *see also* discipline, labour

Index

Institute of the United States and Canada 11, 82, 112
intellectuals: Andropov's contacts with 66, 81–5, 89, 170–1; Czechoslovak 80, 113; Hungarian 201; Soviet 92–3; *see also* dissent
Ipekci, Abdi 132
Iran, Soviet relations with 111, 175, 192
Ishkov, Aleksander 148
Israel 130–1, 172, 175, 195–8

Jaber, Adnan 130–1
Jakobson, Max 24
Jalloud, Major Abdel 196
Japan, Soviet relations with 128, 188
Jaruzelski, General Wojciech 120, 147, 202
Jews: emigration of from USSR 95, 103–5, 172–3; human rights 103
John Paul II, Pope 131–5, 201
Jordan, Soviet relations with 196–7

Kadar, Janos 16, 51, 52–60, 62, 65, 201–3
Kamenev, L.B. 22
Kampiles, William 124
Kampuchea 176, 191
Kania, Stanislaw 120
Kapitsa, Pyotr 84, 191
Kardelj, Edvard 69
Karelia: Andropov in 11, 15, 16, 24, 26–43; Andropov's intelligence work 32–6, 88; post-war administration 38–43; public criticism of Andropov 16, 40–3, 68; Soviet-Finnish war 24–38; war with Germany 25–38
Karmal, Babrak 119, 193–5
Karyakin, Yuri 83
KGB (Committee for State Security) 10, 86–8, 145–6: Andropov as head 1–2, 6, 13, 14–15, 40, 63, 67, 80, 82, 86–108, 109, 113–20, 122–7, 137, 139, 141–2, 144, 159, 162, 168, 170–2; Andropov's effect on 17, 93–4, 99, 108, 110–12, 124, 128; in Eastern Europe 112–18, 120–1; Fifth Directorate of 17, 103, 109; in Hungary 56, 61; internal activities 90–108, 127; methods of 90–1, 93–4; overseas activities 17, 109–31, 133–5; and NATO 110, 112, 121–9; Service A 128; and terrorism 130–1; and Third World 112–13, 129–31

Khrushchev, Nikita 16, 83, 100, 140, 151, 153, 158, 208: and China 70–5, 77–8, 80–1; and Cuban missile crisis 77, 80, 155, 174, 206; downfall of 66, 80–1, 83, 86, 87, 110, 205; and Eastern Europe 65–6, 69, 77–8, 189–90; and Hungarian uprising 51, 56–7, 59, 62, 155; and liberalisation 45, 67, 70, 76, 77, 82, 92, 103, 155; opposition to 68–9, 80; *see also* USA
Kiraly, General Bela 60–2
Kirilenko, Andrei 137, 142–3, 145, 149, 151, 162, 168–9
Kirillov, Igor 150
Kirov, Sergei 22
Kiselev, Ambassador 7, 46
Kissinger, Henry 194
Kohl, Helmut 4–5, 12, 14, 174
Koivisto, Mauno 38, 181
Kolevatov, Anatoly 142
Komsomol (Young Communist League) 20–2, 40, 89: Andropov as head in Karelia 24, 26–35, 43; Andropov as local official 15–16, 22–3; Stalin's purge 23–4
Kondakov, Alexander 43
Konstantinov, Fedor 73
Kosygin, Alexei 11, 12, 81
Krasin, Viktor 40, 98–100
Krol, Cardinal John 134
Kunaev, Dinmukhamed 145
Kupriyanov, General Gennadi 24, 28, 32, 35, 38–43
Kuusinen, Otto 26–7 31–2, 37–8, 43, 68–9, 82
Kuzichkin, Vladimir 111, 118–19
Kuznetsov, Vasily 2

Lebanon 175, 196–8
Lee, Andrew 123–4
Leino, Yrjo 37
Lenin, V.I. 19, 70, 71, 78–9, 143, 154, 187, 189
Levchenko, Stanislav 111–12, 128
liberalisation 48: Czechoslovakia 113, 118; Hungary 45, 51; USSR 67, 76, 77, 81, 84, 92, 155, 172; *see also* de-Stalinisation
liberation movements 71, 113, 129–30, 198
Liberia, Soviet relations with 129–30
Libya, Soviet relations with 196–7
Livius, Judit 8
Lyalin, Oleg 111, 121–3

Lysenko, T.D. 83
Lyubimov, Yuri 10

McMahon, John 130
Madrid, *see* European Security Conference
Maisky, Ivan 84
Makeyev, Valentin 161
Malenkov, Georgy 57
Maleter, Pal 8, 61
Mao Zedong 70-2, 74, 77-8, 81: Andropov's attitudes towards 16, 75, 79, 189
Markov, Georgi (Bulgarian emigré) 134
Markov, Georgy (Soviet writer) 173
Marosan, Gyorgy 8, 56-7
Masaryk, Jan 114, 116
Mauroy, Pierre 1
Medunov, Sergei 148-9
Medvedev, Roy 4, 66-7, 171
Medvedev, Zhores 83-4, 93, 96-7
Mendel, Gregor 83
Meretskov, General K.A. 28
Mexico, Soviet relations with 129, 200
Micunovic, Veljko 69
Middle East, Soviet policies in 18, 175-6, 195-8, 203
Mikhailov, Mikhail 161
Mikoyan, Anastas 51, 54-6, 67, 69
Mitterand, François 125, 174
Mlynar, Zdenek 115-16
Molotov, Vyacheslav 75-6
Mongolia, expulsion of Chinese nationals from 191-2
Moroz, Valentin 106
Mubarak, President Hosni 195
Munnich, Ferenc 57, 59
Myagkov, Alexei 111

Nagy, Imry 7, 45-8, 50-8, 60-3, 69
Nakasone, Yasuhiro 186
Namibia 198
nationalism 76: Chinese 79; Hungarian 52-3, 54-5; Polish 133; USSR 90, 92, 106
NATO, KGB activity in 110, 112, 121-2; and nuclear weapons 107, 177-81; *see also* Britain; USA; West Germany
New Economic Policy, *see* economy, Soviet
Nicaragua, Soviet relations with 175, 199-20
Nixon, Richard M. 1, 4, 155, 187
North Korea, Soviet relations with 64
North Vietnam, Soviet relations with 16, 64, 81

Novikov, Ignaty 161
Novotny, Antonin 113
nuclear weapons 70-1, 73, 77, 174, 177-83, 201, 203-4, 206-7: cruise missiles 177, 181; Pershing-II 177, 181; SS-4 181; SS-5 181; SS-20 107 177-81, 183
Nuclear Test Ban Treaty 1963 77-8
nuclear-free zones 128, 181
Numeiry, President Jaafar 129

Ogarkov, Nikolai 34-5, 185
Orlov, Yuri 107
Ortega, Daniel 199

Pakistan 130: and Afghanistan 176, 192-5, 202
Palestine Liberation Organisation (PLO) 130-1, 196-8
Palme, Olof 181
Panyushkin, Alexander 68-9
partisan movement, Karelia 15, 28-32, 34
Pasternak, Boris 87
Pathé, Pierre-Charles 128
Pavel, Josef 144
Pavlovsky, Ivan 161
peace groups 181: Hungary 201; USSR 172; Warsaw Pact 175
peasants 155, 159, 164-5, 167: in Hungary 49, 50, 52; 1920's 19-21
Peinsipp, Walter 5, 8-9, 62
Pelshe, Arvid 151, 168
Petersen, Arne Herlo 128
Petrenko, Colonel 98
Philby, Kim 111
Pigarevich, General B.N. 28
Plisetskaya, Maya 84
Plyushch, Leonid 106
Poland 44, 53-4, 120, 133-5, 147, 201: martial law 120-1, 139, 175-6, 201; 1956 56, 65
Politburo 64, 87, 92, 95, 103-7, 118-20, 138, 149, 151, 155, 169: Andropov as member 35, 40, 88-9, 95-6, 101-2, 108, 114-15, 120, 122, 137, 139, 142-8, 176; relations with Andropov 43, 134, 145-6, 168, 170, 192, 205, 207
Ponomarev, Boris 11, 69-70, 73-4, 78
Presidium 43, 68, 171: Andropov as President 5, 168-9
Prime, Geoffrey 124
propaganda: anti-Soviet 122, 183; Soviet 43, 109, 117, 128

Index

psychiatric abuse 17, 91, 92-3, 94-5, 99, 106, 171
Pym, Francis 1

Qian Qichen 190

radio, foreign 6, 17, 103, 106
Rajk, Laszlo 51, 54
Rakosi, Matyas 48, 50-4, 58-9, 113
Rappoport, Yakov 27
Rawlinson, Sir Peter 122
Reagan, Ronald 105, 108, 112, 134, 177-9, 182-4, 186, 187, 188, 194, 197, 200, 205
Reddaway, Peter 90-1, 104
reform, post-Stalinist: Czechoslovakia 80, 113-15, 117-18; Hungary 9, 45, 47-8, 50-2, 80; Poland 65; USSR 18, 83, 157-8
'reformism': in Czechoslovakia 80; in Hungary 45; in Poland 65; in USSR 66, 79, 82, 83
Repin, Valery 172
re-Stalinisation 66, 67, 77, 84, 99
'revisionism': in Czechoslovakia 80; in Hungary 52; Sino-Soviet dispute 71-2, 73-6, 79; in Yugoslavia 77
Rockefeller, Nelson 124
Romania, Soviet relations with 56, 76
Romanov, Grigori 162
Rositzke, Harry 121
Rostokvsky, Semyon (Ernst Henry) 84
Rowny, General Edward 177
Rudenko 100
Rumyantsev, Alexei 83
Runge, Yevgeny 110
Russian Orthodox Church, and human rights 103, 106
Ryzhkov, Nikolai 161

Sakharov, Andrei 84, 94, 106-7, 171
Salisbury, Harrison 6
Salynsky, Afanasy 10
dos Santos, President Jose Eduardo 199
Saudi Arabia, Soviet relations with 196
Savinkin, Nikolai 88n.
Savonenkov, Lt.-General 37
Schapiro, Leonard 17
Scharegin, Nikolai 97-8, 100
Schmidt, Helmut 14
Seitmuratova, Aishe 100-2
Semichastny, Vladimir 86-8, 110
Serov, General Ivan 56-7, 61-2

Shatrov, Mikhail 142
Shcharansky, Anatoly 107
Shchelokov, Nikolai 96, 100, 161
Shcherbitsky, Vladimir 145
Shehu, Mehmet 75
Shelepin, Alexander 86-8
Shevchenko, Arkady 12-13
Shibayev, Alexei 143
Shultz, George 185, 197
Sinyavsky, Andrei 84, 87, 92-3
Slansky, Rudolf 116
SMERSH (anti-informer squads) 34
Smirnov, Alexei 172
SMOG (poets' group) 10
Smrkovsky, Josef 117
Solidarity trade union 120, 132, 133, 176, 201
Solzhenitsyn, Alexander 83-5, 92, 102-3, 106, 172
South Korean airliner, shooting down of 185-6
Stakhanov 22
Stalin 17, 45, 48, 50, 75, 88, 99-100, 190, 208: and collectivisation 19-21; and industrialisation 20, 45; purges 22-3, 26, 53-4, 60, 70, 85, 105, 114; war with Germany 25-7; *see also* de-Stalinisation; re-Stalinisation
Struyev, Alexander 161
Sudan, Soviet relations with 129
Supreme Soviet, International Affairs Committee 77
Suslov, Mikhail 11-12, 67, 82, 141-4, 147; Andropov's relationship with 65, 67-8, 137, 147; and China 76-7, 78-9; and Hungary 54-6, 67; and Yugoslavia 69
Svoboda, President Ludvik 115-16, 117
Skyiäinen, Rudolf 30
Syria 130: Soviet relations with 18, 147, 176, 196-8, 208

Tamm, Igor 84
Taraki, Nur Muhammad 119
Tarsis, Valery 92-3, 94
Thatcher, Margaret 128, 174, 180
Third World: KGB in 112-13, 129-31; Soviet relations with 18, 71, 154, 175, 204
Tikhonov, Nikolai 2, 12, 197, 199
Timoskainen, F.F. 32-4
Tito, Marshal 45, 56, 59, 65, 69-70, 189
Tolubeyev, Nikita 133
Trifonov, Yuri 173
Trotsky, Leon 134

Tsvetkov 41-2
Tsvigun, Semyon 141-2
USA, Soviet relations with: Andropov 18, 79, 146, 174, 178-9, 182-7, 194, 196-8, 203-4, 207-8; Brezhnev 105, 107-8, 129, 151, 155, 174, 195; Khrushchev 72-3, 77-8, 155; spying against 123-30; and Vietnam 81 Ustinov, Dmitry 12, 145-7, 150, 151, 169, 191, 207

Vakulkin 41-2
Valenta, Jiri 116-17
Vasarhelyi, Miklos 7-8, 55, 59, 62
Vietnam 77, 81, 130, 176, 191
Vladimov, Georgy 171
Vogel, Hans-Jochen 3, 179
Vorotnikov, Vitaly 170

Walesa, Lech 132, 133, 201
Warsaw Pact 179, 201: Hungary in 58, 202
West Germany, Soviet relations with: Andropov 177, 179-80; Brezhnev 147, 174; Khrushchev 80
Winpisinger, William 184

Yakir, Pyotr 98-9
Yegorov, Alexander 43
Yershov, Anatoly 161
Yugoslavia 45, 53, 56, 59, 69-70, 75, 189: Soviet rapproachement with 65, 73, 74, 77-8

Zamyatin, Leonid 185
Zhou Enlai 80-1
Zia ul-Haq, President 193-5
Zinoviev, G.E. 22